# FAST QUILTS FROM FAT QUARTERS

BARBARA CHAINEY

A DAVID & CHARLES BOOK


David & Charles is an F+W Publications Inc. company
4700 East Galbraith Road
Cincinnati, OH 45236

First published in the UK in 2006



A catalogue record for this book is available from the British Library.

ISBN-13: 978-0-7153-2311-3 hardback
ISBN-10: 0-7153-2311-3 hardback

ISBN-13: 978-0-7153-2462-2 paperback (USA only)
ISBN-10: 0-7153-2462-4 paperback (USA only)

Printed in Singapore by KHL Printing Co Pte Ltd
for David & Charles
Brunel House Newton Abbot Devon

Commissioning Editor Vivienne Wells
Editor Ame Verso
Art Editor Sarah Underhill
Project Editor Linda Clements
Photography Karl Adamson and Ginette Chapman
Production Controller Ros Napper

Visit our website at www.davidandcharles.co.uk

David & Charles books are available from all good bookshops; alternatively you can contact our Orderline on 0870 9908222 or write to us at FREEPOST EX2 110, D&C Direct, Newton Abbot, TQ12 4ZZ (no stamp required UK mainland only); US customers call 800-289-0963 and Canadian customers call 800-840-5220.

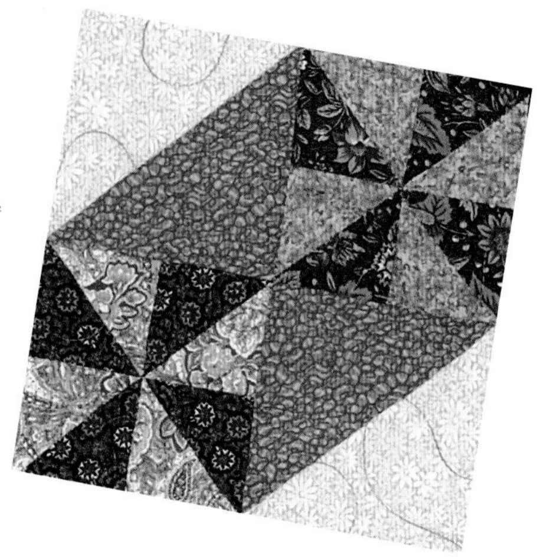

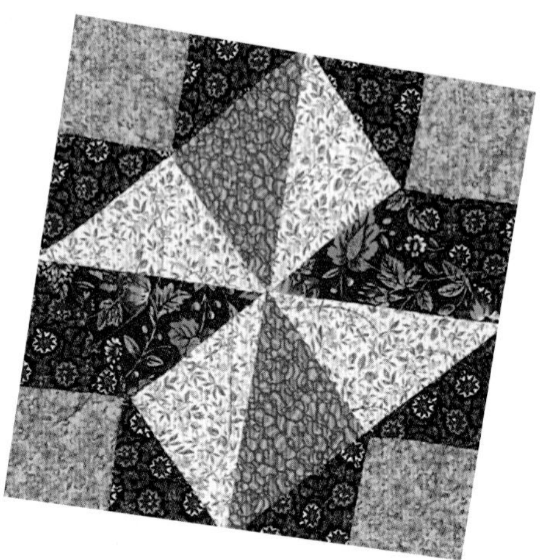

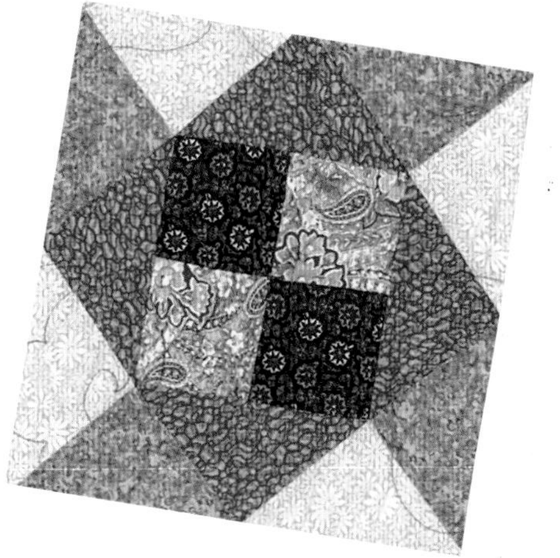

# Contents

# Introduction

Fat quarters feature in every quilter's stash. When quilt shops began cutting fabric this way, which gives four wide (useful) quarters to the yard rather than four thin (less useful) ones, they soon found they had a runaway success on their hands. The majority of quilters own more fat quarters than they truly know what to do with – these oh-so-useful cuts of fabric are not only sold singly but also in enticing colour combinations and selections that are impossible to resist. It's a wonderful route to instant fabric gratification – bring home several fat quarters, rather than a yard of one fabric, or even better, acquire two or three colourful selections. Sadly, what often happens is that the quarters stay on a shelf, are patted and stroked from time to time, but become almost too good to use and, before you realize it, they are out of date, out of style and out of favour – but still on a shelf.

The idea for this book came from having my own excellent and extensive five-year collection of fat quarter selections. All of them were delightful to look at, but somehow the right projects for them never came along and so they continued to sit, colourfully, on the shelf. An article by Jean Ann Wright (editor of *Quilt* magazine) described how she had devised a plan for cutting a fat quarter of fabric with minimum wastage and maximum number of basic shapes. These cut shapes were stored in shoe boxes and used as a starting point for making

scrap or multi-fabric quilts. Jean Ann cut her shapes from individual quarters but I wondered what would happen if a whole stack of quarters was cut and then, instead of storing the shapes for future use, why not see what could be made from them, right then and there? Calling on a friendship of fifteen years or so, Jean Ann willingly gave full permission for me to develop her plan further into a scheme that was easy to use and had masses of potential for making unique quilts.

So far, so good: I had a plan and I had fabric, but testing and exploring the plan called for more than one pair of hands and more than my personal fabric choices. Enthusiastic members of Cosby Quilters and a surprising number of good quilting friends were 'volunteered' to make the many quilt tops that finally made this book possible.

The results of their efforts are fifteen fully described quilts, and interspersed with these are a further twenty quilts, appearing in gallery features throughout the book. These gallery pictures and brief descriptions will give you some idea of the enormous range of quilts possible using this cut-first-decide-later approach. Most of the quilts use the main cutting plan on page 17, and because I love the idea of cutting everything out at once, the last three quilts use the same principle but follow a slightly different route.

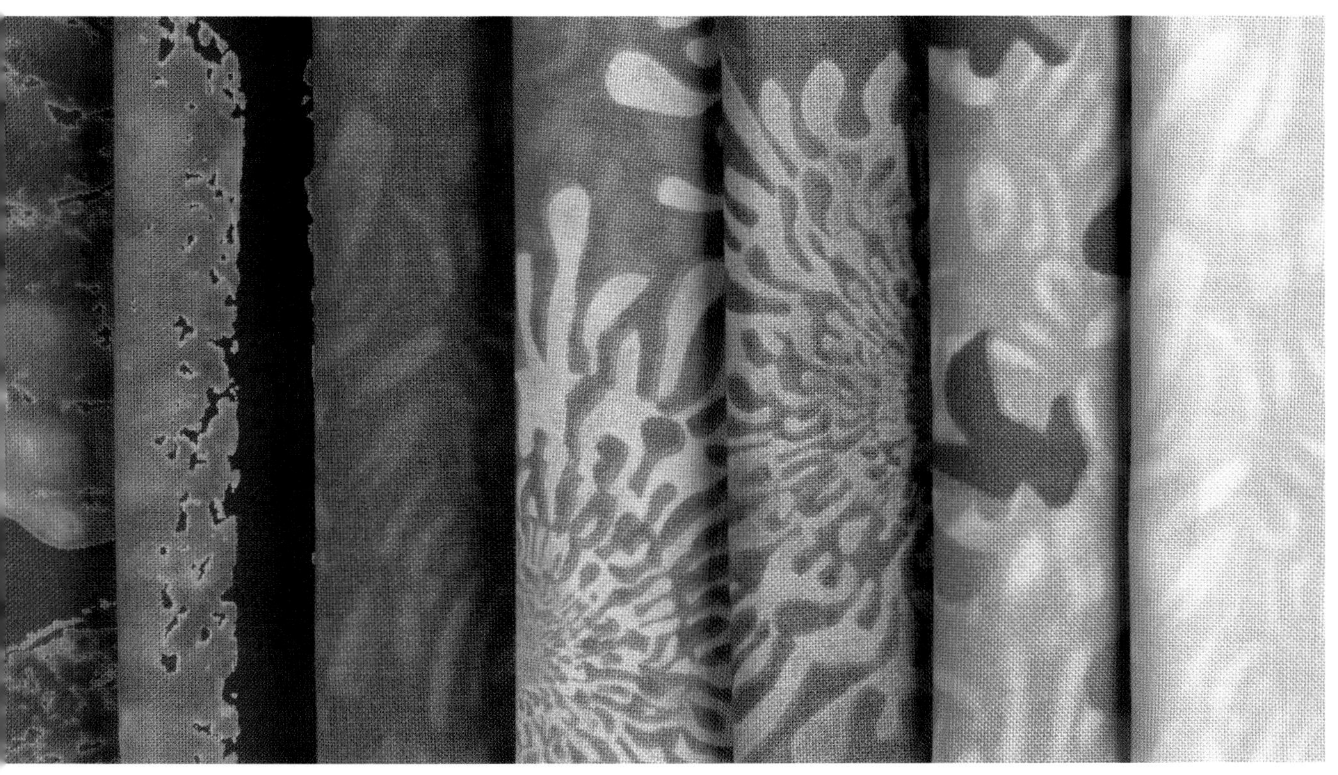

# Using this book

In the following pages you will find information and advice on equipment and the all-important topic of choosing fabrics, before being introduced to the main cutting plan and some of the practicalities of using it. A taste of just some of the plan's potential is given in block formats in Discover the Possibilities on pages 24–29, followed by the individual quilt projects. Advice and suggestions on settings, quilting and simple finishing techniques can be found on pages 111–119.

From the first 'light bulb' moment to the final draft, this book was always going to be about a freestyle approach to quilt construction – take fat quarters, cut them up, then decide what you will make from the resulting pieces, rather than purchasing specific yardage and following a project to the letter. The results will be uniquely yours – whether formal blocks in a regular setting or an overall arrangement; the challenge and the fun of this 'cut-first-decide-later' approach is something I hope you will find creatively rewarding.

**June's Gem**

June Lovatt really entered into the spirit of the main cutting plan and cut up *lots* of quarters from her stash. The finished quilt has terrific 'olde worlde' cottage charm and you can see how much fun June had piecing and setting all the different blocks and units together.

# Equipment

## Rotary cutter

There are many different brands of these essential tools to choose from. If you don't already have a preference and are about to acquire one, ask for advice at your local quilt shop or group. Try before you buy and opt for the best you can afford. Comfort and ease of use are issues of great importance. Some brands have an automatic safety mechanism to shield the blade when the cutter is not in use. If you frequently cut through six layers or more it is best to acquire a large blade cutter, which makes light work of cutting through multiple layers.

## Cutting mat

This should have clear markings and be of a sturdy thickness. It is a good idea to use a mat and ruler from the same manufacturer if you are looking for maximum accuracy. Do not leave your mat near any heat source, in a hot place or in direct sunlight – it could warp quickly and permanently. Of course it will need replacing eventually. Buy the biggest you can to fit into your working space, and add a smaller one to take to classes. For projects based on the cutting scheme in this book a cutting mat bigger than 20in x 20in will be much easier to work with.

## Rulers

There are many rulers to choose from, with many widths and lengths. Look for good visibility, clarity of markings and a practical size. An 18in x 3in or 4in is a good choice for general use. When you are measuring and making the first few cuts through a number of stacked fat quarters it will be helpful if you have a ruler that is bigger and wider than this, so you do not need to move the ruler along the fabric as you are cutting. In the interests of accuracy, if you own a variety of rulers, do not switch back and forth between brands during the same project.

## Sewing machine

Piecing and construction require only the most basic of sewing machines – steam-driven or hand-cranked will do the job. Something rather more sophisticated will be needed if you will be quilting and finishing the project yourself – a walking or even-feed foot will be needed for simple machine quilting and binding, a darning or embroidery foot and the capacity to lower or cover the feed dogs for free-machine quilting. Whatever the make or style of your machine, be kind to it and keep it lint free, oiled and regularly serviced and use a new needle at the start of every project.

## Sewing thread

For best results use good quality, fine cotton rather than general-purpose sewing thread. There is now a huge choice of brands: the general view is that finer thread (50s or 60s count) 'sits' better in the seam, lies flatter and generally makes for more accurate piecing. Neutral colours, such as medium grey and dark cream, are good choices that fit in with most colour schemes.

## Needles

Get into the habit of starting each project with a fresh needle in your hand or your sewing machine.

## Scissors

Invest in several pairs of scissors and make sure you know their whereabouts. Devise a plan to ensure that there is always a pair right next to your sewing machine. Keep the blades sharp by refusing to use them for anything other than snipping threads – which is easier said than done!

## Pins

Choose pins that are fine and have a long shank, such as flower-headed pins or silk pins. Avoid thick or chunky pins – they may distort fabric when in position.

## Fabric markers

The line made by a fine HB mechanical pencil or a chalk wheel will be visible on most fabrics. I would advise against using a fadeout pen or waxy markers. You need to make a fine, visible line that is going to be easy to remove, so test, test, test. Remember, you will be stitching on some marked lines, cutting on others. You will not be marking on 'open' fabric during the construction process, although you might want to mark quilting lines on the completed top. The beauty of the cutting plan featured in this book is that it minimizes the amount of marking on fabric before constructing blocks or units, so you will be thinking mostly in terms of a marker for quilting lines.

## Portable layout sheet

Fold-out boards used for jigsaw puzzles make excellent 'keeping' surfaces for laying out blocks or units and carrying them between sewing machine and ironing board.

## Design wall

A design wall or board is the perfect place to set out arrangements of the cut pieces. A length of flannel or needlepunched cotton batting can be taped to a wall or portable board. A large piece of lightweight foamcore board is another popular, inexpensive and easily available choice. Interfacing printed with a grid might be helpful for setting out all-over or 'non-block' arrangements, or you could mark up such a grid yourself on a piece of plain interfacing.

## Iron

A light- to medium-weight iron, with steam and dry settings and a smooth soleplate that is easy to clean, is recommended. For most of my work I like to use a small homemade pressing board (made from two fabric bolt inners covered with a clean old towel), using a regular domestic ironing board only for the longer border seams and final pressing.

## Starch

Advocated by an illustrious line-up of quilting authorities, starch is both cheap and useful – once you've tried it you may find it impossible to revert to piecing with unstarched fabric. Spray starch is widely available (in the laundry section at supermarkets) or you could mix up your own formula of liquid starch and water to use in a garden spray bottle. Be careful of fallout when you spray fabrics and protect as many surfaces as possible, including the floor. Spray with restraint – excessive spraying may encourage the wet fabric to distort as it is being pressed and may also build up a residue on the iron's soleplate, as well as little white flakes on the fabric itself. I spray each fat quarter lightly and press it smooth before stacking the quarters ready for cutting. If a fabric seems particularly lightweight I will perhaps spray it and press it twice before it goes into the stack.

## Light

It may be last on this list of equipment but this is possibly the most important item of all. Good light to work by is essential. Full spectrum or daylight lamps are available in lots of different shapes, sizes and prices. I have one for the space where I choose and cut fabrics, another close to the sewing machine and a third by my chair for handsewing moments.

*Checks, swirls, florals, stripes – so much to choose from!*

# Choosing Fabrics

Choosing fabrics for any quilt project is exciting and frustrating in equal measure. It never seems to be a problem for any of us to acquire fabric in great quantities, but there is the perennial question that we all come up against – which fabrics will look good/ better/best together? Which choices will guarantee not only success and your satisfaction but also the admiration of other quilters?

Deciding on a selection of fabrics that will look great and work effectively together is something that you always want to get absolutely right, whatever the project. You may feel even more pressure when you use the cutting plan on page 17 since the whole concept here is that you will be cutting up all your fabrics *before* going on to make any construction choices. Of course this means that you will not be following the usual excellent advice to make a sample block before committing to cutting. A sample block is usually a great way to start a large project or indeed any project – it offers you an opportunity to check out your colour and fabric and it also gives you the chance to check that you have understood all the cutting and piecing directions. Working with a cutting plan means that you dive right into the whole thing, which is a completely different way of going about things, and it certainly forces you to think a little bit more 'outside the box' because you will be choosing from a finite number of cut pieces, rather than cutting specific pieces as required. You will be surprised at how much you learn about colour and value, and your personal preferences, as you work your way along from stacked fabrics to cut pieces to pieced units, blocks and finally a quilt.

# Where to start

First of all, the one major rule – choose what pleases you. Seems so easy and obvious doesn't it? After all, if you don't absolutely love the colours or the style of prints you've selected then it's a fairly sure thing that you won't enjoy making the project and you won't care for the finished piece. Colour moods and preferences change almost from day to day – sometimes you might gravitate to choosing warm, country colours teamed with muted neutrals, other times you'll automatically select any amount of blue fabrics; sometimes it's brights, sometimes it's pastels, and so on.

For your first project with the main cutting plan (or indeed, for any other quilting project), you can make a great start by choosing a colour family you particularly like. Gather up as many fat quarters as possible in this colour, including prints and solids, dark, medium, light, and bright values and use these as the starting point for your project. Choose two light, two medium and two dark values as the basis of your selection and add to these as you please – I would strongly recommend keeping to this evenly divided proportion of value irrespective of the final number of fat quarters you decide to work with.

Don't forget to take a long look at the huge number of different selections to be found in quilt shops and catalogues – there are so many gorgeous options available and they are a great starting point for suggesting a main colour theme or a style of fabrics.

*Fabrics with the same style, colourings and value*

Feel free, as I always seem to do, to acquire several selections – purely in the interests of quilting research and inspiration!

Think about what type of look you are aiming for: again use your personal preferences as a guide – scrappy and multicolour with lots of different styles of fabric, designer style and co-ordinated with a particular colour or theme as a focus, e.g., nursery prints, Thirties prints, batiks, jungle, documentary – the possibilities are tremendously varied. One really easy way of 'getting it right' is to find a multicolour print you love and use it as your keynote fabric, then choose roughly similar numbers or proportions of each colour as it appears in the fabric.

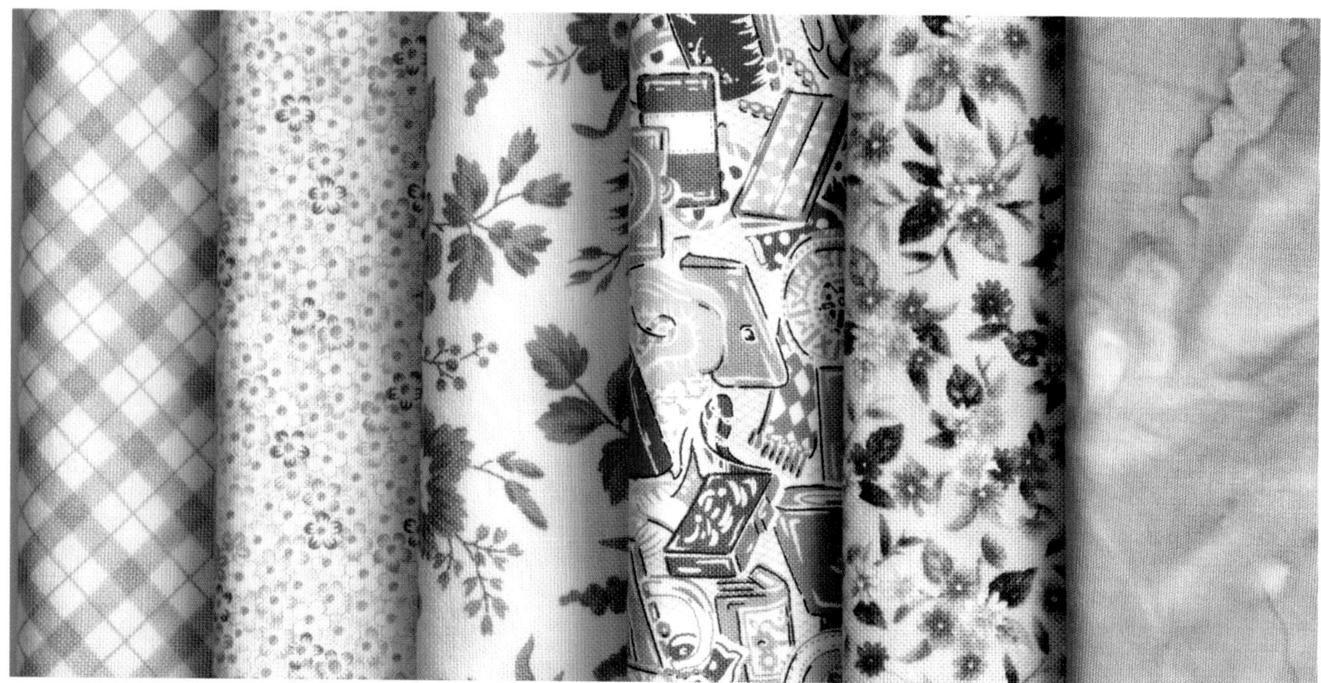

*From plaid to marbled via floral and quirky – a scrappier style selection*

# Colour

Acres of print and countless pictures have been devoted to colour – how to choose it and how to use it. No matter how well it is described and explained, sometimes the whole 'colour' thing can seem totally intimidating for most of us – and puts everything on to a technical rather than intuitive level. We still feel that there is a right and a wrong to every colour selection and preference and we're just waiting for the Colour Police (Quilting Division) to arrive and arrest us. In every class and in every quilt shop the heartfelt wail 'I'm no good with colour' is heard, and every quilter can empathize with that particular feeling of inadequacy! Once you begin talking about the colour wheel and the different relationships between colours it can all start to seem very complex and perhaps too rigid for comfort. Maybe if we just got hold of the idea that the colour wheel (Fig 1) is there as a tool for us to use, rather than as a set of rules to be followed, we would fare better in our colour quest.

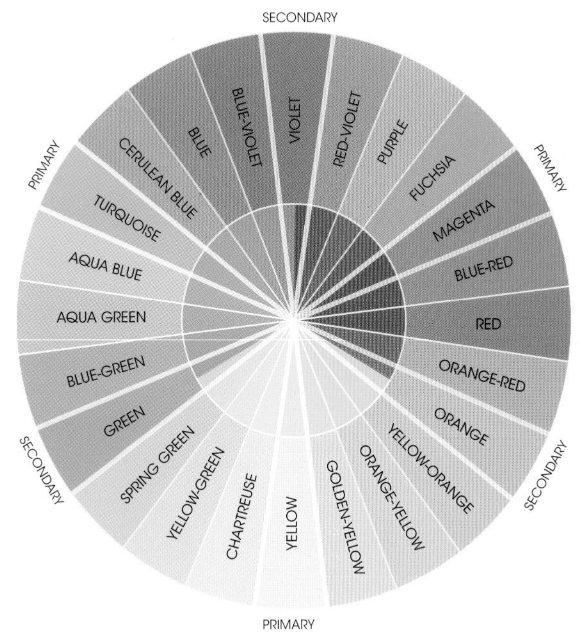


**Fig 1** *Studying a colour wheel and the relationships between the colours can help with planning your fabric selections*

# Colour terms

Here are some very basic terms and suggestions for you to consider along with the colour wheel in Fig 1 and the examples shown in Fig 2.

- A hue is a colour. A tint is a hue with white added making it lighter. A shade is a hue with black added making it darker. A tone is a hue with grey added.

- Value describes the lightness or darkness of a particular hue. Warm colours are based on red, orange and yellow; cool colours are based on blue and green.

- A monochromatic colour scheme is based on one colour or hue and can also include different shades, tints and tones (see Fig 2).

- An analogous colour scheme includes colours that are adjacent to each other on the colour wheel, for instance green and yellow.

- A complementary colour scheme is one that has colours directly opposite each other on the colour wheel, for example aqua blue and orange-red.

**Fig 2** *Same quilt, three different colour schemes – monochrome, analogous and complementary*

# Value

During the fabric selection process for several of the quilts in this book I learned a lot about my own preferences when making value choices. To begin with I wanted to use lots of those wonderfully graded selections of dyed fabrics and other yummy selections of quarters that were all very close in value and quite low in contrast. If you want to produce a 'blended' piece of whatever style then choosing these close values and low contrasts will work very well. However, you may prefer to have a little more clarity and definition in your work, which will mean some selecting out from your first choices. I would also suggest that, particularly when using the cutting plan concept in this book, it is more important to have balance and contrast in the values of your fabrics rather than worrying about 'correct' or 'good' colour choices.

*Similar style of fabric in dark, medium and light values*

*Good contrast between dark, medium and light*

*Lower contrast fabrics*

# Contrast

Contrast is what it implies, for instance red and blue contrast – one is warm, one is cool. Pale pink and navy blue contrast, not only as warm against cool, but as light against dark. Small amounts of contrast, whether in colour or value, or both, will provide a highlight or accent – imagine a quilt that has mostly blues from light to dark values with a generous dash of sunshine yellow. The colour contrast in this case sharpens up the yellow and lifts the blue (see Sunshine Team, page 73).

*Light background fabrics contrast well with warm or cool colours*

# Background fabrics

These are intended to give space and breathing room to the main fabrics by adding contrast. If you decide to use this cutting plan approach with the aim of making a traditional-looking quilt based on traditional blocks, your light-value fabrics will be used as backgrounds. In the interests of clarity try to choose backgrounds that are much lighter or darker in value than any of your other choices.

To achieve a scrappy or random look you could use a number of different background fabrics similar in value and scale – this often works really well.

Alternatively, use just one background fabric that is a strong contrast in value and scale with all of the other fabrics – this will give a very crisp, more traditional feel to the project. If you decide to use several backgrounds, I would recommend that you acquire them as fat quarters and use the cutting plan. However, if you prefer to have a single background fabric it may be more economical to buy as regular yardage. In this case you will need to cut equivalent numbers of each shape from full-width strips of the appropriate measurement.

*Same fabric selections but dark background choices – such a difference!*

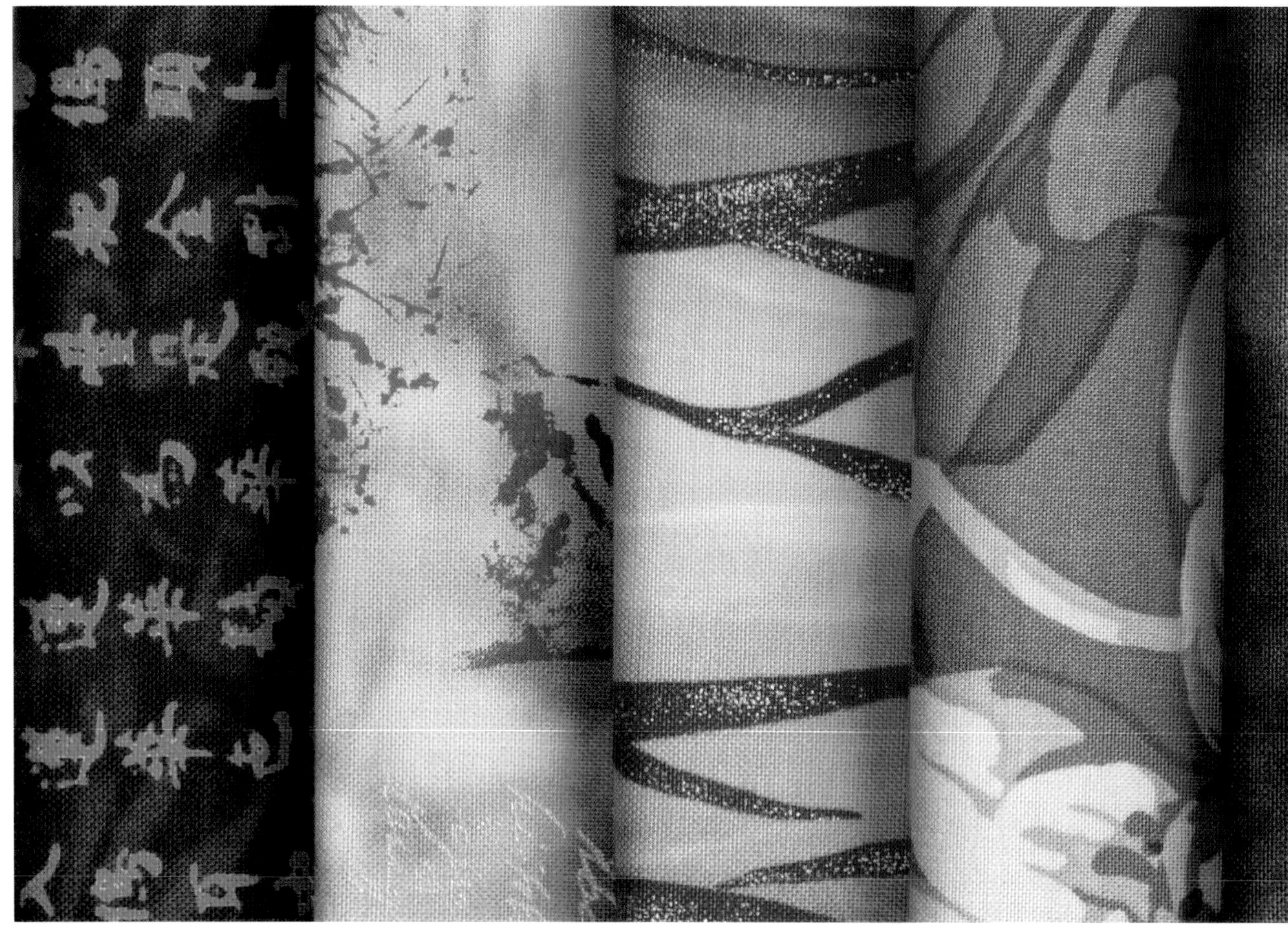

# Fabric variety

Single colour or monochromatic schemes work well only if there is good range of dark, medium and light fabrics within that chosen colour. The same principle applies to multicolour schemes – if the values are too similar the result will be muddy. Likewise, whatever the number of quarters you choose, take care not to include fabrics that are very similar in scale and colour – the differences will be barely distinguishable when they are cut up into small shapes.

Remember that value is just a smart term for dark, medium and light tones. You will want to have some variety in the values you choose – aim for roughly equal quantities of dark, medium and light fabrics to begin with. So, for a selection of six fat quarters have two light, two medium and two dark fabrics.

Variety of scale is also something to think about. There is no point in choosing six large-scale prints, even if they are divided fairly satisfactorily into dark, medium and light values. The similarity in scale will make it difficult to distinguish one cut piece from another. It is much better, and more interesting, to vary the scale of the prints across small, medium and large. A good variety in the visual texture of your chosen fabrics will help to give the finished project more interest and pace. So, rather than choosing two large-scale floral prints, two medium-scale floral prints and two small-scale floral prints, a livelier choice might be a large-scale floral print, a large-scale splashy abstract print, a medium-size check or plaid, a medium-scale floral print, a small tone-on-tone print and a small stripe or 'blotch' print.

*Dark, medium and light values, and variety in the scale and style of print*

# Fabric quantities

It was generally agreed among the volunteers testing the cutting plan in this book that a minimum workable number of fat quarters was six. Obviously the potential size of a project depends on the quantity of fabric that is cut to begin with – fewer than six quarters means much less variety and interest in the blocks or units made from the plan and thus a smaller quilt, although there is no limit to the amount of further yardage that can be added in later for sashings, settings and borders.

A selection of twelve fat quarters will give lots of variety and interest and makes a bigger quilt if all (or nearly all) the cut pieces are used – further yardage for settings still remains an option here to make the quilt even bigger. For larger-scale projects you could choose only six different fabrics and have two fat quarters of each. Or you may like to work with, say, a total of twelve fabrics but repeat two medium and two dark value choices. Be aware that this inevitably puts more emphasis on the repeated fabrics, so make sure that any repeats are fabrics you really want to feature.

# Additional fabric

There is a stated assumption throughout this book that fat quarters, in any number and combination, are used to construct blocks, units and basic components only as the starting point from which a quilt can grow. The quantity of fat quarters is not usually intended to include sufficient fabric for sashings, settings, borders, backing or binding. Once the blocks or units are stitched you can experiment on a design wall with various settings and arrangements and at this point be open to adding other fabrics to complement and further enhance your original choices. See Finishing Your Quilt (pages 111–119) for further information.

# Concept and Cutting Plan

The formula offered here is a particular way of working – cutting regular basic shapes and using certain basic ingredients, that is, stacked fat quarters of fabric rather than full-width yardage. The result is almost certainly guaranteed to make you think, as well as making the creation of interesting, unique quilts fast and easy. Just stack up your selection of fat quarters, cut according to the plan in Fig 3 (opposite) and begin composing blocks or units to make your quilt.

You can use the squares, rectangles and triangles to make traditional four-patch or nine-patch blocks or maybe invent some of your own. Alternatively, you could make up random pieced units of the same size that can be treated as blocks, or set pieced units together in a random or formal all-over design. Unlike other stack-and-cut techniques, where the result is a number of identically structured blocks that differ only in the way the fabric is placed, this concept gives you freedom to construct a wide range of blocks and styles limited only by your imagination.

If you choose to work with a traditional-style block format, which is familiar to most of us, you will rapidly discover that there are never sufficient numbers of certain shapes to make repeated blocks of near-identical fabrics. Instead, you will be forced to make all sorts of substitutions, choose alternatives and generally be creative. I like to think of this as being very much in the spirit of the earliest years of quiltmaking – which it is – the starting point is simply different here, being from a position of plenty rather than from one of scarcity.

The benefits of using the cutting plan in this book include the following. It more or less guarantees a good mix of fabrics across a project. It is easy to make something sparky and quirky with an individual touch. It gives an understanding of how shapes, colours and values work together. It gives freedom from looking at a picture/plan of a project and working back to cutting out pieces required and then assembling – this way, all cutting is done first, assembly second, finished plan last. There is also the excitement of working in a formal yet free way, not needing to know from the outset exactly what the finished piece will look like.

## How the plan works

The cutting plan (Fig 3) makes optimum use of the area of an average fat quarter of fabric (calculated here as 22in x 20in). With portrait orientation rather than landscape, the cutting plan divides the area first into strips then into squares and rectangles and lastly into half-square and quarter-square triangles (see Fig 4 and the photographs overleaf for the stages of cutting). So from each fat quarter you will have:

A squares x 2 (4½in)
B squares x 4 (2½in)
C half-square triangles x 4
D quarter-square triangles x 8
E half-square triangles x 18
F squares x 2 (3⅜in)
G rectangles x 4 (4½in x 2½in)

These shapes will allow you to create a multitude of simple units, which can then be built up into a myriad of quilt patterns. See Fig 5 on page 21 for some examples of simple units that can be pieced from the shapes in the cutting plan.

When the shapes are pieced together, allowing for ¼in seam allowances, the spatial maths works out like this:

A = 4½in square
2 x G = A
4 x B = A
8 x E = A
4 x D = A

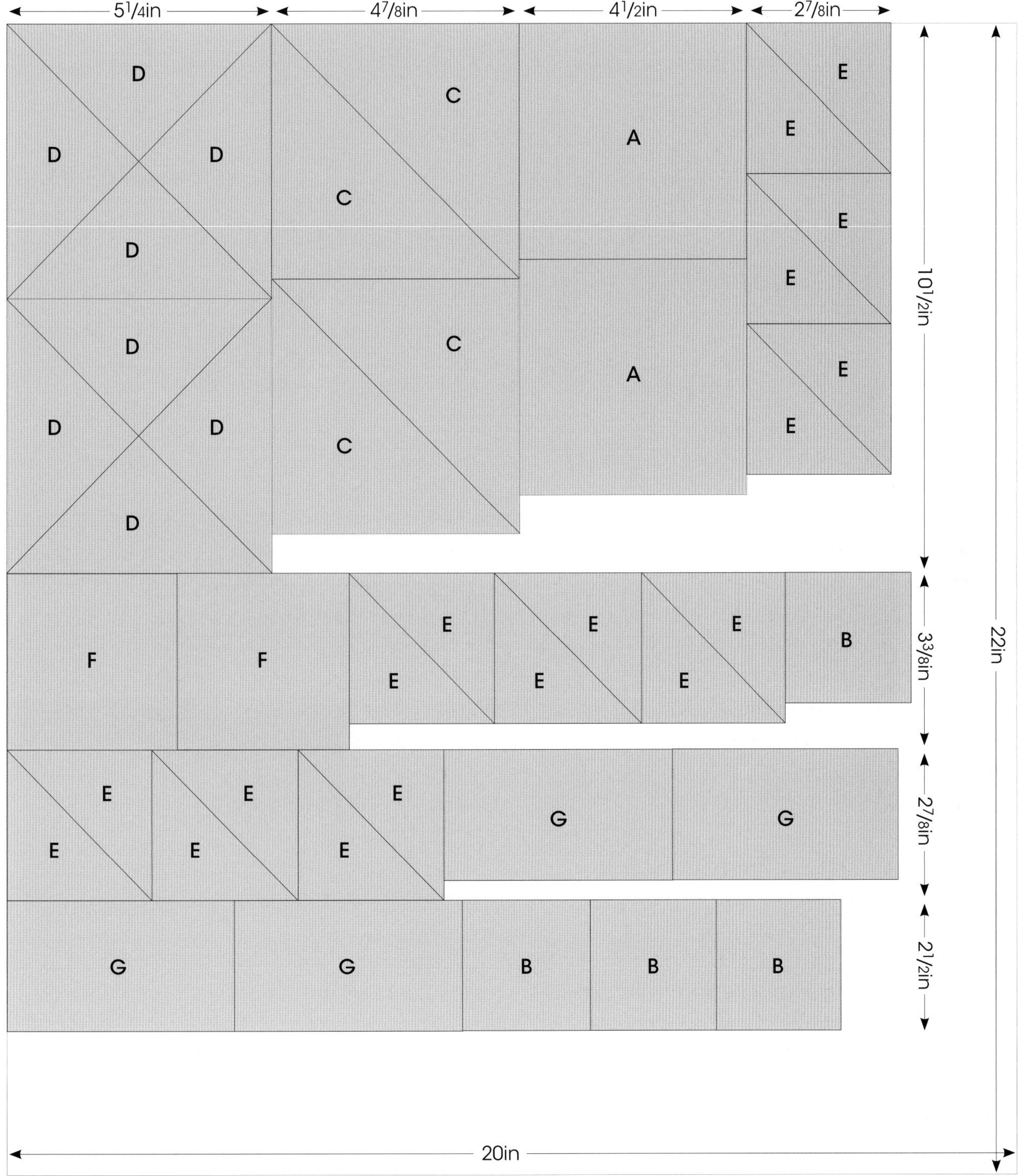


**Fig 3 – the cutting plan**
*This plan for fat quarters is the starting point for most of the quilts in this book (except the last three). Copy it out on to thick paper following the measurements given here and overleaf in Fig 4, which also shows the sequence for cutting all the shapes. Mark all the measurements on your paper plan*

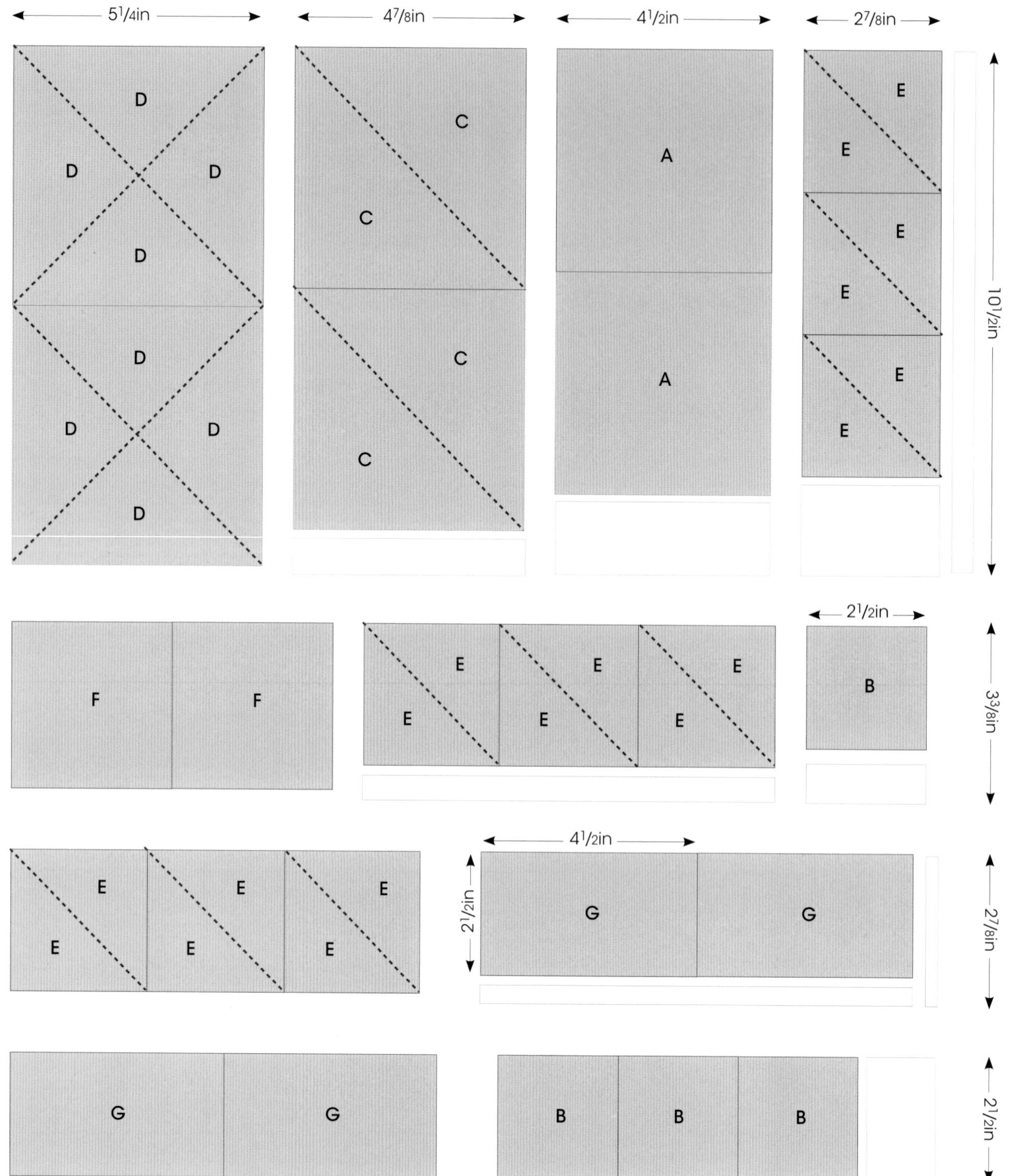


**Fig 4** *Cutting plan showing the sequence of fabric cuts (see also the photographic sequence opposite). Fat quarters can vary considerably in size so you may have differing amounts of 'waste' fabric after you have cut all the shapes according to this plan – you may even have sufficient of some fabrics to cut extra B squares and E triangles*

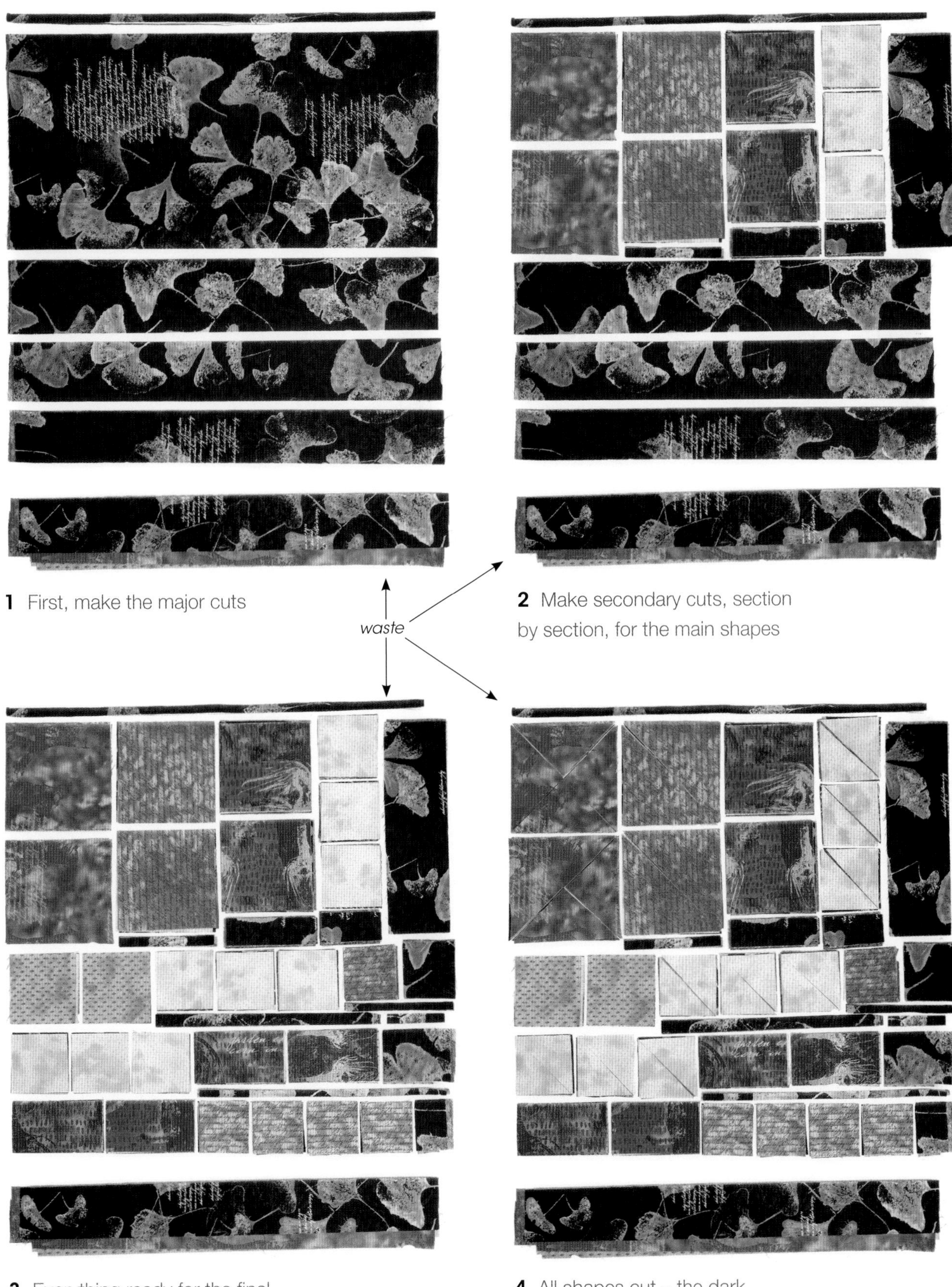


**1** First, make the major cuts

**2** Make secondary cuts, section by section, for the main shapes

**3** Everything ready for the final cutting of triangles D, C and E

**4** All shapes cut – the dark print shows waste fabric

# Fast Quilts in Easy Stages

This section describes how to make quilts using the cutting plan, including making a paper map of the plan, cutting your fat quarters according to the plan and how to best construct the blocks.

### 1 Prepare your fabrics

To wash or not to wash – that is the question when it comes to fabric. Quilters tend to divide into two directly opposed camps on this particular topic – those who have to wash, press and fold any fabric before it gets into their stash and those who just have to acquire fabric and own it. You will have your own preferences and my advice is to follow them. Personally, I'm in the acquisition-only camp.

Washed or not, you may find that spray starching your fabrics before laying them out and cutting will make for easier handling and perhaps improved accuracy in piecing. The extra weight that starch adds helps to minimize shifting of layers as you are cutting and also as you stitch pieces together. Starched fabric is less susceptible to fraying and distortion, which is something to consider, especially as the cut pieces are likely to have a fair amount of handling as you set blocks out and try different combinations of shapes and units. One of the things I like about working with starched fabric is that the cut edges look so sharp and crisp that you feel you can produce sharp and crisp-looking work – it certainly improves my accuracy and helps my piecing skills. You can use liquid starch, mixed in roughly equal amounts with water in a small garden spray bottle, or a regular commercial brand of heavyweight spray starch (see also Press Your Work, page 23).

First of all I spray each fat quarter, then press carefully at a high heat and steam setting. When I stack the quarters I usually layer them all together and press from the top before moving the stack to the cutting board – that final pressing helps to keep the layers together.

### 2 Make a cutting plan

A good majority of the quilt testers found that making a full-sized paper 'map' of the cutting plan helped them to focus well when they came to the cutting process. They also found that measuring and marking the geometric shapes on to paper gave them an understanding of how they would be cutting their fabrics and the sequence of cuts required for the plan. Later on, the paper map also served as a good organizational aid to keep track of the cut shapes. One or two of the experienced and confident testers said that they felt the map made little difference to them, but certainly for the first time you work with this cutting plan I would strongly recommend taking the time to draw out a full-sized map – it really will help you to see how everything works and can avoid cutting goofs with the stacked fabrics. You only need to make the map once rather than for every single project!

To make your own cutting plan use any cheap heavyweight paper, such as shelf paper or wallpaper, and cut a piece that is slightly larger than 22in x 20in. Measure and clearly mark an area 22in x 20in on the paper. Referring to Fig 3 on page 17, mark off all the main cutting lines and shapes together with identifying letters and actual measurements.

The working life of your paper map can be extended by laminating or covering it with adhesive library film, which will give a smooth, flat surface that is easy to use and facilitates picking up the smaller cut pieces. Many of the testers found that cutting out the shapes according to the plan and putting the stacked shapes into position on the paper map helped them to keep track of the shapes and locate the right size of triangle for a particular block or unit. Early on you will probably begin to remember the letter names of the shapes and using the map reinforces this learning.

### 3 Cut your fat quarters

For the scheme that is at the heart of this book cutting the fabric is the single most important step so take care to read and understand these instructions before you start!

Lay the stacked fat quarters out completely flat on a cutting mat that exceeds their size, i.e., bigger than 20in x 20in, so you can measure and make the first cuts with ease (and a long ruler!). Lay the stack out in a portrait (lengthways) orientation not landscape (widthways).

With a normal rotary cutter you should be able to cut up to six layers accurately; if a quilt requires a bigger stack, simply split the stack into more manageable layers. Have your paper map close at hand and refer to it frequently, following the well-used maxim of 'measure twice, cut once'. Check, check and check again the measurements before you cut each strip or shape. Refer to Fig 4 and the photographs on the previous pages – and take your time. If you find that, despite all this close attention, you have goofed and measured and cut incorrectly, do not despair. Put the goof strip or pieces to one side and complete as many of the remaining cutting steps as you can.

Now return to the offending items and assess the best way to proceed. If you have cut a strip wider than required it's a simple matter to re-cut it to the correct size. If you've cut a smaller strip than required then take a look at the plan and see if you can use it to re-cut one of the other sizes or shapes. For a worst case scenario, use the offending strips or pieces to make setting strips, sashings or borders. Even if something does go 'wrong' look on it in the same way as running out of fabric – just another creative opportunity!

## 4 Set up your machine

You do not need a fancy machine to work with this cutting plan for fat quarters – any machine that makes a good straight stitch is fine. Set the stitch length for general stitching as recommended by the manufacturer, or based on your own preference and experience – I have mine set at about 2 on a scale of 0–4.

Since you will be stitching through a variety of colours, a combination of neutral-coloured sewing threads for the top and the bobbin is probably the best choice – a pale grey and a dark cream always seem to work well together. It is certainly worth taking the time to wind a couple of spare bobbins as you are setting up your machine to avoid the frustration of discovering that you have been stitching for ten minutes or more without any thread in the bobbin.

## 5 Lay out the blocks

Use a cutting mat, a piece of foamcore board, needlepunched batting, a tray or any other suitable, portable work surface to try out various arrangements of pieces in block format. I like to have a smooth surface for this, which makes it easy to slide and switch pieces around and then carry the arrangement over to the sewing machine to stitch, so my preference is to use a large sheet of white foamcore board and a few pins to fix final arrangements.

**Fig 5** *Some of the simple units that can be made from the shapes cut from the main plan. These units can be arranged into larger blocks according to your preference (see Discover the Possibilities, page 24)*

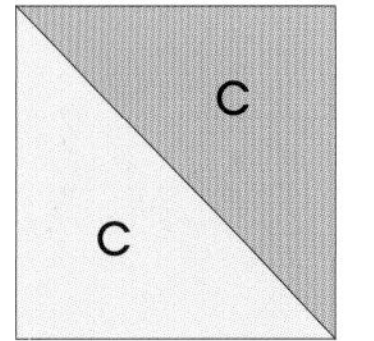

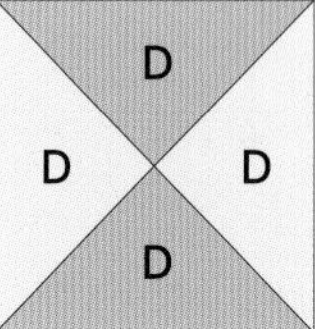

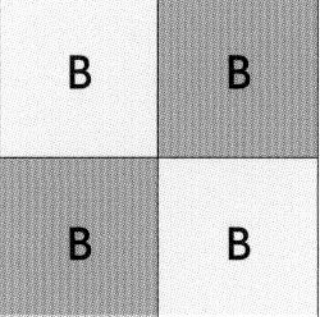

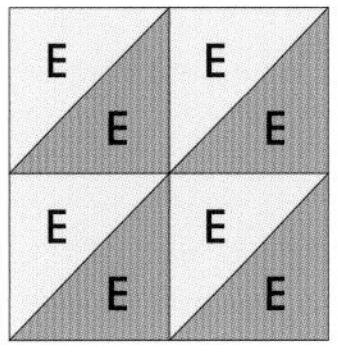

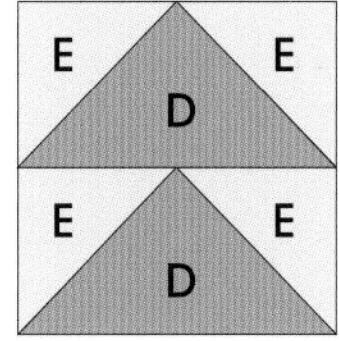

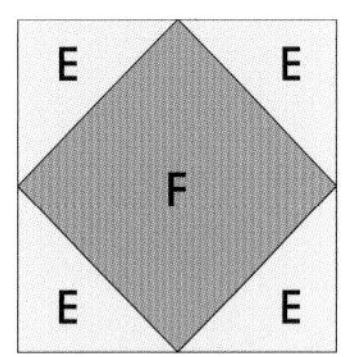

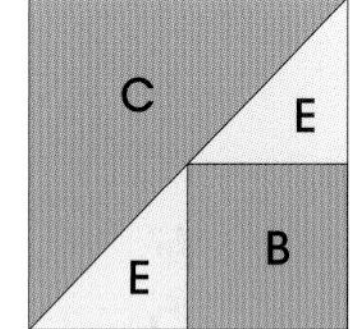

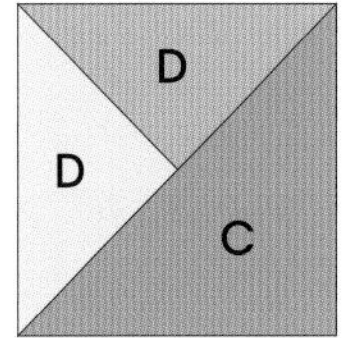

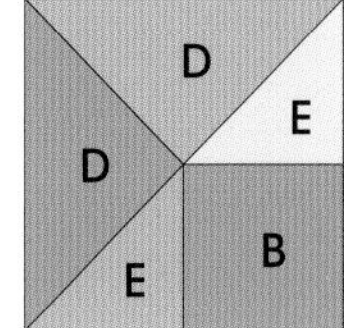

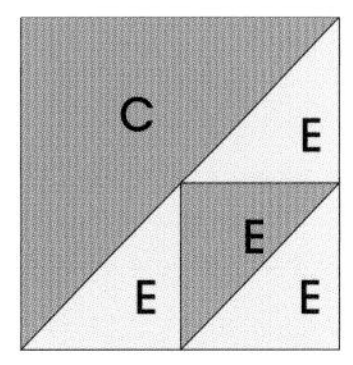

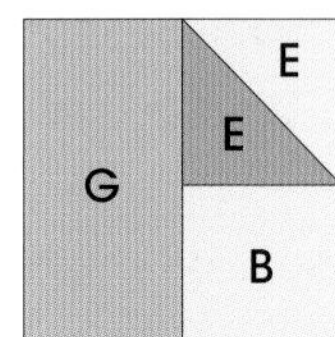

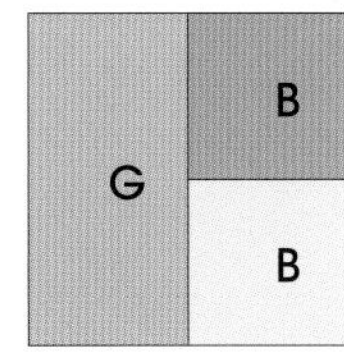

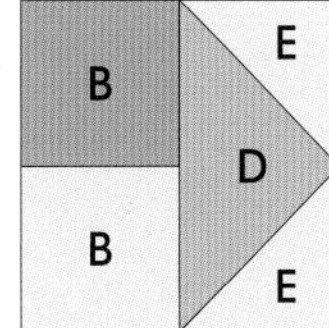

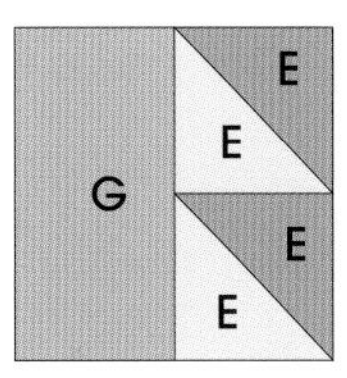

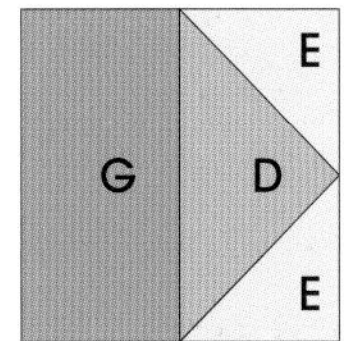

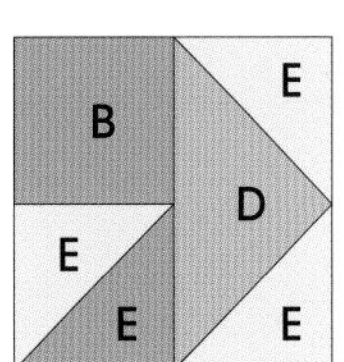

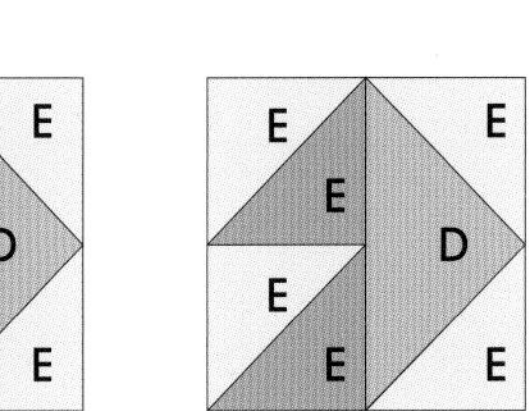

### 6 Begin block construction

Begin at the very beginning, with small units only! Fig 5 on the previous page shows some examples of simple units that can be made from the cut shapes. Refer to Fig 6 to see the sequence of steps for constructing a simple four-patch block and Fig 7 for piecing a nine-patch block. Piece all of the smallest units first, pressing all seams and trimming threads with care before moving on to the next step. The photographs opposite show the fabric pieces arranged into blocks.

All of the blocks used in the main project quilts in this book are similarly explained with diagrams throughout the quilt chapters, both as an 'exploded' view showing all the pieces and an assembled view. Discover the Possibilities (pages 24–29) shows a selection of traditional four-patch and nine-patch blocks that you can make using shapes from the cutting plan.

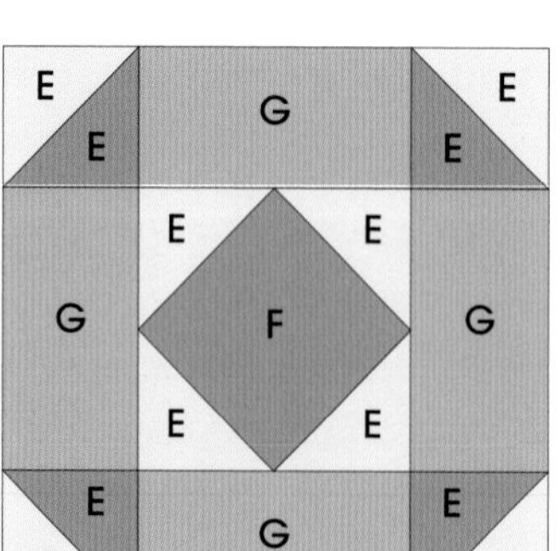


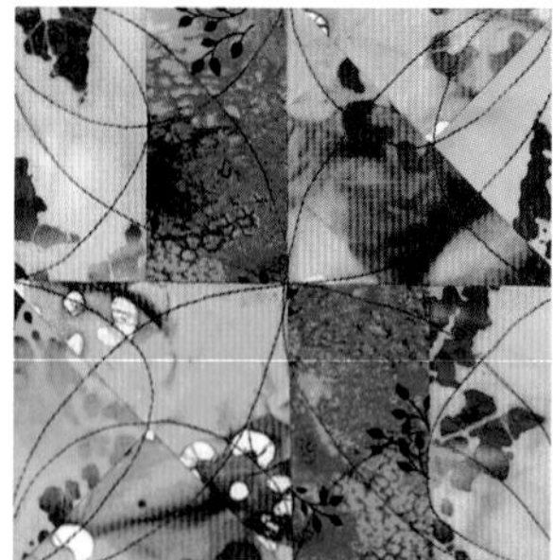

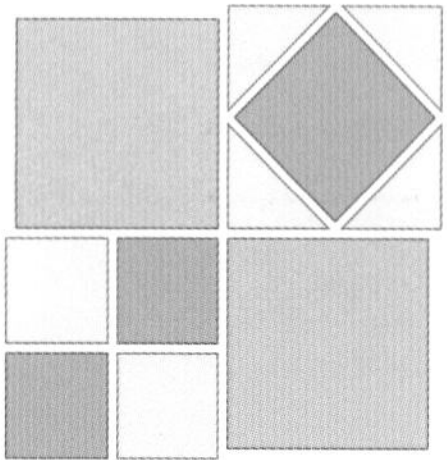

**Fig 6** *The sequence for constructing a four-patch block*

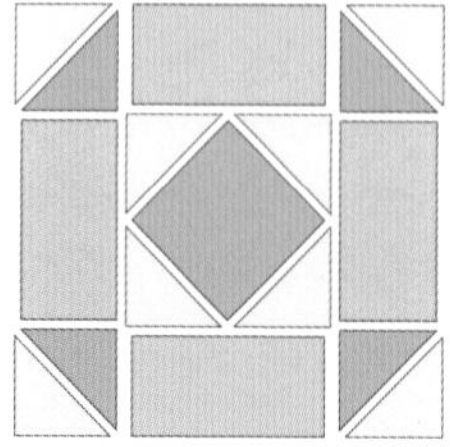

**Fig 7** *The sequence for constructing a nine-patch block*

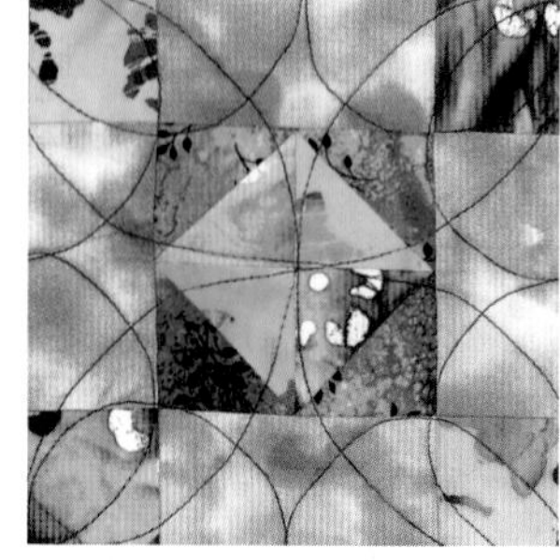

## Chain piecing

You can minimize stopping and starting and keep the sewing process smooth and productive by using a chain piecing technique (Fig 8). Begin by stitching across a small snib or piece of folded fabric then feed paired patches through without pausing to pull out or snip threads. This method is neat, speedy and economical with thread. The lengths of paired pieces are snipped apart before they are pressed.

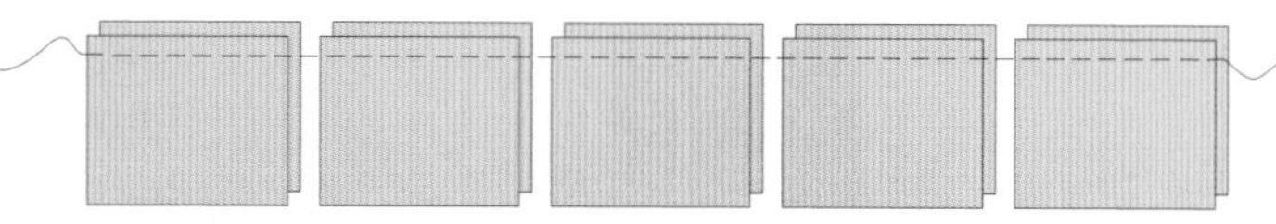

**Fig 8** *Chain piecing is a sensible and time-saving method of dealing with seams to make units and blocks in small or large quantities*

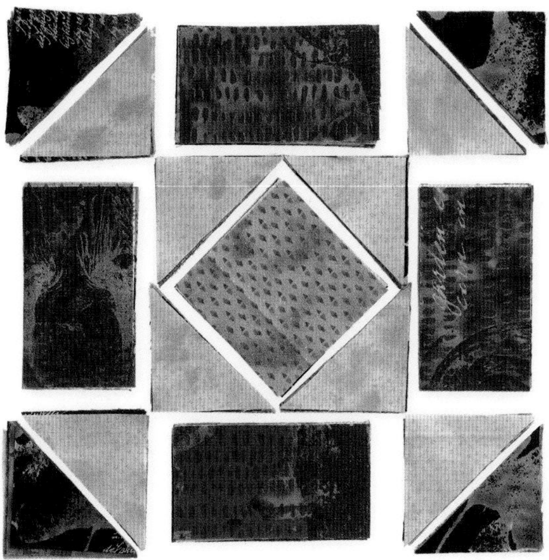

*First arrange stacks of the cut shapes into one simple block format . . .*

*. . . then use the remaining stacked shapes to make a second block. All the variations of both blocks will look good together because they are based on the same fabrics in different combinations*

**7 Press your work**

Attention to pressing can improve the appearance and accuracy of your piecing. Finger pressing uses the warmth and pressure of finger and thumb to flatten down a seam. There is also a nifty little wooden pressing tool that you can use to flatten and smooth seams without using heat. Using the heat of an iron for pressing seams means that you should always remember that you are not ironing shirts – the difference is that seams are *pressed* flat without moving the iron around, whereas ironing involves moving and re-shaping. Steam has the ability to distort, particularly with too much movement of the iron, so dry heat is generally considered to be the preferred option. Steam pressing may be more useful for the final pressing of a block.

Press seams flat first (as they come from the machine), to set the line of stitching and also to minimize the depth of the seam. Then press, either open or to one side, depending on your preference. If you opt to press seams to one side, it is usual to press both seam allowances towards the darker fabric. Pressing to one side also requires that you pay attention to where the bulk of the seam will fall and plan ahead so that when you come to join units or sections of blocks together, the seams will fall in opposing directions – this makes it easier to match for accurate joins.

**8 Assemble your quilt**

Instructions for joining all the blocks together are given with each quilt. Some block settings are suggested on pages 24–29. Finishing your quilt, including advice on sashing and borders, is dealt with on pages 111–119. So, now it's time to select your fabrics, cut them according to the cutting plan and get stitching!

# Discover the Possibilities

The following pages show just some of the amazing number of traditional blocks you can make using shapes from the main cutting plan. Instead of making formal blocks you can construct multiples of simple units and arrange them into block format, as I did for the quilt on page 100 – see ideas on page 29. Use the units and blocks here as a starting point and you'll soon be making quilts in a fraction of the normal time.

## Four-patch blocks

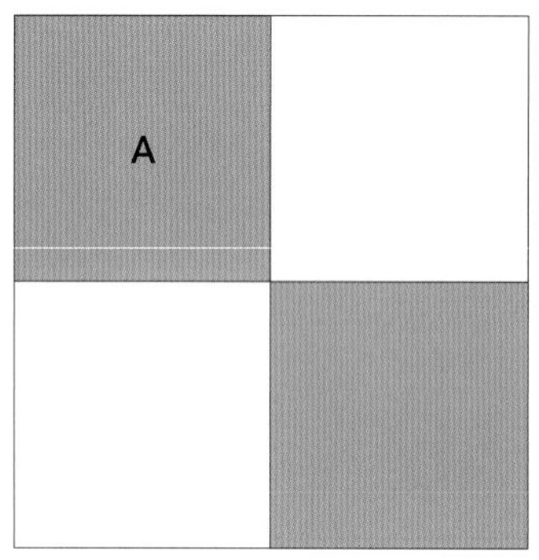


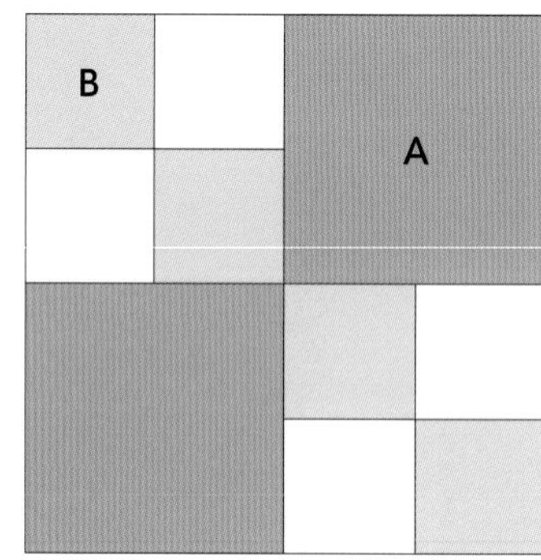


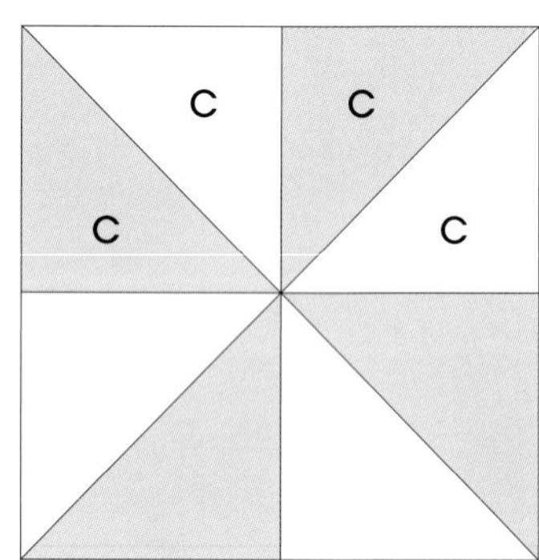


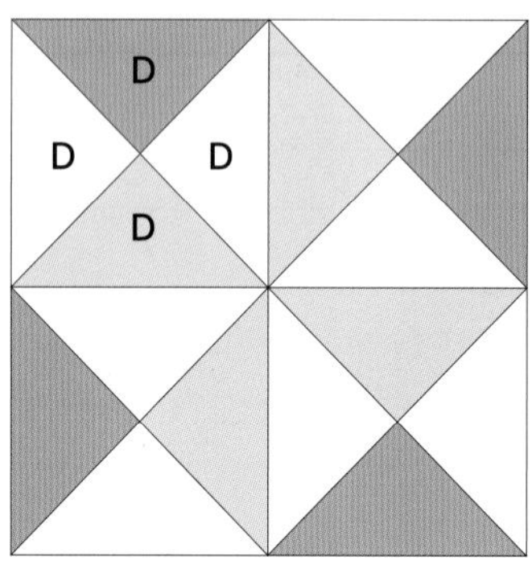


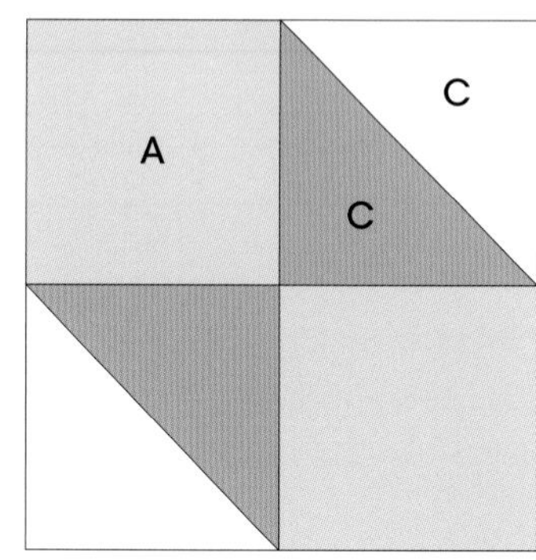


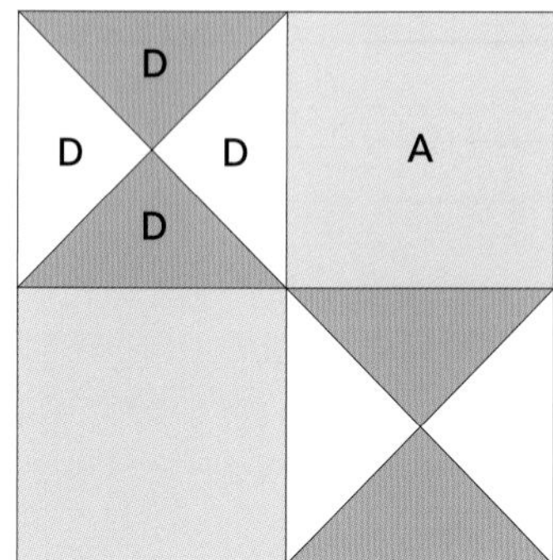


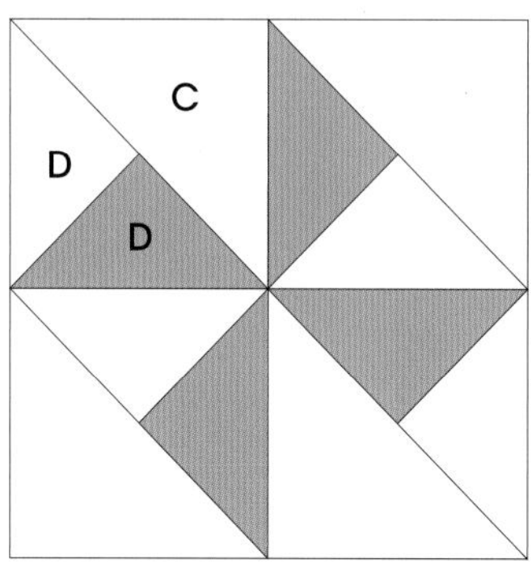


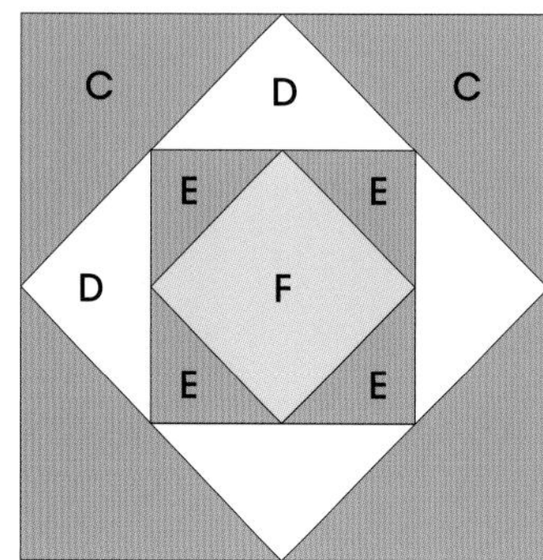


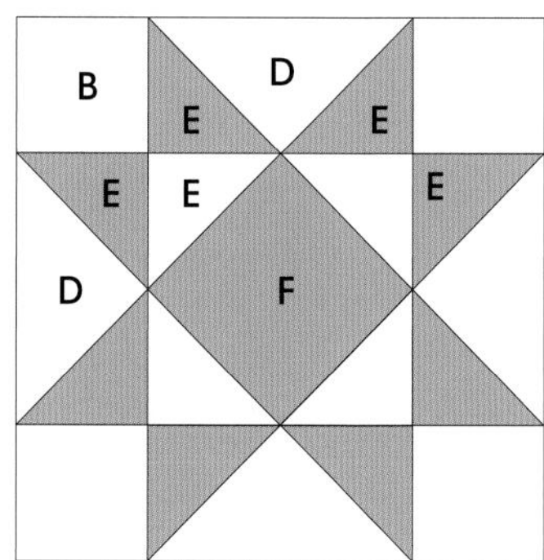

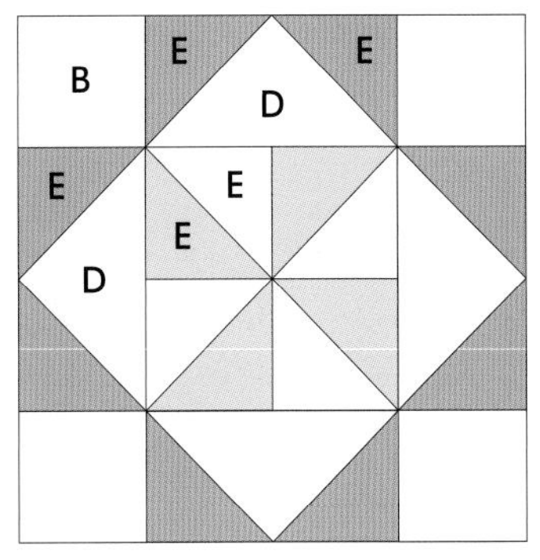
B
E
E
D
E
E
E
D

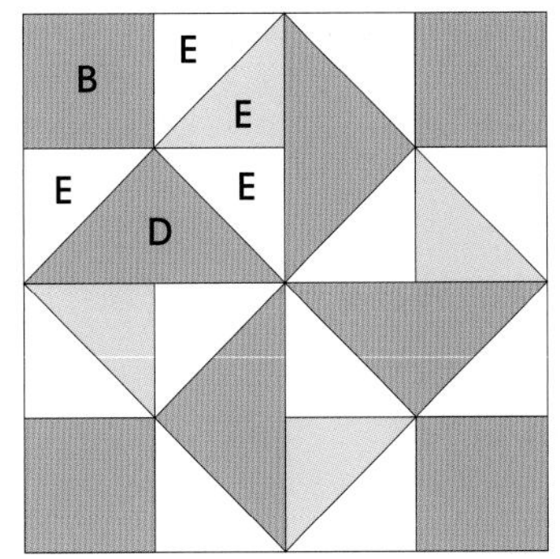
B
E
E
E
E
D

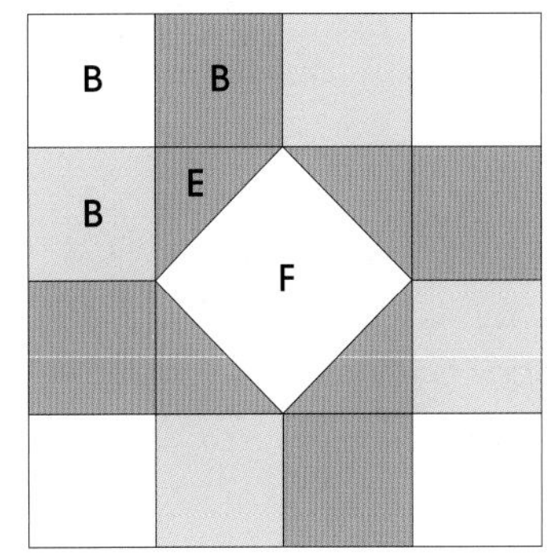
B
B
B
E
F

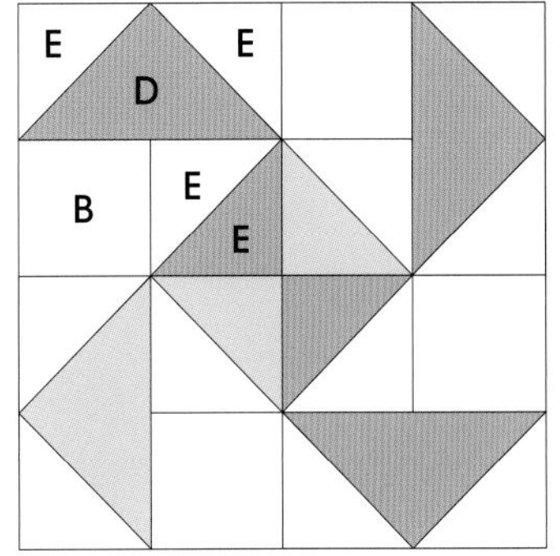
E
E
D
B
E
E

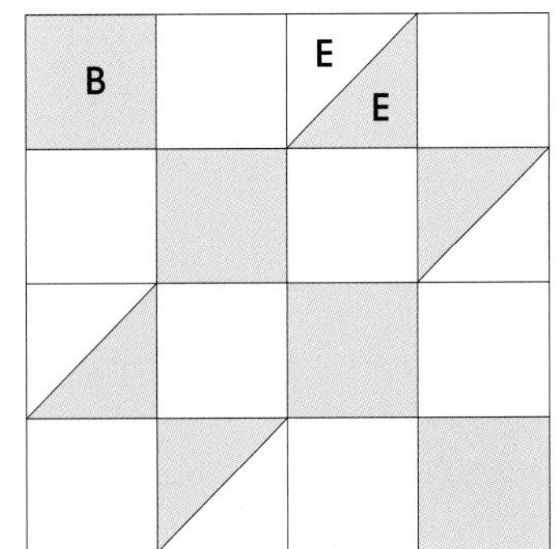
B
E
E

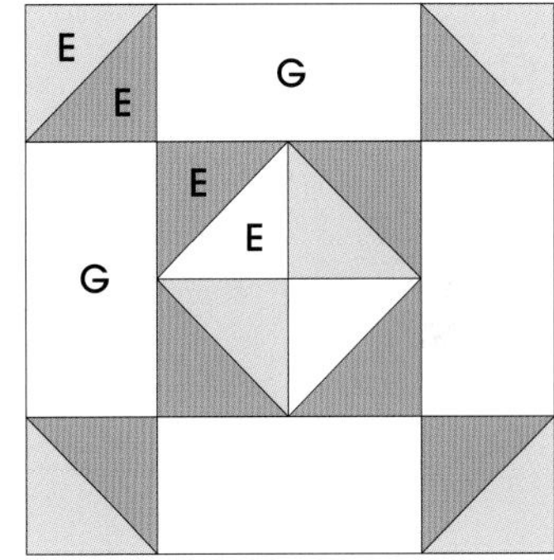
E
E
G
E
E
G

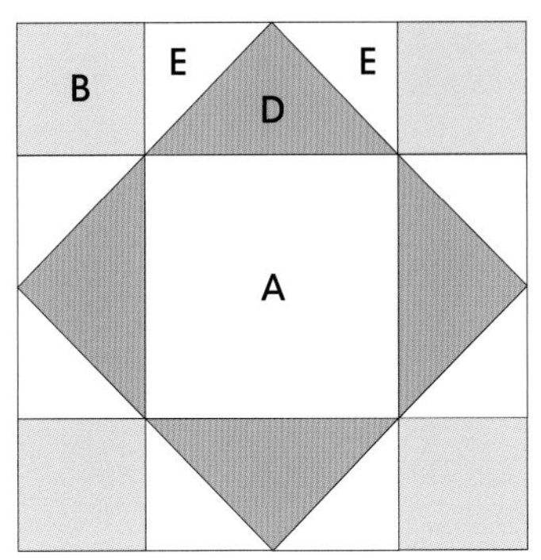
B
E
E
D
A

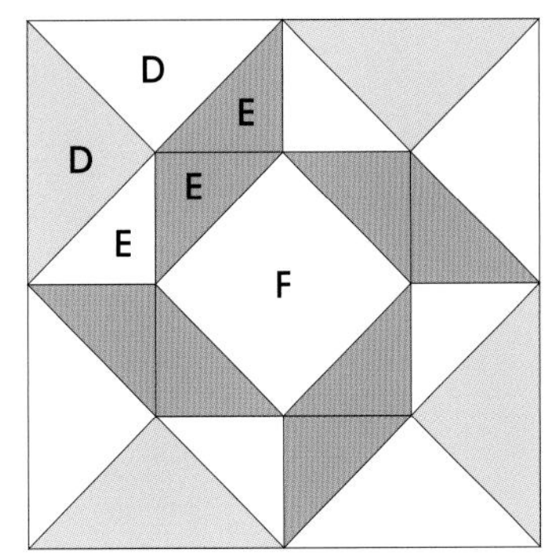
D
E
D
E
E
F

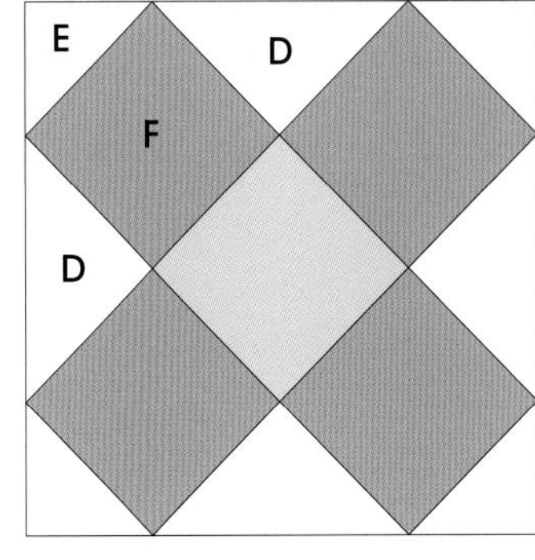
E
D
F
D

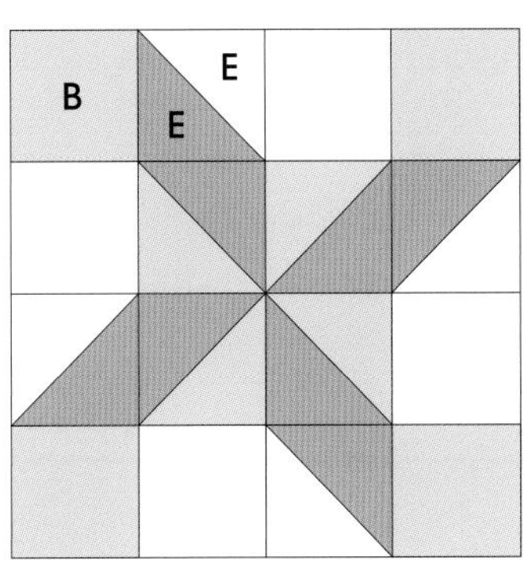
B
E
E

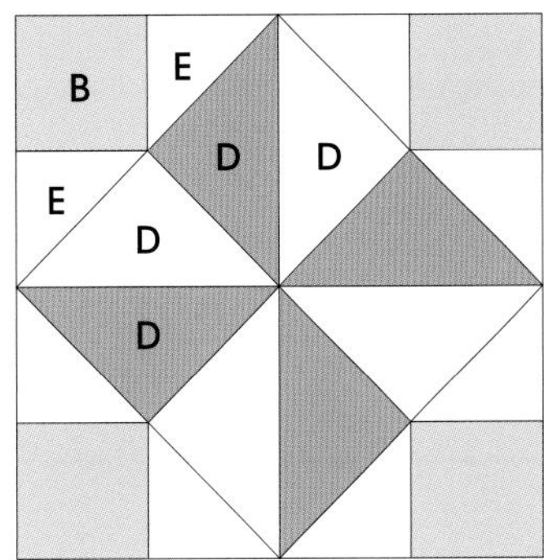
B
E
D
D
E
D
D

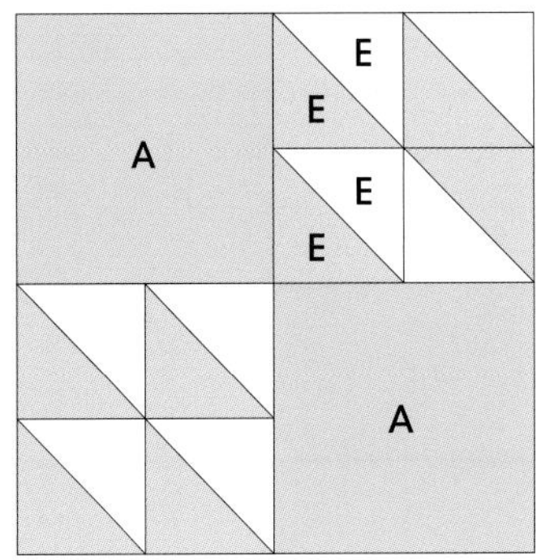
A
E
E
E
E
A

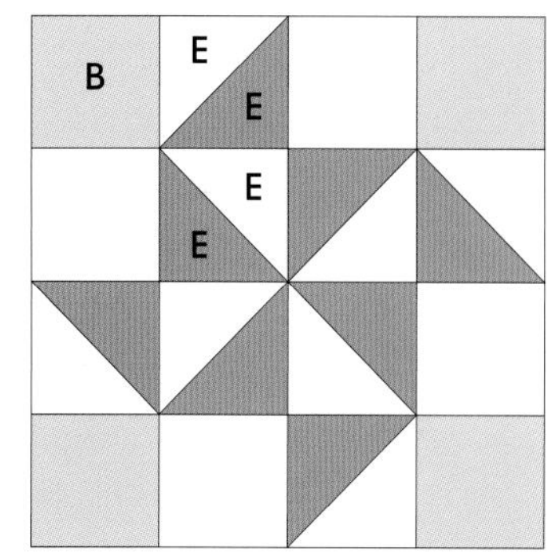
B
E
E
E
E

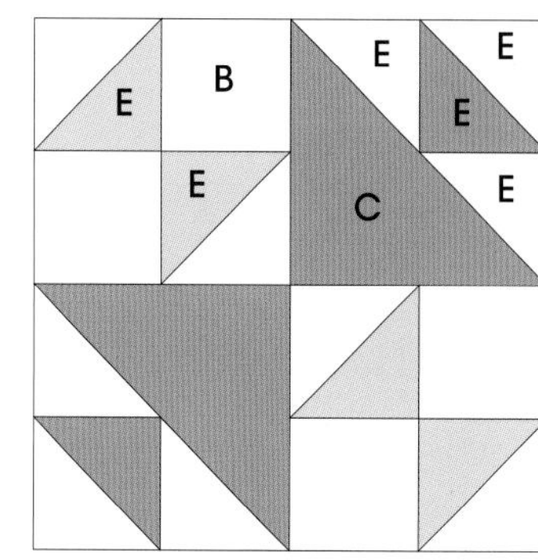
E
B
E
E
E
E
C
E

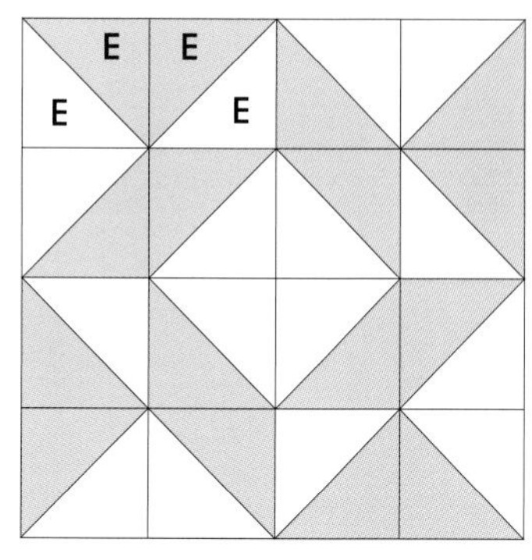
E
E
E
E

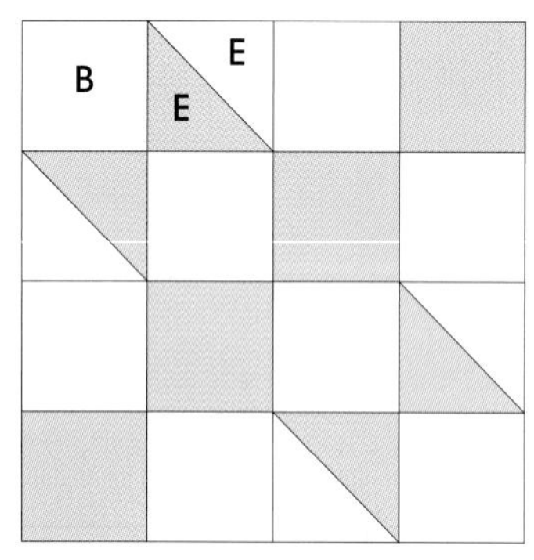
B
E
E

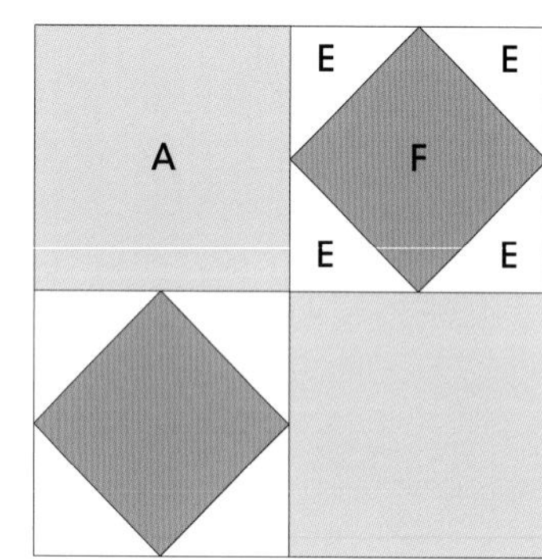
E
E
A
F
E
E

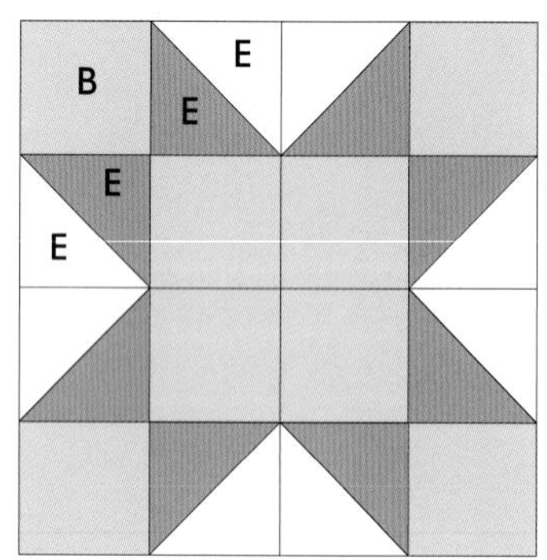
B
E
E
E
E

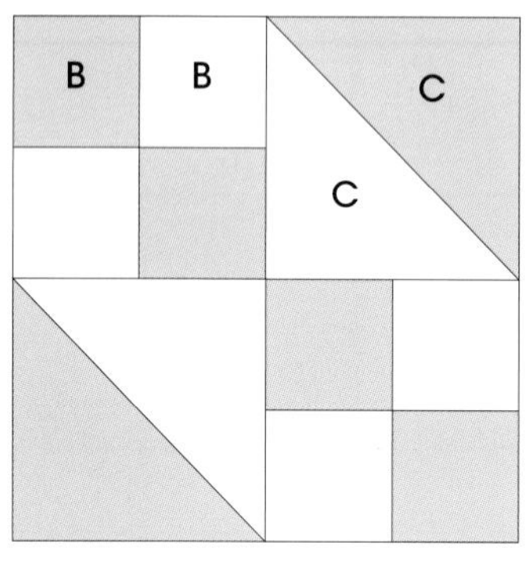
B
B
C
C

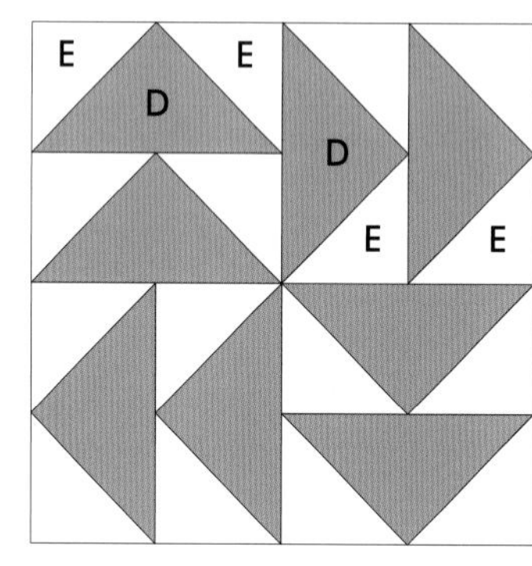
E
E
D
D
E
E

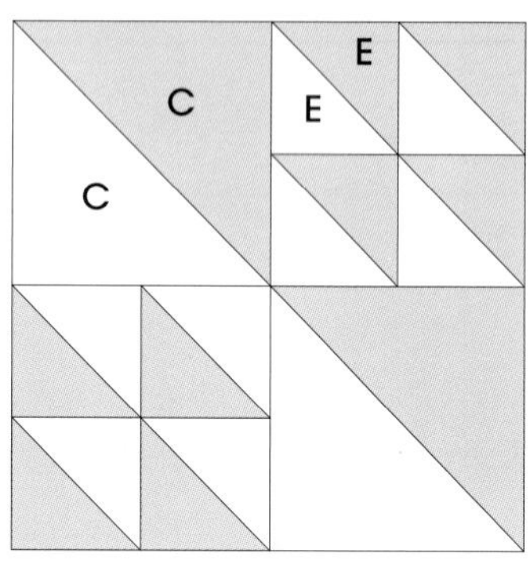
C
E
E
C

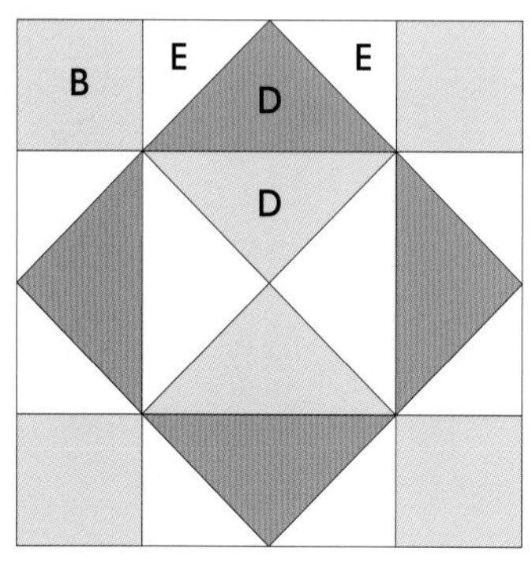
B
E
E
D
D

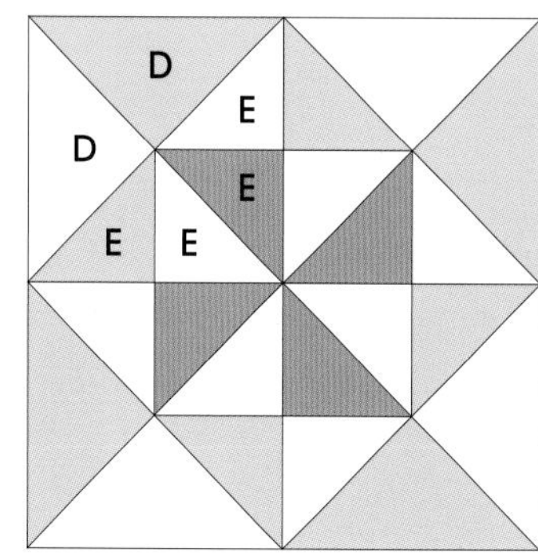
D
E
D
E
E
E

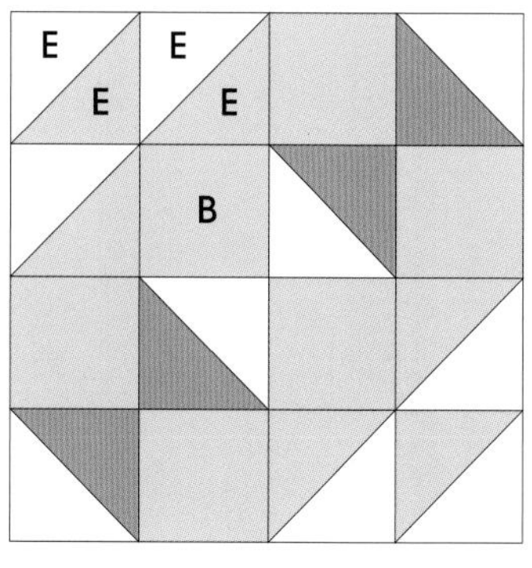
E
E
E
E
B

# Nine-patch blocks

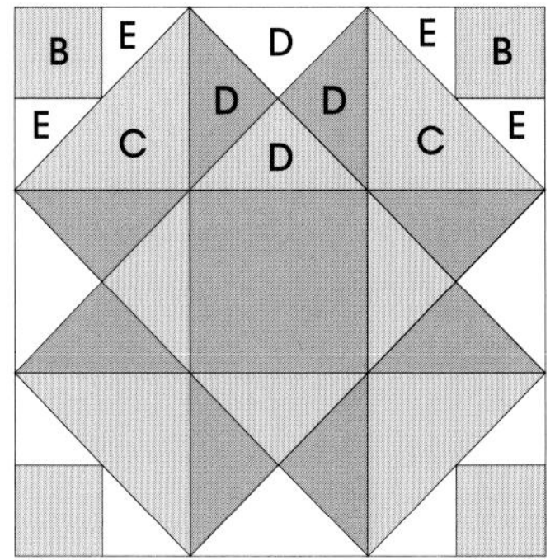


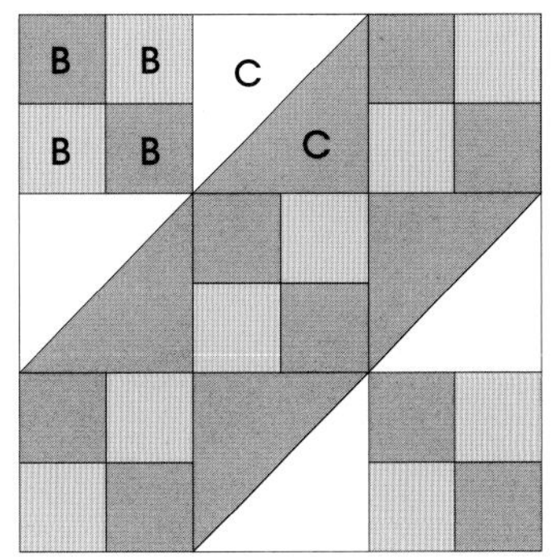


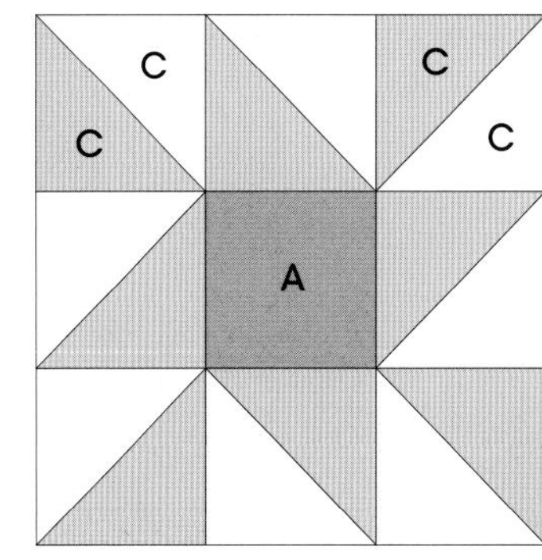


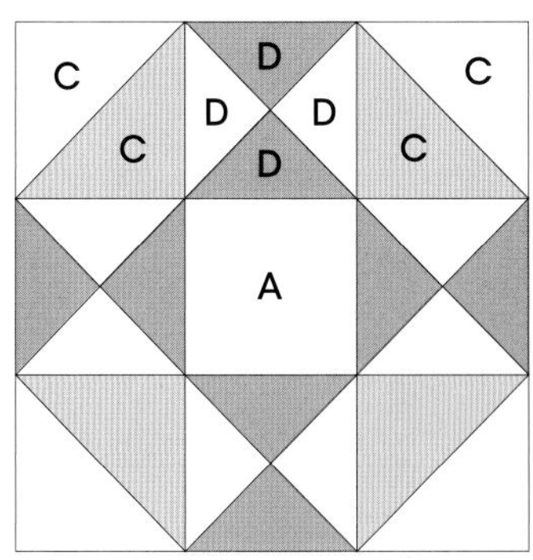


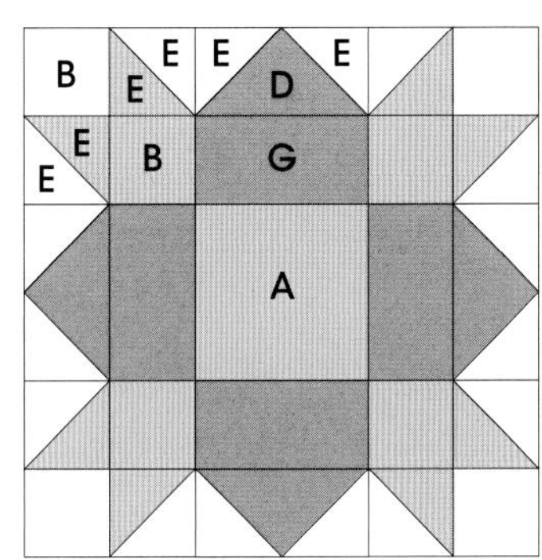


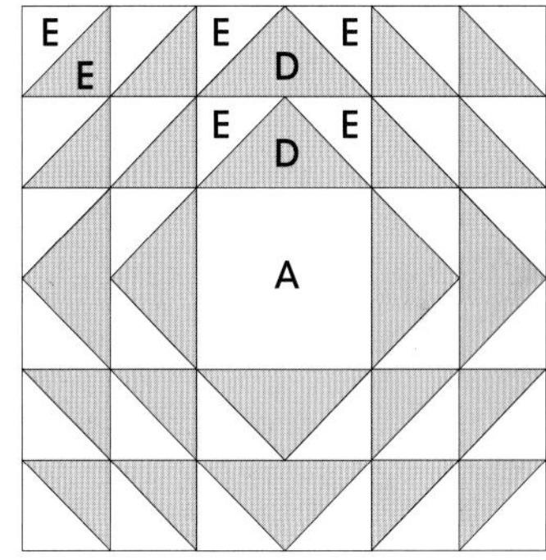


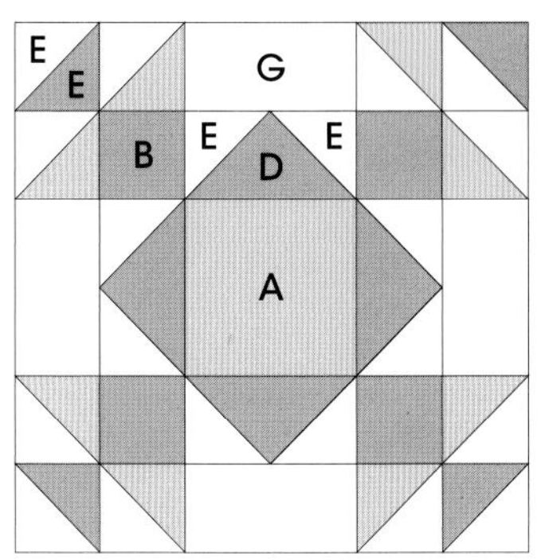


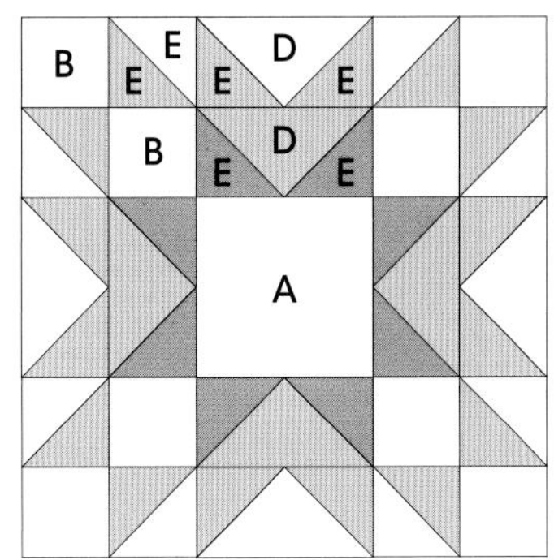


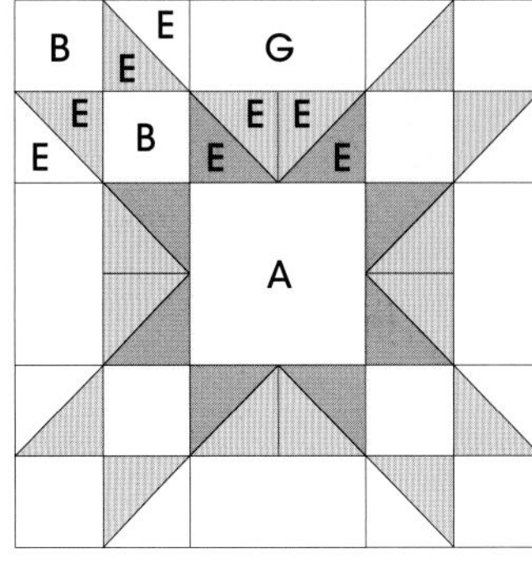


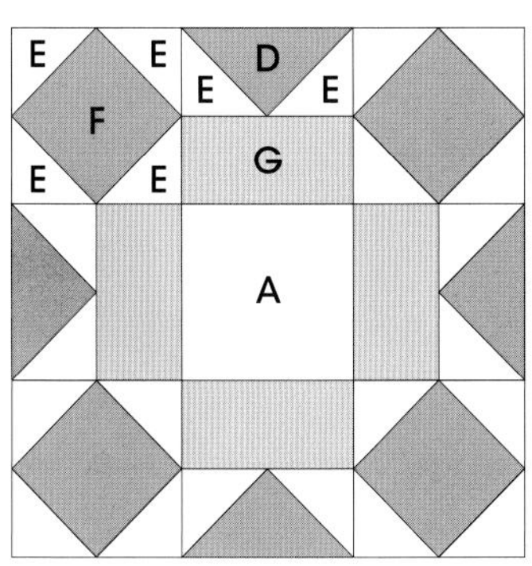


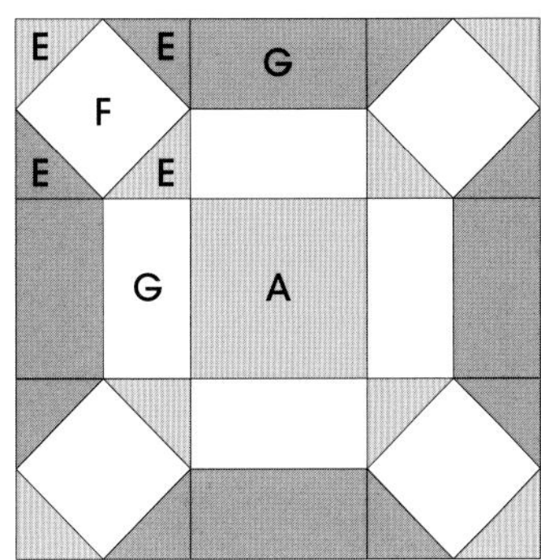


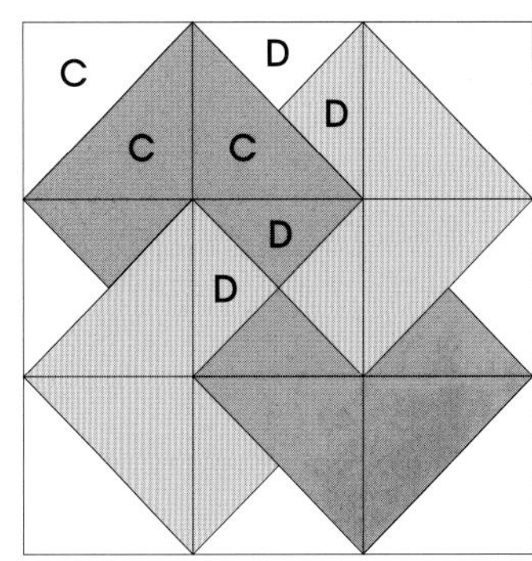

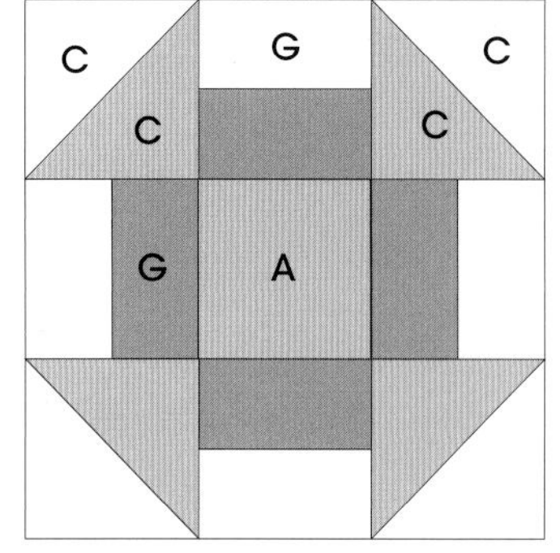
C G C
C C
G A

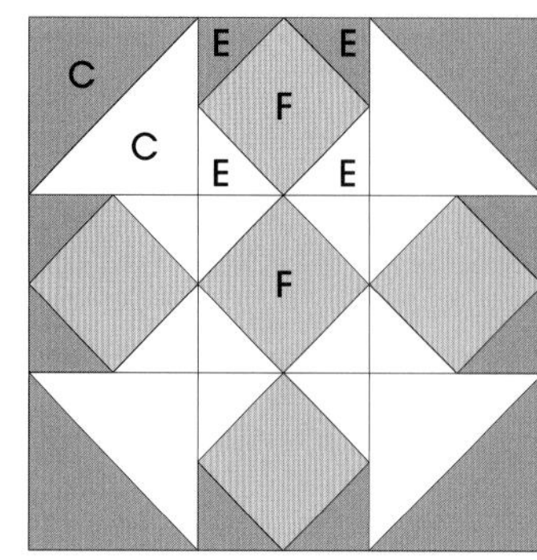
E E
C F
C
E E
F

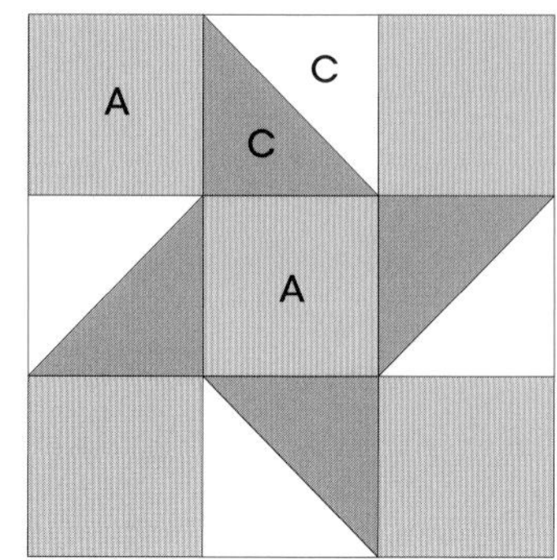
C
A
C
A

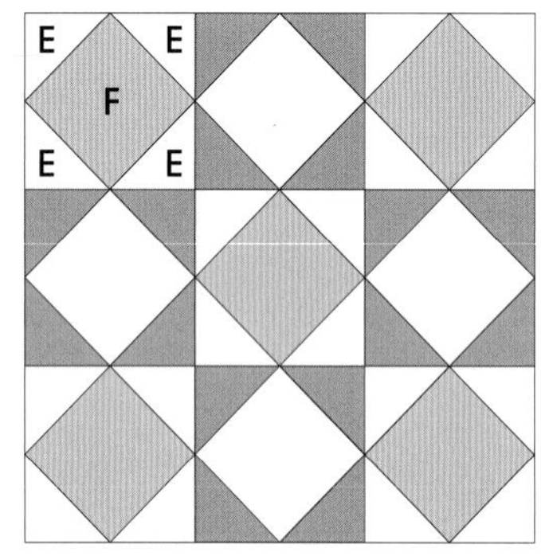
E E
F
E E

B E E E
F
E
C
E E

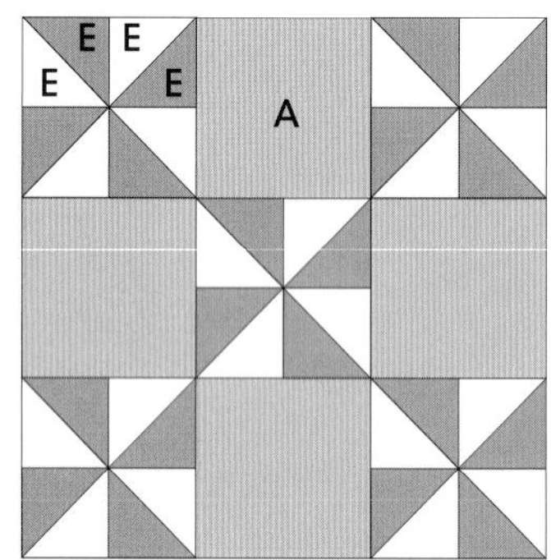
E E
E E
A

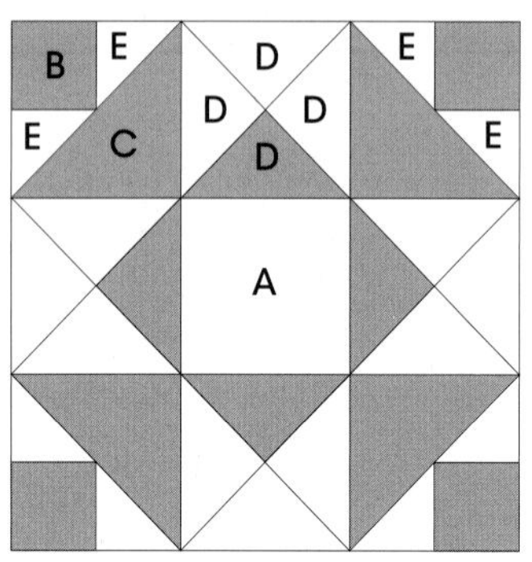
B E D E
D D
E C D E
A

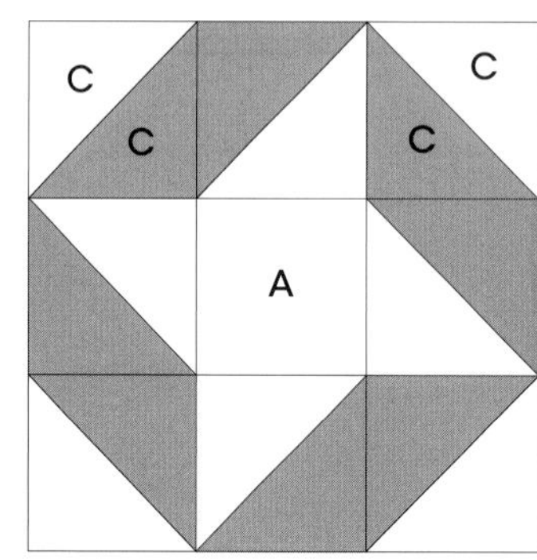
C C
C C
A

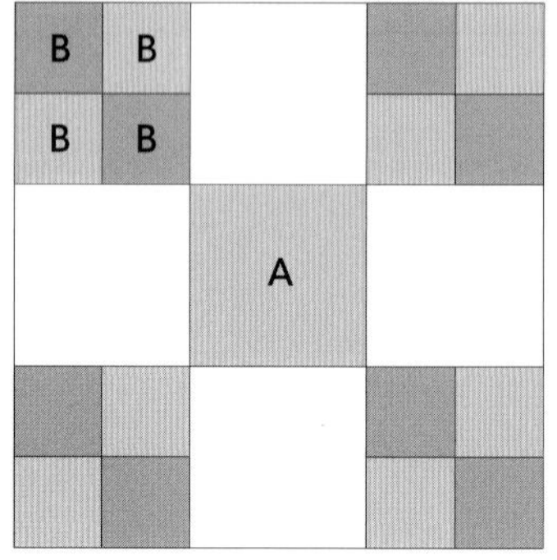
B B
B B
A

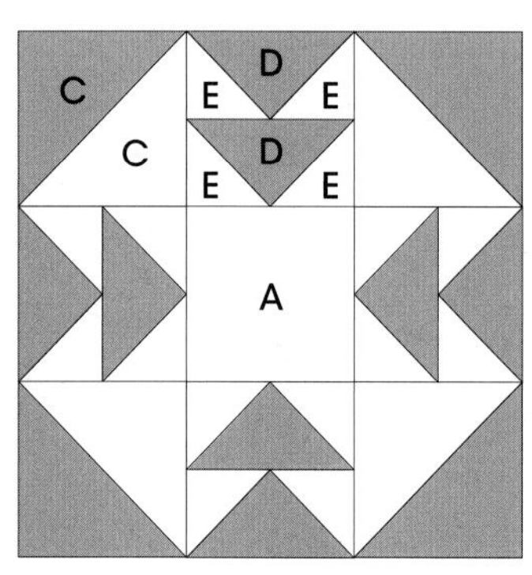
D
C
E E
C D
E E
A

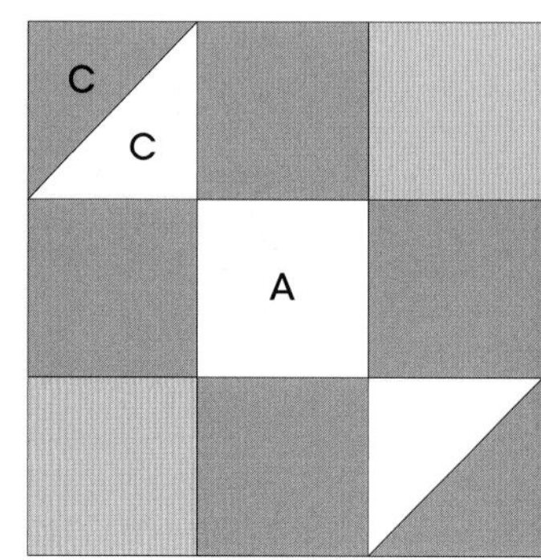
C
C
A

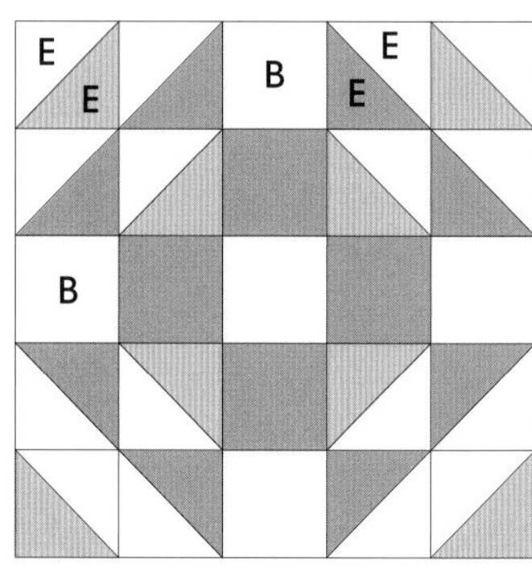
E E
E B E
B

# Simple units

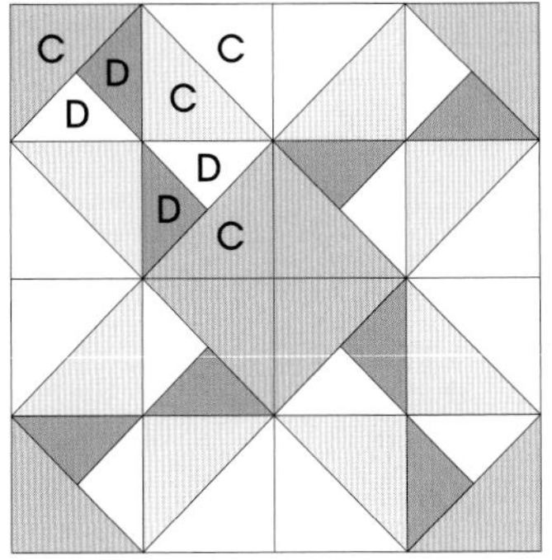


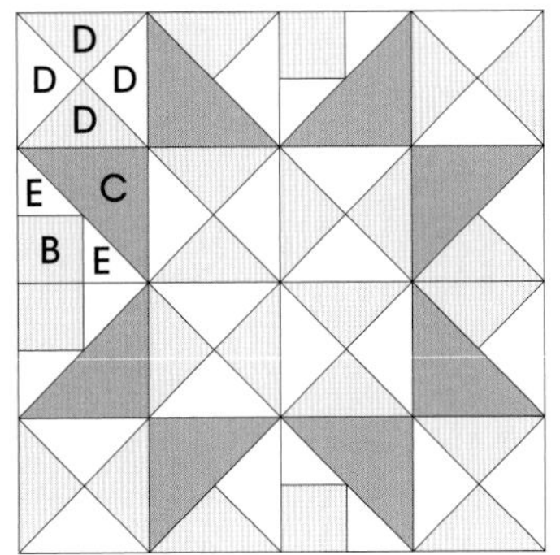


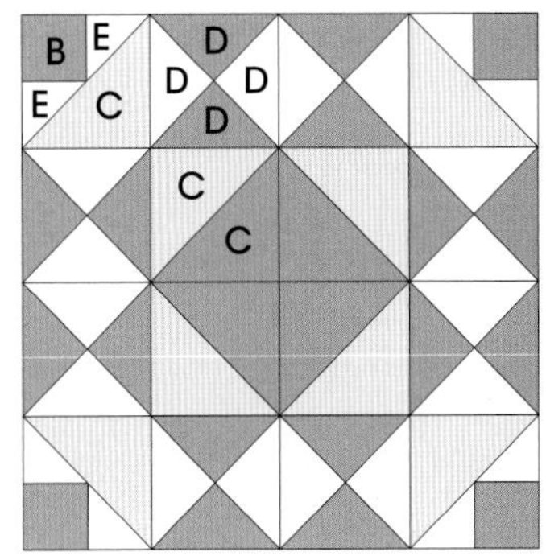


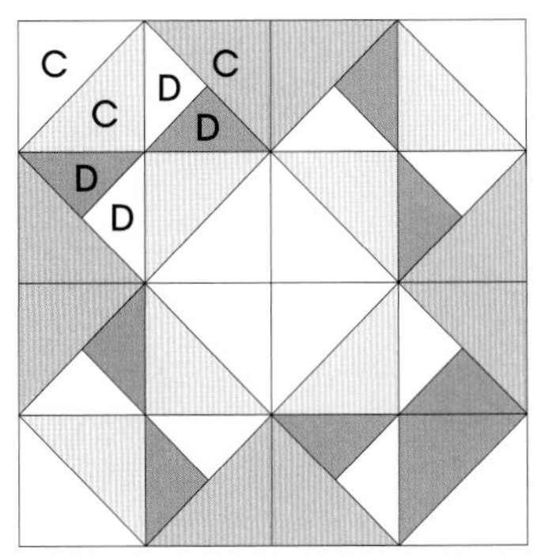


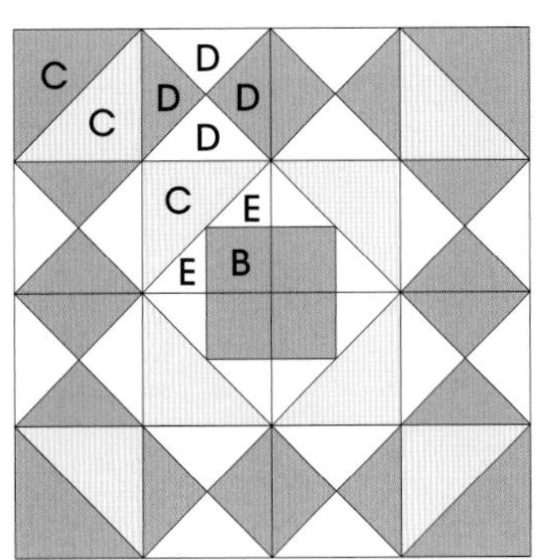


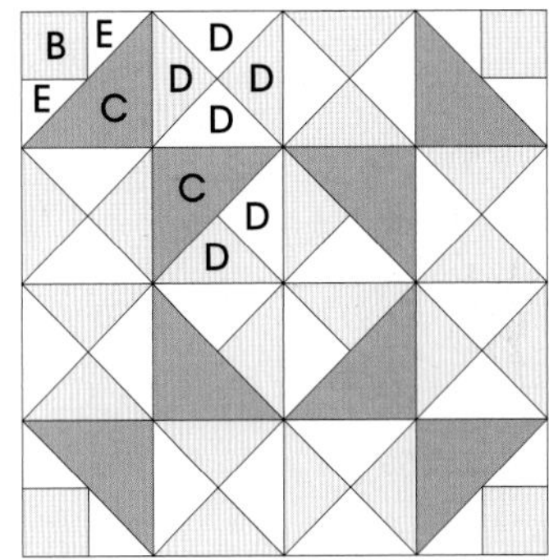


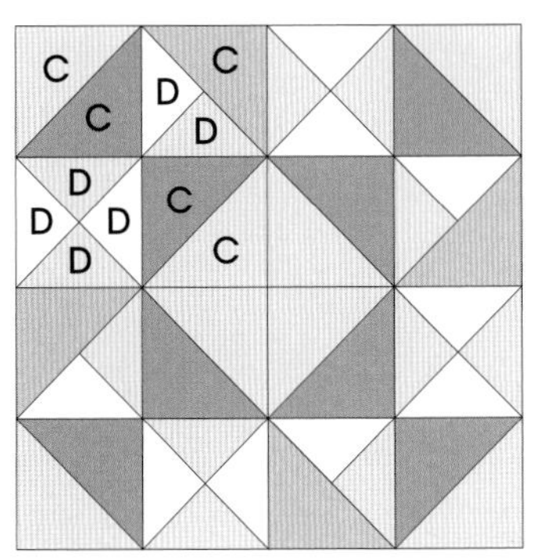


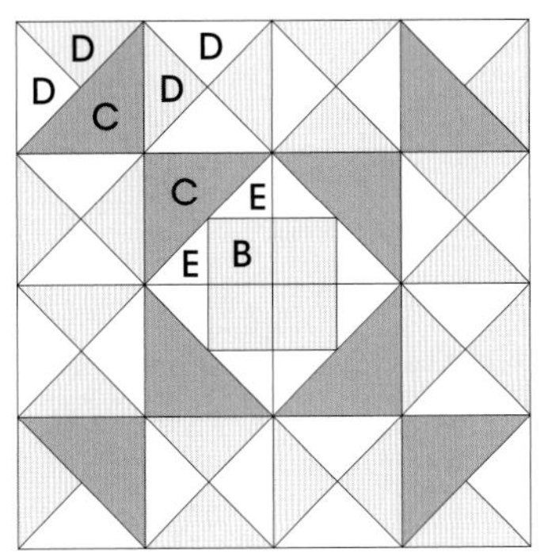


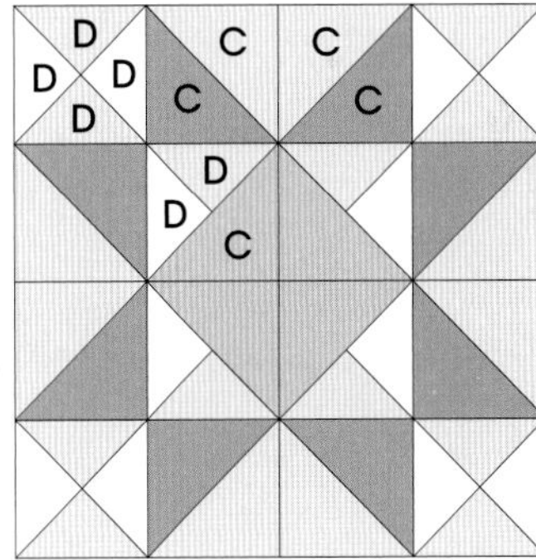


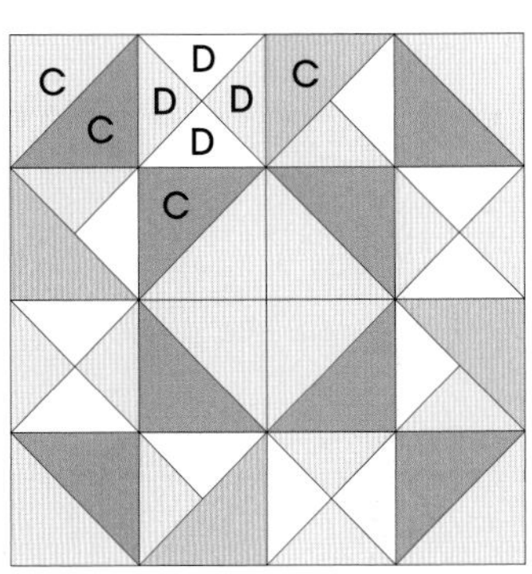


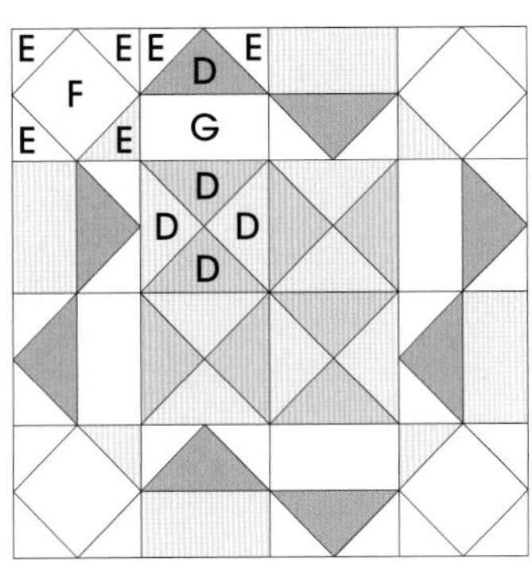


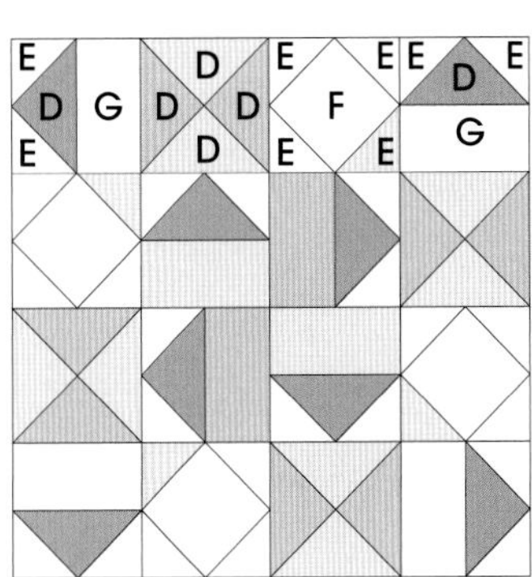

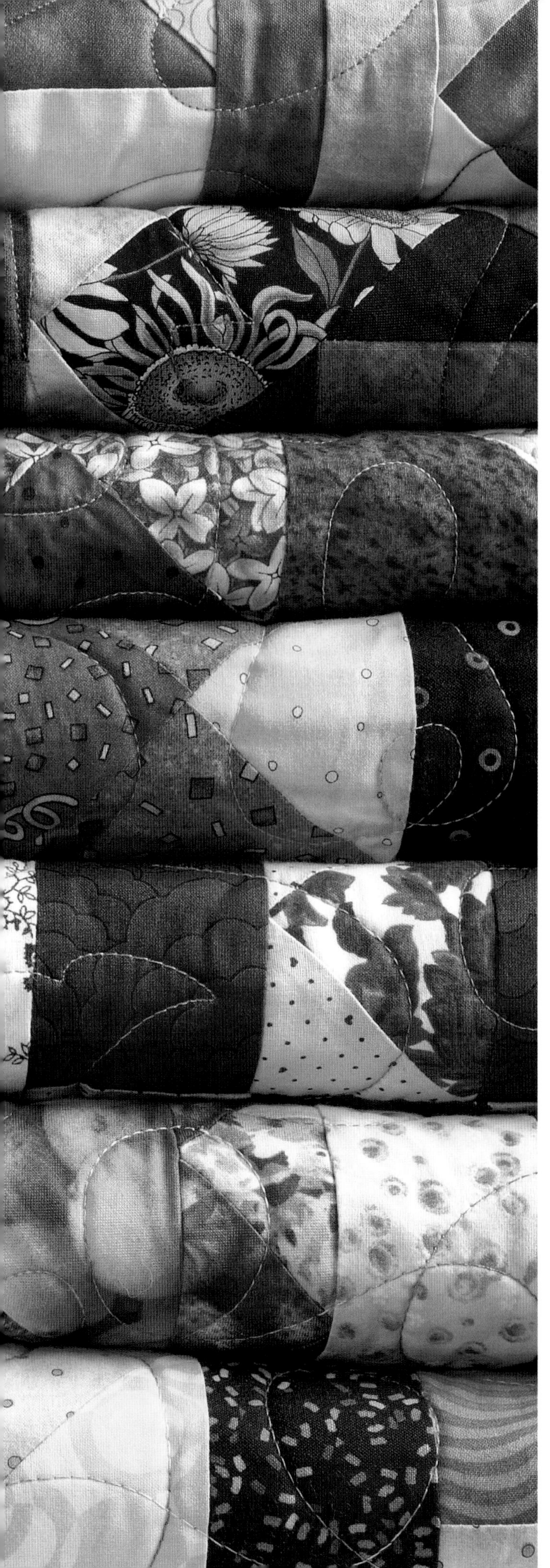

# Fast Quilts

In the following pages you will find twelve quilt projects of varying sizes and styles, all of which were made using fat quarters and the cutting plan on page 17. Amongst these feature quilts are pictures of a further twenty quilts, briefly described, which give you some idea of the exciting range of possibilities the cutting plan provides.

From pages 100–110 three extra projects are described, showing different aspects and developments of the 'cut-first-decide-later' concept. African Adventure is an example of a quilt made by cutting all the fat quarters into one single shape, while Tessellating Ts and Churn Dash show how you can cut all the specific shapes for a single block from stacked quarters.

# Blue and Lime Delight

This was the first quilt I made using the prototype cutting plan and concept and I found it both fast and fascinating to do. If I had begun in the traditional way, cutting specific shapes from chosen fabrics to make pre-selected blocks, several hours would have been spent choosing fabrics and several more precious hours deciding on the position of those fabrics in the blocks and so on and so forth. It was so much fun just making up easy four-patch blocks almost at random from the cut shapes that I couldn't wait to begin on the next project using the same principle! When I had put the blocks together with their surrounding strips and 'piano key' border I began to realize that this 'cut-first-decide-later' idea offered an effortlessly simple way to mix and balance fabrics – magic!

*Designed and pieced by Barbara Chainey, quilted courtesy of The Bramble Patch*

*"This is the quilt that started it all. Once the pieces were cut from a selection of lively fat quarters it all went together in super-quick time – almost instant gratification!"*

**You will need**

- Six fat quarters for the blocks
- Four fat quarters in co-ordinating prints for the setting and border
- Backing fabric, 54in x 44in
- Batting/wadding, 54in x 44in
- Binding fabric (see page 118)

| | |
|---|---|
| **Quilt size:** | 51in long x 41in wide |
| **Block size:** | 8in square finished |
| **Skill rating:** | Easy |

# Making the blocks

1 Spray starch and press all quarters carefully, select the six quarters you want to use for the blocks and set aside the remaining four quarters.

2 Stack the six quarters on your cutting board and follow the cutting plan (Fig 3 on page 17). Because this quilt was made from the prototype cutting plan I made a number of mistakes, one of which was to be over-selective of shapes and fabrics to use in the blocks – this meant that there were a lot of pieces left over. You might plan to make extra blocks and use these for matching cushions or pillows – or even to start another project.

3 Place all the cut shapes on to your full-sized map (see page 20) then you can begin arranging selected shapes into simple blocks. It is a good idea to lay out several blocks at once rather than one at a time as this avoids undue repetition and helps you to get a good feel for how the shapes work together. The blocks for this quilt are shown on these two pages, and you can either refer to these or make other block arrangements of your own. Note that two of the blocks (1 and 8) are repeated. Use the 'exploded' diagrams shown below each of the pieced blocks to guide you in construction and refer to pages 20–23 for cutting and piecing guidance.

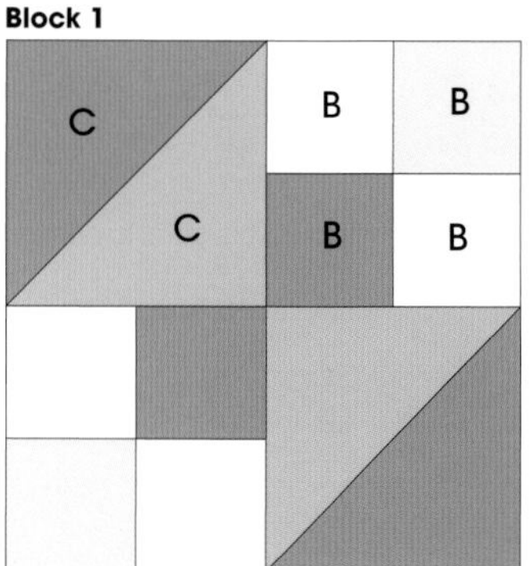


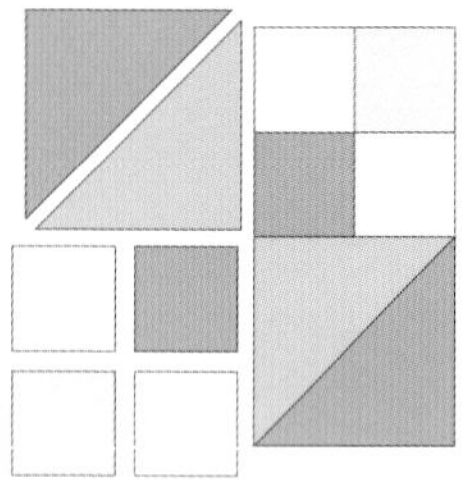

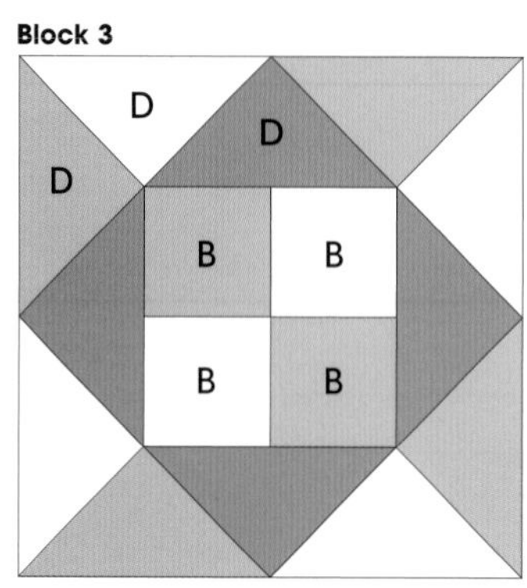


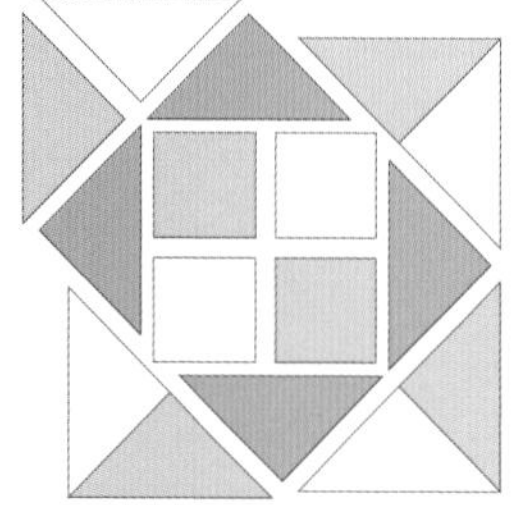

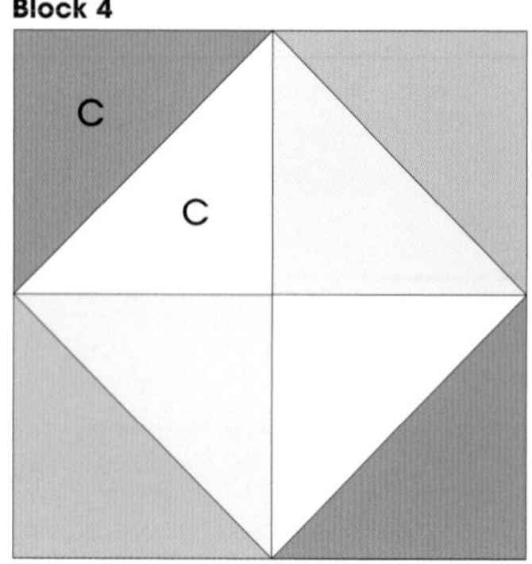


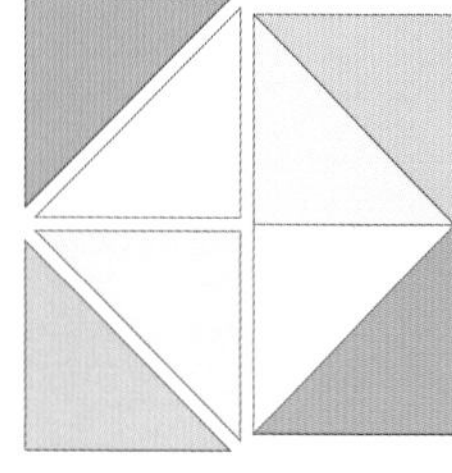

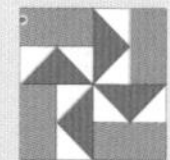

### Block diagrams

Blue and Lime Delight uses ten blocks, shown here. Blocks 1 and 8 are repeated (see layout, page 36). See the 'exploded' diagrams for block construction.

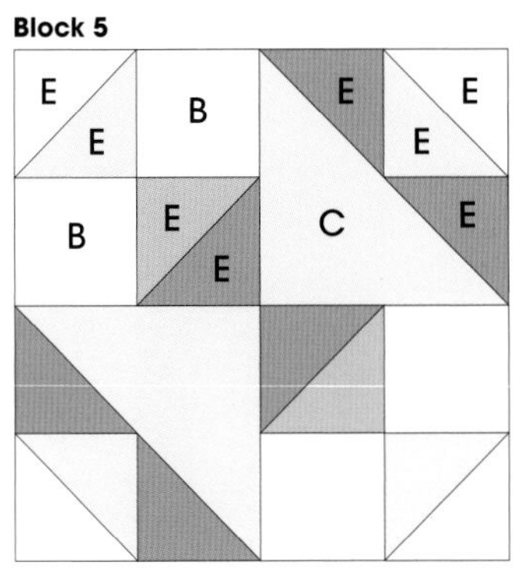


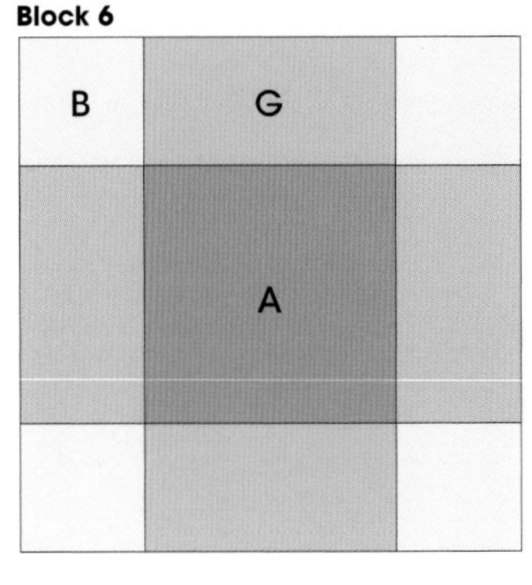


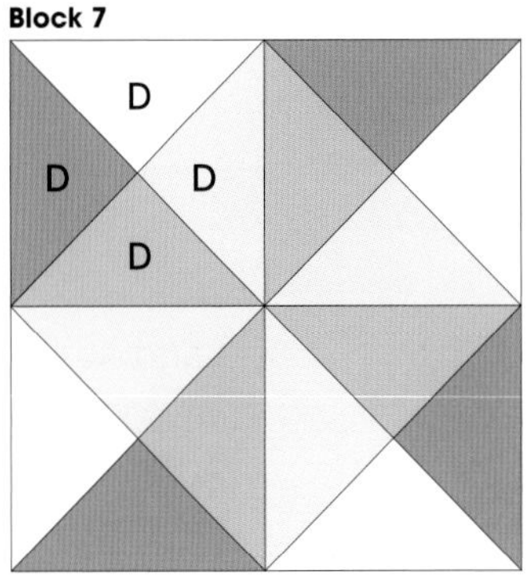


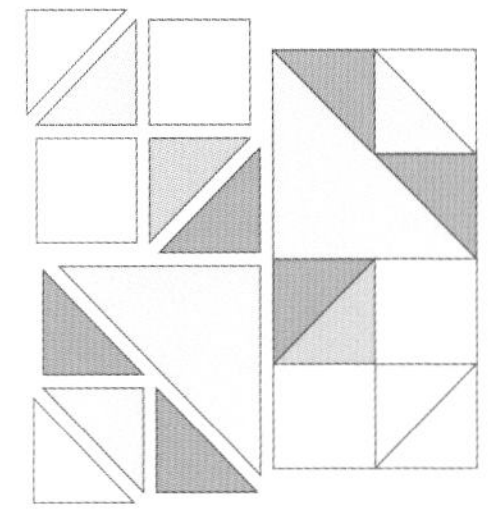

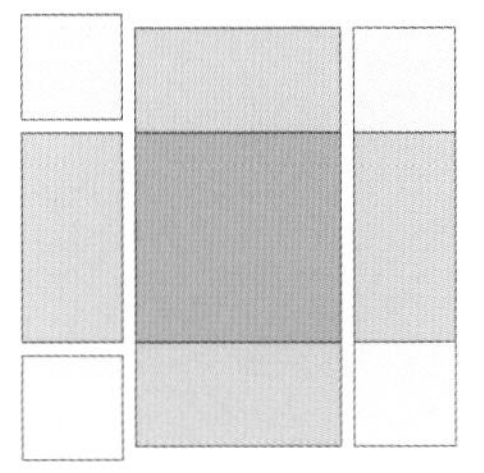

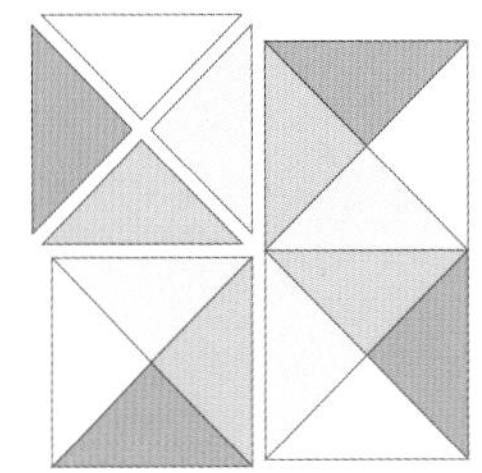

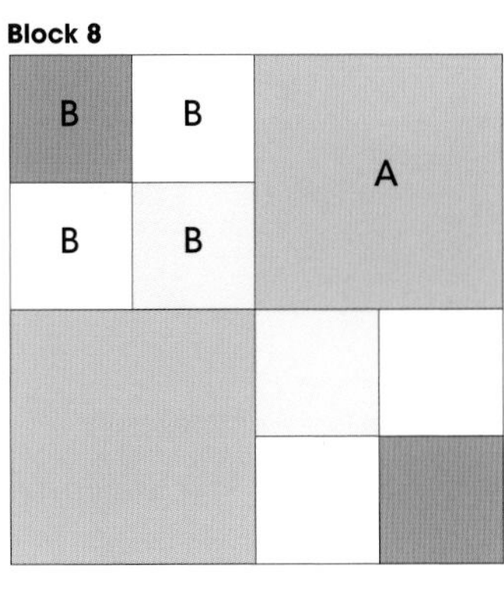


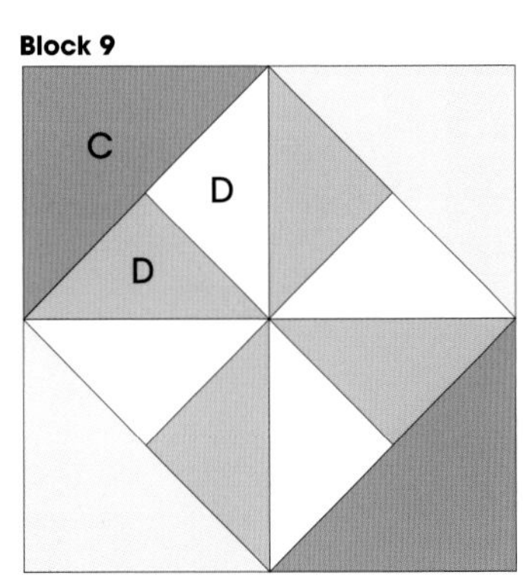


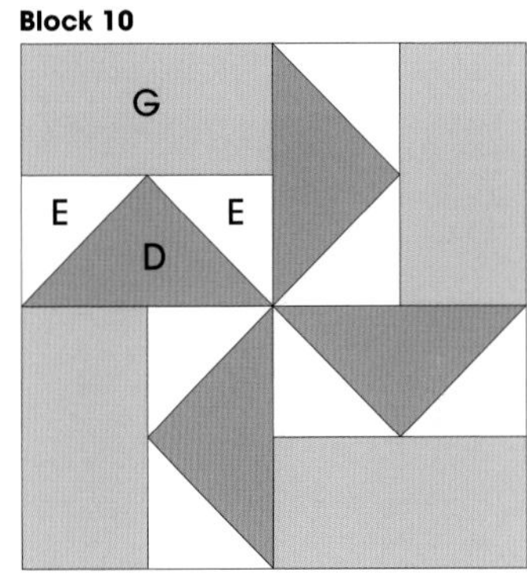


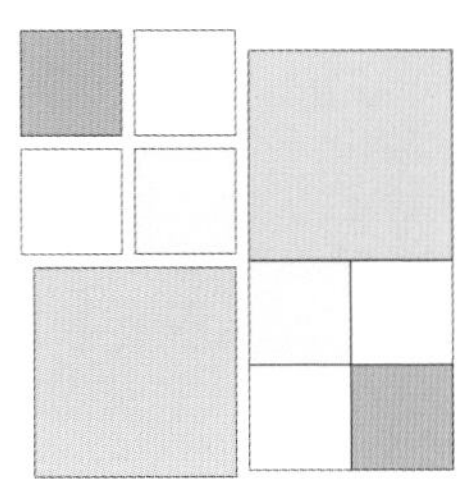

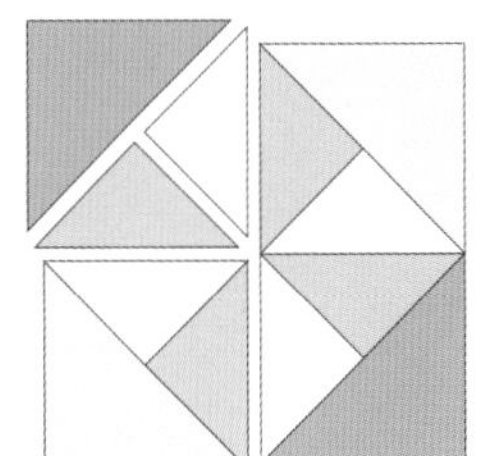

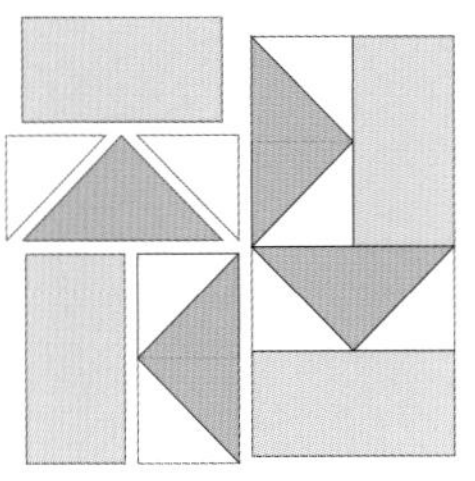

## Putting it all together

4 When all the blocks are complete, give them a spritz of starch and press carefully. Trim away any remaining threads, then check the measurement of the blocks, trimming and squaring up if required.

5 Set the blocks out on a design wall or similar planning space and move them around until you are completely satisfied with the arrangement. From each of the four fat quarters you set aside earlier cut 1½in wide strips to use as frames for the blocks – I chose to use a different print for each side of each block. (See page 111 for further framing ideas.) Press and trim the framed blocks.

6 Join the blocks together into four rows of three, then join these four rows together (see Fig 1). From the inner border fabric cut 1¾in wide strips and stitch first the two sides and then the top and bottom strips into position. The colour confidence feature, opposite, shows the same layout but using three different colourways.

7 Cut all remaining fabric into strips 1½in and 2½in wide and piece these strips together to make stripped bands which can be used to make the quilt borders. I chose to vary the width of the strips and arrange colours and widths randomly because this was an easy way to include leftover strips from the block frames. To do the same you will need two pieced border strips 5½in wide x 42in long and two border strips 5½in wide x 53in long – these measurements are approximate and have a small margin for error. I recommend that you work with the specific measurements of your own quilt for this final stage – you may, for instance, be able to cut slightly deeper borders or prefer something narrower for your quilt.

8 Stitch the border bands into place, then trim edges and threads as necessary before pressing the completed quilt top.

**Fig 1** *Layout of Blue and Lime Delight with sashing and borders*

*The traditional four-patch blocks used in this quilt were fast and easy to piece but the position and placement of the fabric values are not what I would normally have chosen. Making blocks from a finite number of cut shapes meant that I had to be freer and more creative with my choices and it certainly got me thinking!*

## Finishing off

9 Layer the quilt backing, batting and quilt top together and baste or secure the layers according to your preference (see page 117) for the method of quilting you will be using. Quilt in your chosen style (see page 118).

10 Finish by binding and labelling your quilt (see page 118).

## Colour confidence

Here you can see how this design would look in three different colourways: first in warm, cheerful reds; then in neutral, cool and crisp bright blues and finally in a softer palette of sage and heather tones. The colours in these illustrations are not precise like-for-like replacements from the original quilt but they do give a good feel for the sometimes surprising changes and effects that colour can make. Why not try out your own variations and see how your colour choices affect the result?

# Country Charm

I wanted to see what would happen if I laid out just two traditional-style blocks and made as many of these as possible from the cut shapes. Halfway through making the blocks this seemed to be a really great idea, but when all the blocks were finished and laid edge to edge in a basic alternating set the whole thing just looked boring – something to do with the medium and dark tones of the fabrics I had chosen perhaps. Eventually this on-point strippy solution presented itself and had far more appeal than the first plan.

*Designed and pieced by Barbara Chainey,*
*special thanks to Ann Jermey for the hand quilting*

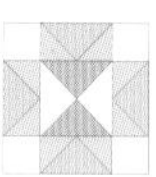   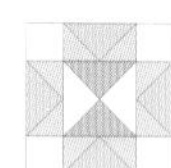

*"Plaids, checks and warm country colours are always appealing and over the years I've often felt the need to buy 'just a few' and add them to a growing section of my stash. This quick quilt provided the perfect excuse to start using some of them."*

**You will need**

- Nine fat quarters for the blocks
- Fabric for setting triangles for blocks, thirty 7in squares
- Sashing fabric, four strips 2½in x 57in
- Inner border fabric, two strips 2½in x 44in
- Outer border fabric, two strips 6in x 60in and two strips 6in x 54in
- Backing fabric, 74in x 58in
- Batting, 74in x 58in
- Binding fabric (see page 118)

**Quilt size:** 70in long x 54in wide
**Block size:** 8in square finished
**Skill rating:** Beginner to improver

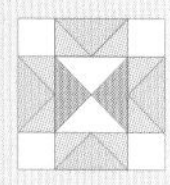

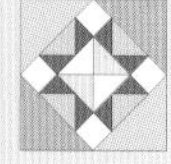

## Making the blocks

1 Starch and press all nine fat quarters before making two separate stacks of five and four fat quarters each. Now use the cutting plan (Fig 3 on page 17) to cut up both stacks.

2 Use the two blocks shown in Fig 1 as a guide and lay out a total of seven of block 1 and eight of block 2. Alternatively, you could refer to the Discover the Possibilities section on page 24 and choose a different pair of blocks.

3 Make up all the blocks using the exploded diagrams in Fig 1 as a guide to construction sequence, referring to pages 20–23 for cutting and piecing guidance. Press all the blocks before measuring and trimming them to size as necessary.

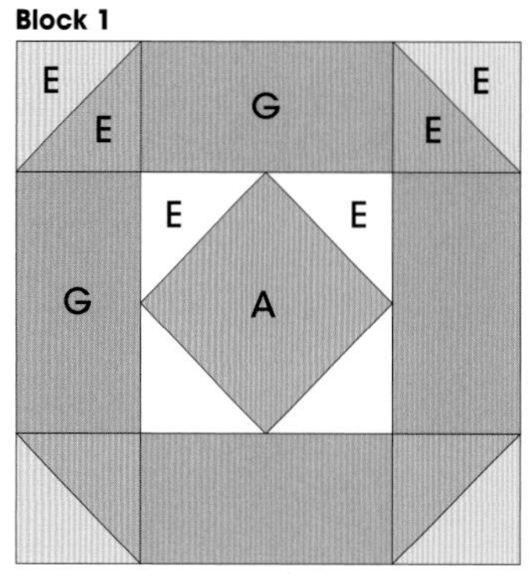


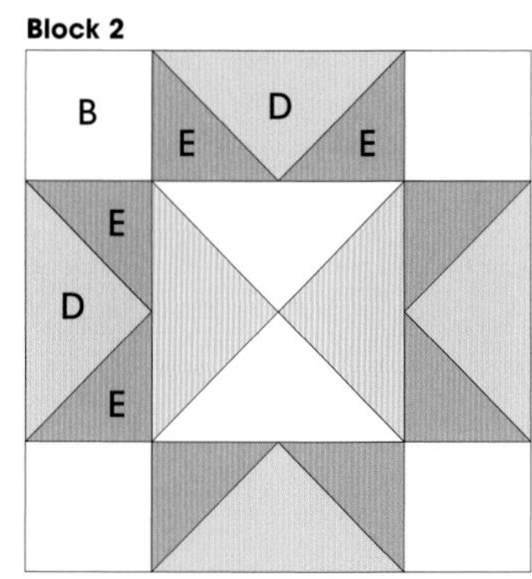


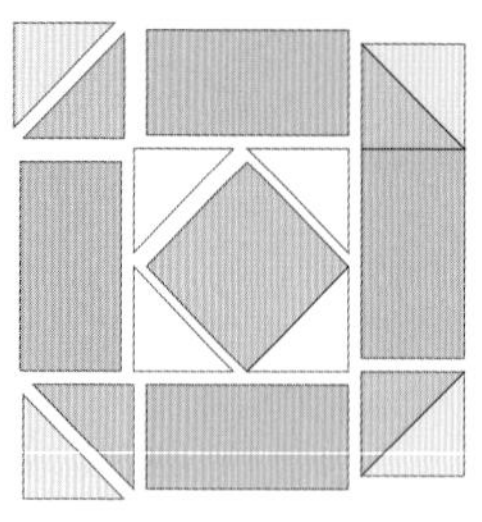

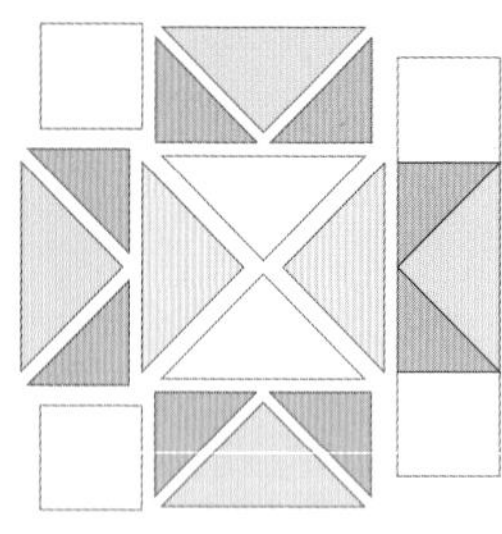

**Fig 1** *The two blocks that make up the quilt showing the pieced blocks and then the 'exploded' view. You will need seven of block 1 and eight of block 2*

## Putting it all together

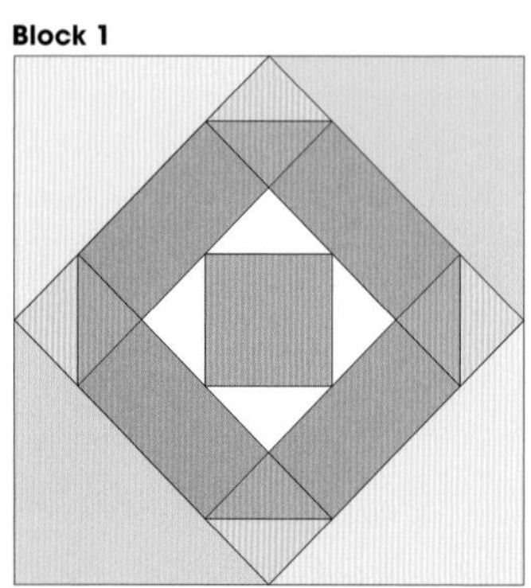


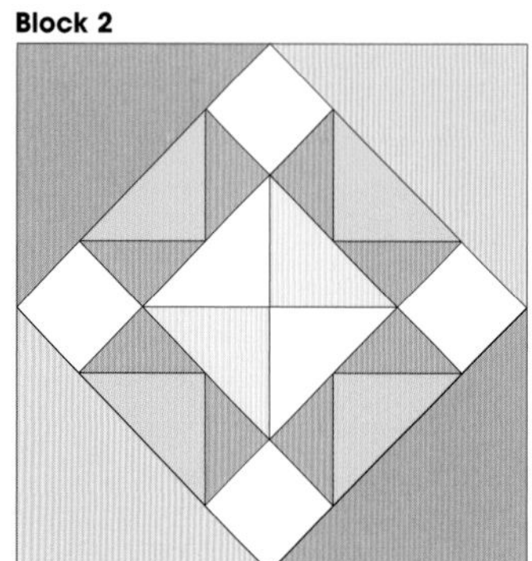


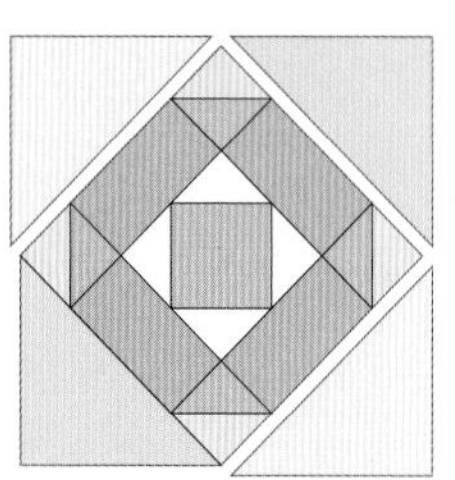

**Fig 2** *Joining the triangles to the blocks*

4 Cut a total of thirty 7in squares from a variety of plaid and check fabrics – I used only eight different fabrics and could easily have used a much wider selection. Cut each of these squares diagonally once to give a total of sixty triangles. Now join four different fabric triangles to each 8in block as shown in Fig 2.

5 Join the blocks into three strips of five blocks referring to Fig 3 for the placement of the blocks. You might prefer to use the alternative placement shown in Fig 4.

Fig 3 *Joining the blocks into three strips of five*

**Fig 4** *An alternative layout for the placement of the blocks*

6 Cut two sashing strips 2½in x 57in and join the three strips of blocks together (see Fig 5). Cut two inner border strips 2½in x 57in and stitch to the left and right sides. Cut two inner border strips 2½in x 44in and stitch to the top and bottom. Cut four main border strips: two 6in x 60in for the left and right sides and two 6in x 54in for the top and bottom. Stitch all border strips into place and press.

## Finishing off

7 Give the quilt top a final press, remembering to trim any remaining loose threads before layering with the batting and backing and quilting according to your preference (see pages 117 and 118).

8 Finish by binding and labelling your quilt (see page 118).

**Fig 5** *Layout of Country Charm with sashing and borders*

# Nine by Nine

Jean Ann got very excited when she saw how her initial cutting plan had been developed and was determined not to miss out on any of the fun of making quilts for this book. Always a prolific quilter (her all-time record during a visit to my home, is nine quilt tops in five days), she quickly pieced three quilt tops using the amended version of her plan! Jean Ann played with various block layouts and finally decided to make just one basic block and see what small variations could be made within it. Can you spot the repeated blocks? This self-imposed restriction of a single block layout meant that she did not use every single piece that was cut from the stack of ten whimsical bright prints. All the leftover pieces were quickly put to excellent use to make a baby quilt.

*Designed and pieced by Jean Ann Wright,*
*quilted by Shannon Baker*

*"Prolific quilter Jean Ann Wright used a collection of sunny yet sharp-coloured fabrics to give her trademark zing and zest to this stylish interpretation of the traditional Ohio Star block."*

**You will need**

- Ten fat quarters for the blocks
- Sashing fabric, twelve strips 2¼in x 13in
- Inner border fabric, four strips 2¼in x 44in for inner border
- Outer border fabric, cut or piece four strips 4½in x 52in
- Backing fabric, 54in square
- Batting/wadding, 54in square
- Binding fabric (see page 118)

**Quilt size:** 50in square
**Block size:** 12in square finished
**Skill rating:** Beginner to improver

# Making the blocks

1 Spray starch and press your chosen fat quarters then stack them on your cutting mat and cut according to the cutting plan (Fig 3 on page 17).

2 Use the seven blocks shown on these two pages as a guide to laying out a total of nine Ohio Star variation blocks. Jean Ann made three differently coloured versions of block 1 to complete her nine block arrangement. Once you have made your own block arrangements the piecing can begin – use the 'exploded' blocks shown below each pieced diagram as a guide for the construction sequence, and refer to pages 20–23 for cutting and piecing guidance. Press all blocks before measuring them and trimming them to size.

## Block diagrams

Nine by Nine uses seven blocks, shown here. Block 1 is repeated three times (see layout diagram, opposite). See the 'exploded' diagrams for construction.

Block 1

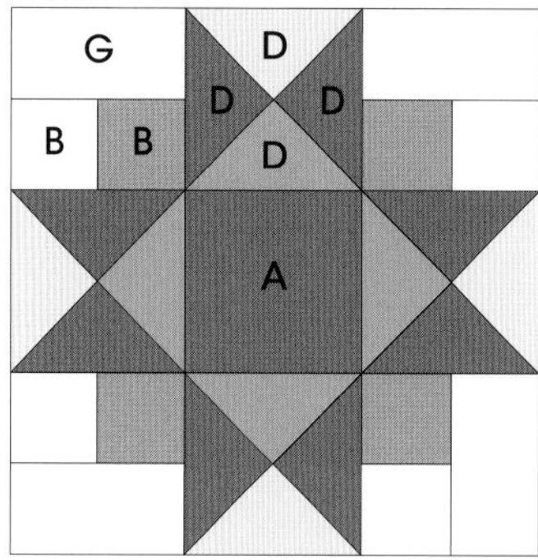


Block 2

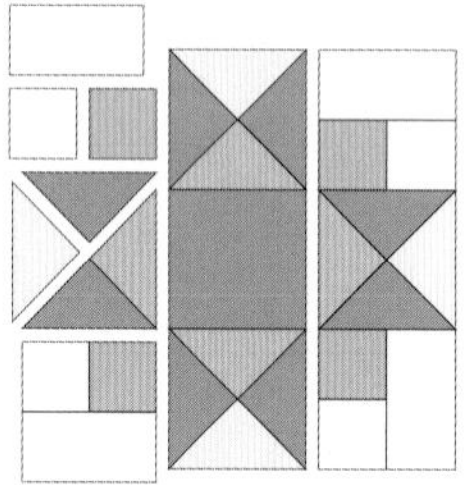

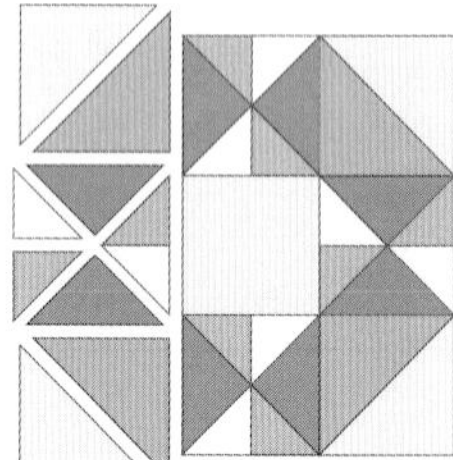

Block 3

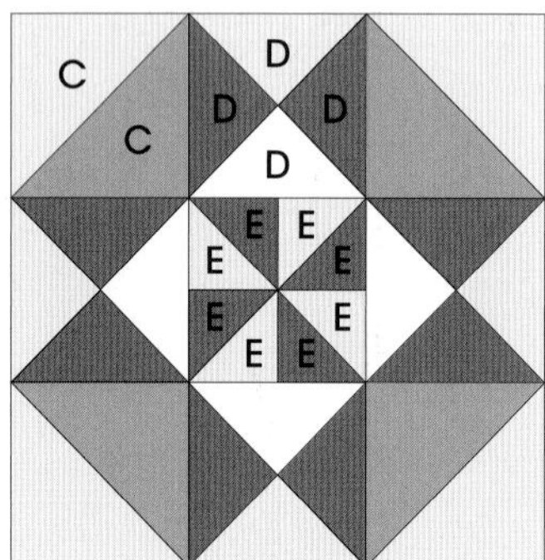

Block 4

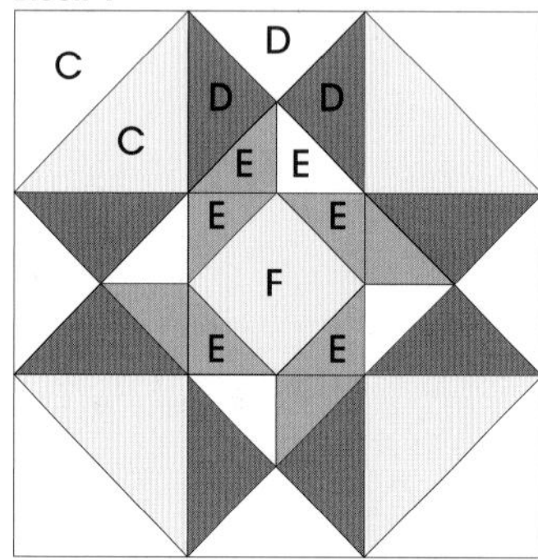


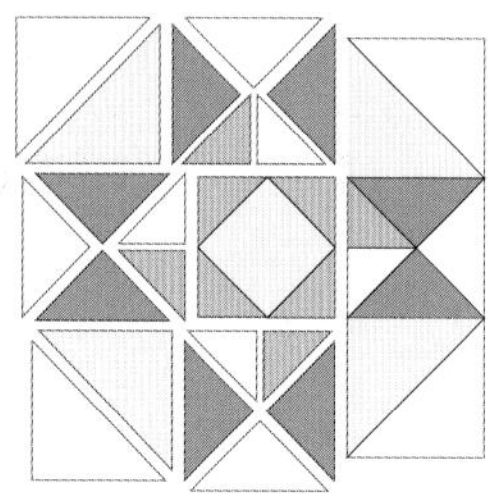

Block 5

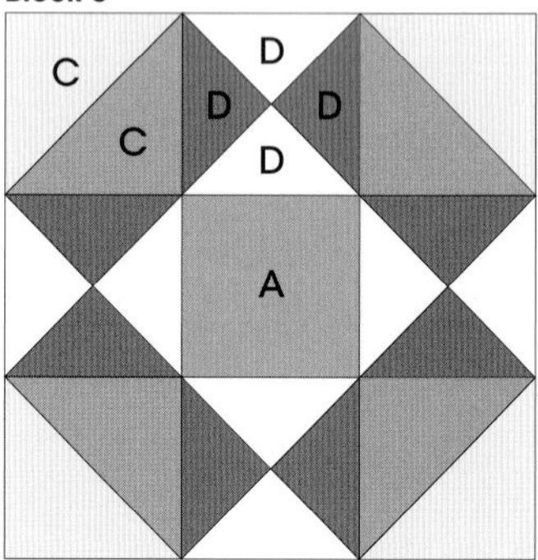


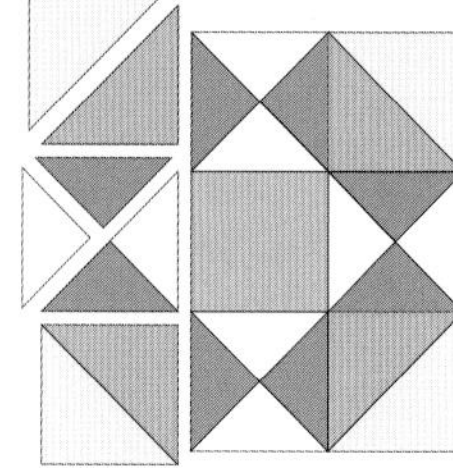

**Block 6**

C C D D D D E E E E E E E E

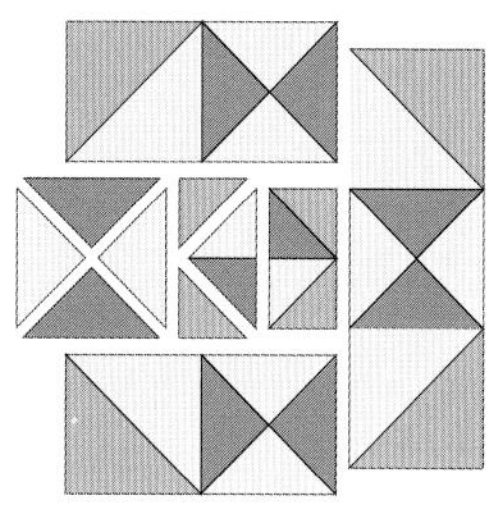

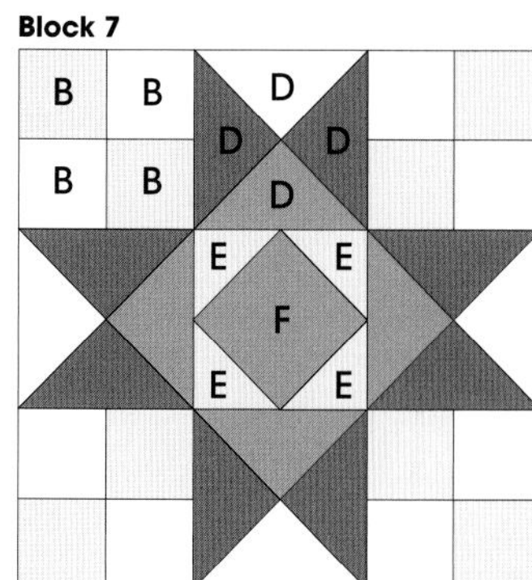


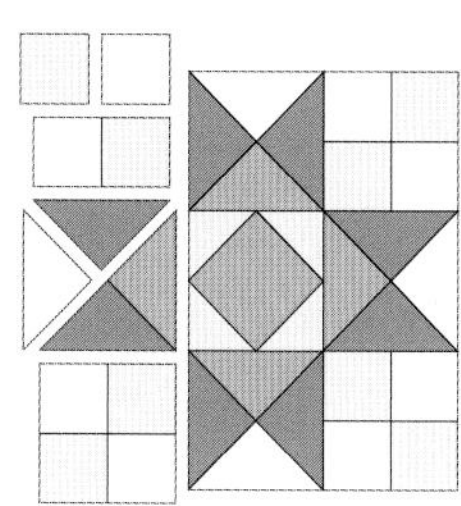

## Putting it all together

3 From the sashing fabric cut twelve strips 2¼in x 12in minimum. Stitch the three-block strips together. Following the Fig 1 sequence, join the sashing strips to the blocks.

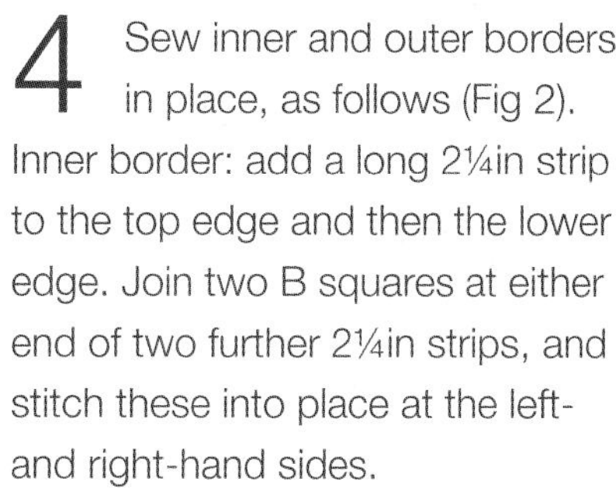

4 Sew inner and outer borders in place, as follows (Fig 2). Inner border: add a long 2¼in strip to the top edge and then the lower edge. Join two B squares at either end of two further 2¼in strips, and stitch these into place at the left- and right-hand sides.
Outer border: consider incorporating any leftover shapes into a pieced border. Alternatively, cut four strips of border fabric 4½in x 52in (or the width of your quilt top) and stitch into place – sides first followed by top and bottom. Press the top, trimming loose or long thread ends.

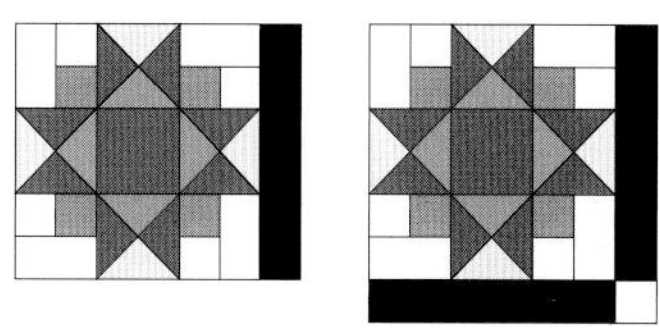

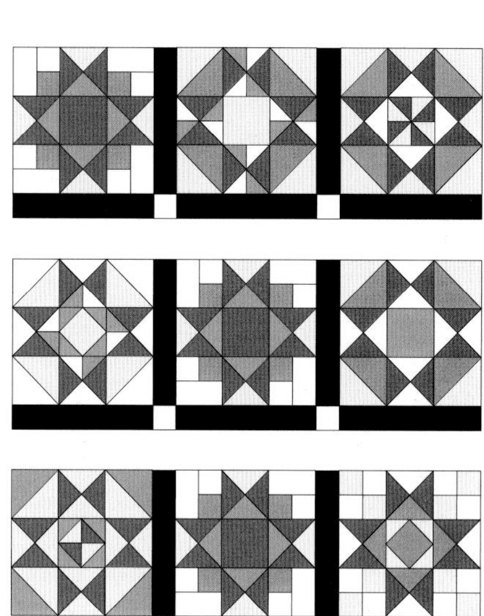

**Fig 1** *Joining the blocks in strips with sashing and setting squares*

**Fig 2** *Layout of Nine by Nine, with borders added*

## Finishing off

5 Layer the quilt top, batting and backing and baste together before quilting (see page 117). The quilting is an overall pattern of swirls to complement the bright fabrics.

6 Finish by binding and labelling your quilt (see page 118).

# Christmas Sampler

All quilters seem to have a fondness for Christmas projects. I thought a sampler-style Christmas quilt would be a great idea and found that using the cutting plan and nine fat quarters of festive fabrics as a starting point gave just the result I was looking for. The whole process went remarkably quickly, although I will admit to making an error in the final stages of the cutting – definitely a case of more haste, less speed! The blocks were laid out in pairs, two or more pairs at a time. As I was putting the twenty-four blocks together it occurred to me that this could be considered an Advent sampler. Narrow sashings of dark green set the blocks together and the narrow red inner border made a good accent for the wider soft green border.

*Designed and pieced by Barbara Chainey, quilted courtesy of The Bramble Patch*

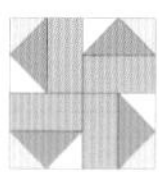 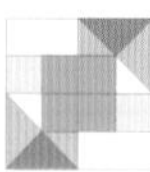  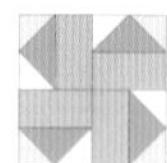

*"Twenty-four blocks and simple narrow sashing make a sampler quilt perfect for the festive season. I began with the idea of making pairs of blocks and having made eight pairs had sufficient shapes left from cutting the original selection of nine fat quarters to make eight individual blocks."*

**You will need**

- Nine fat quarters of Christmas fabrics for the blocks
- Wide outer border, two strips 5in x 57in or length of top and two strips 5in x 49in or width of top
- Narrow inner border, two strips 1¼in x 55in or length of top and two strips 1¼in x 39in or width of top
- Sashing fabric, strips cut 1½in
- Backing fabric, 70in x 52in
- Batting, 70in x 52in
- Binding fabric (see page 118)

**Quilt size:** 66in long x 48in wide
**Block size:** 8in square finished
**Skill rating:** Beginner to improver

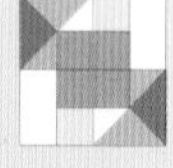
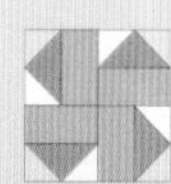

## Making the blocks

1 Starch and press all fat quarters carefully. Working with nine fat quarters you might find it easier (and more accurate) to stack and cut five layers first and then cut the remaining four layers. Use the cutting plan (Fig 3 on page 17), putting the shapes in position on your full-sized paper map before laying out blocks of your choice.

2 The sixteen blocks I chose for this quilt are shown in the diagrams here and overleaf. Eight of the blocks are repeated as pairs in the final quilt layout but you could make twenty-four individual blocks if you prefer. Alternatively, look at Discover the Possibilities on pages 24–29 for lots of other block options and ideas.

Block 1

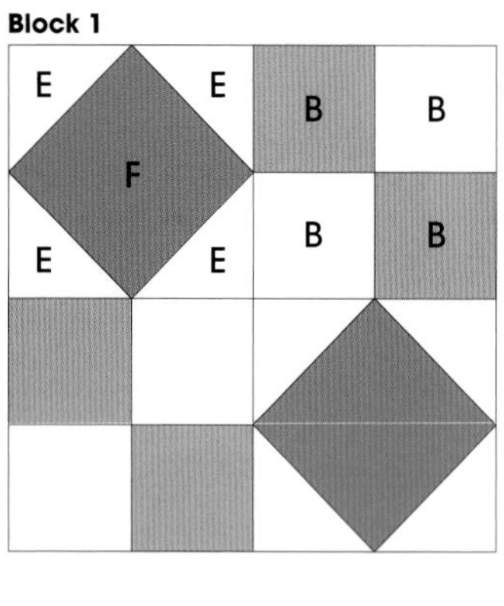


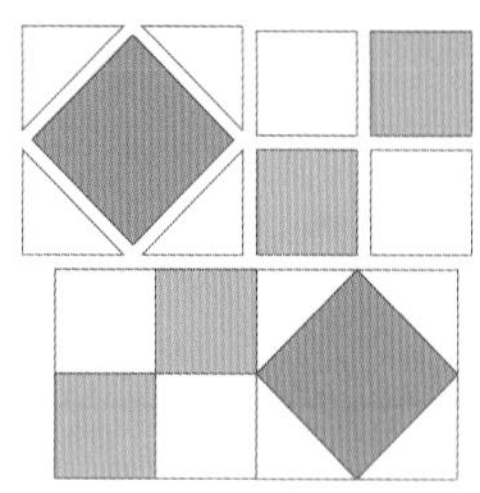

Block 2

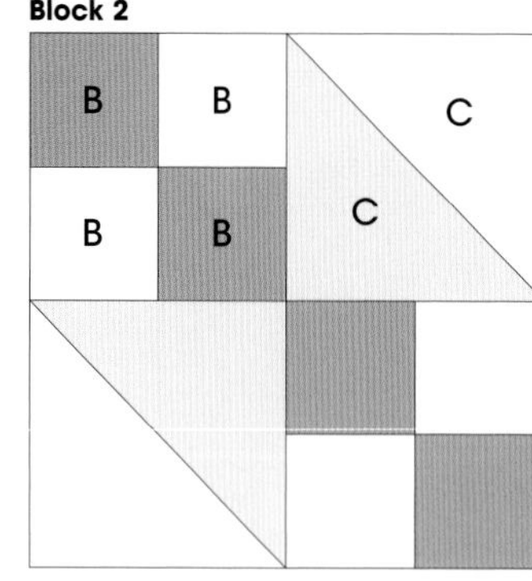


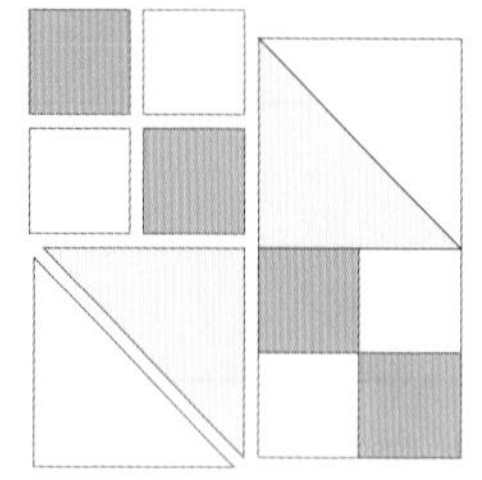

Block 3

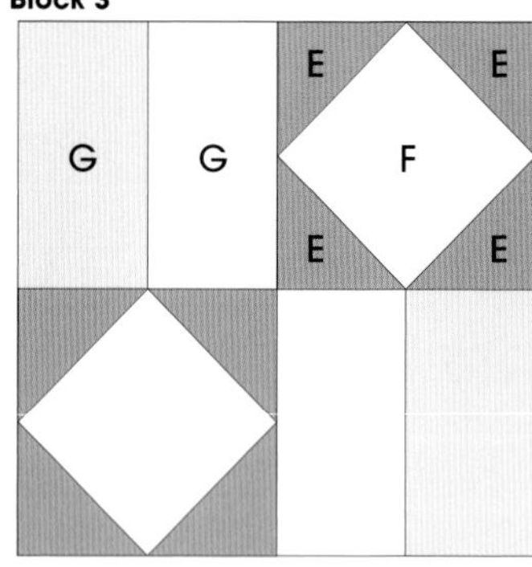


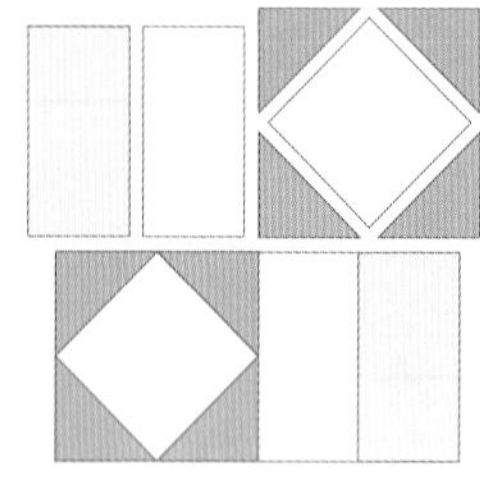

Block 4

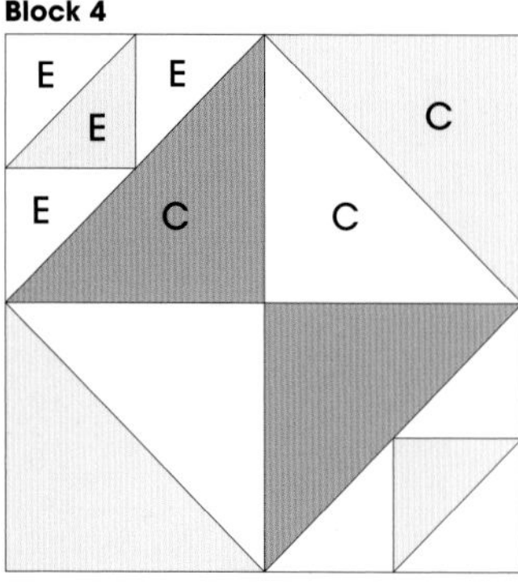


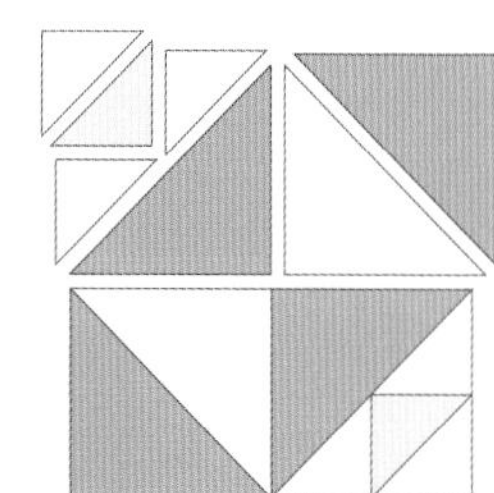

Block 5

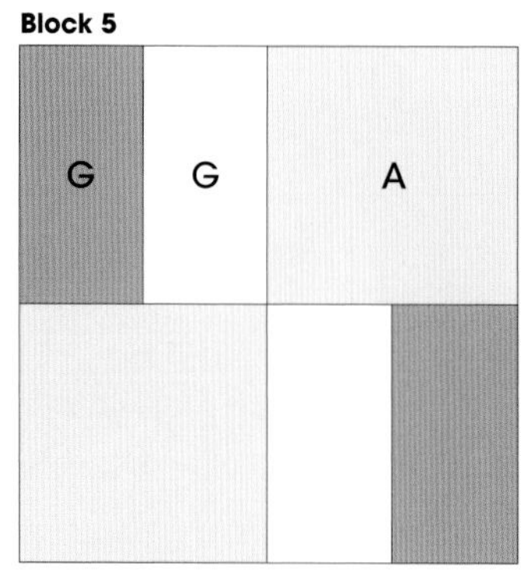

Block 6

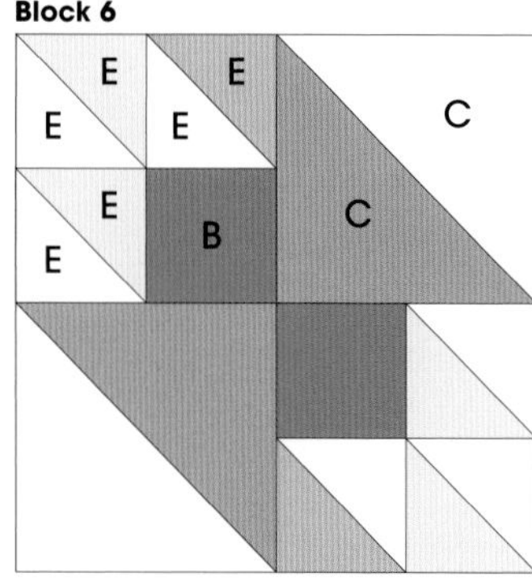

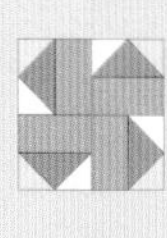

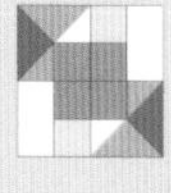

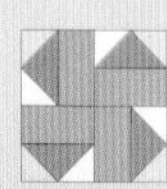

## Block diagrams

The Christmas Sampler uses sixteen blocks, shown here and overleaf. Blocks 1, 2, 8, 9, 10, 11, 13 and 14 are paired blocks. See the 'exploded' diagrams for construction.

**Block 7**

C
D
E
D
C
B
E

**Block 8**

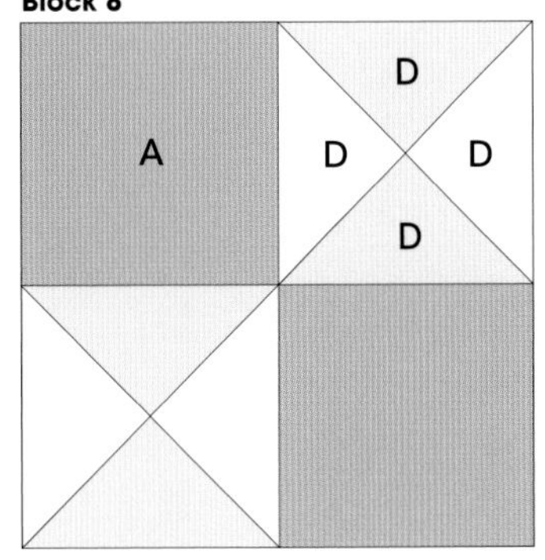


**Block 9**

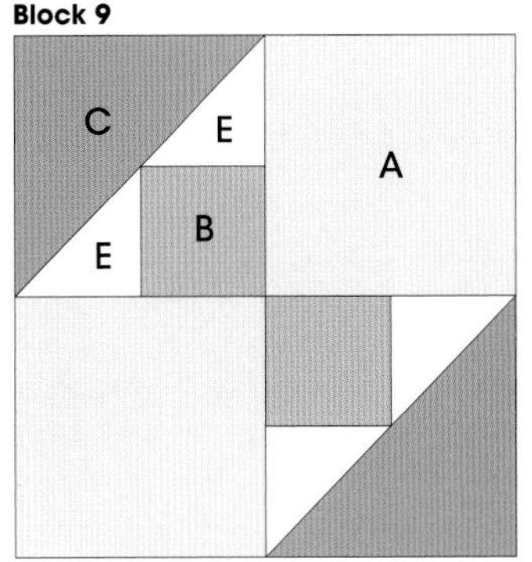


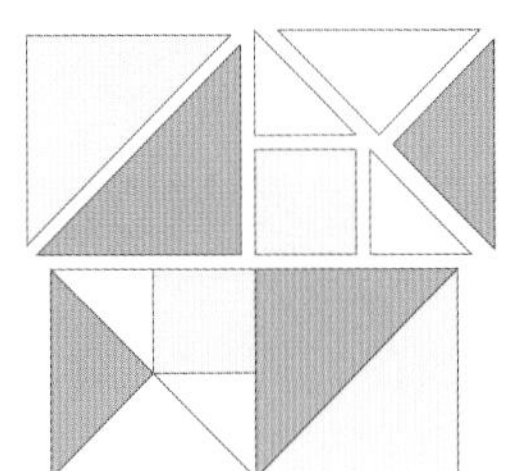

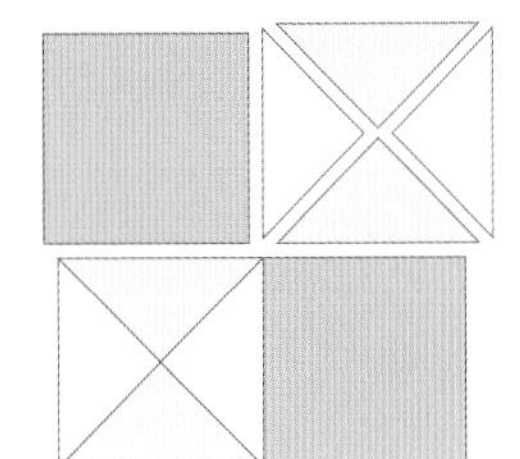

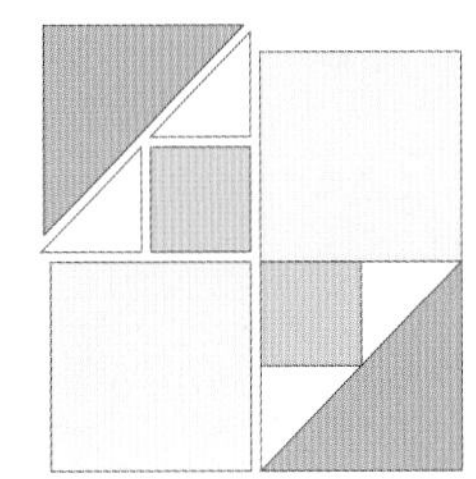

**Block 10**

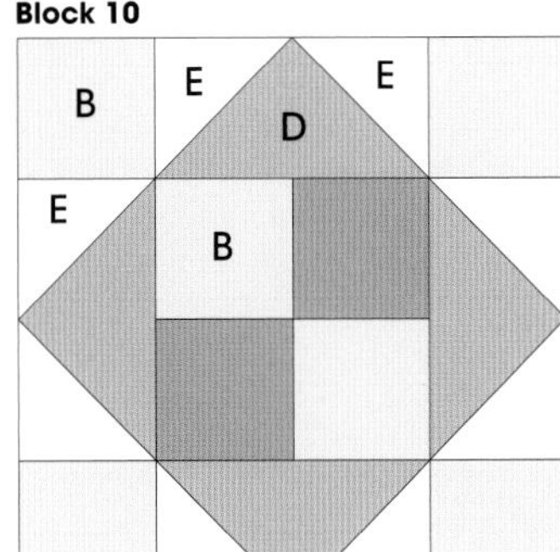


**Block 11**

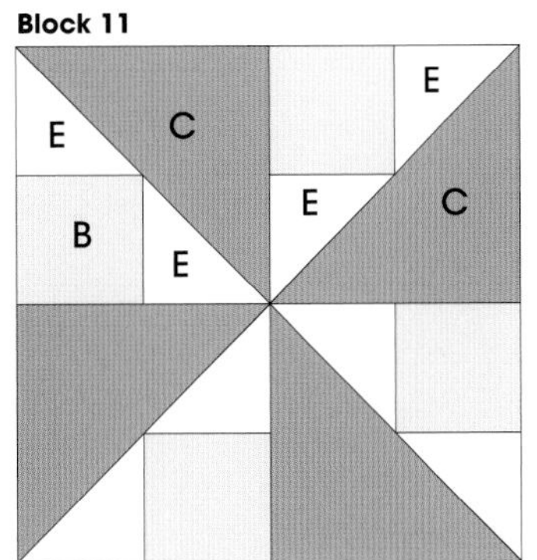


**Block 12**

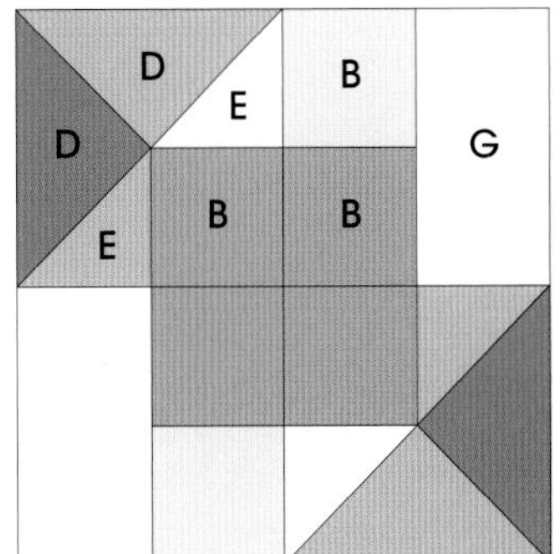


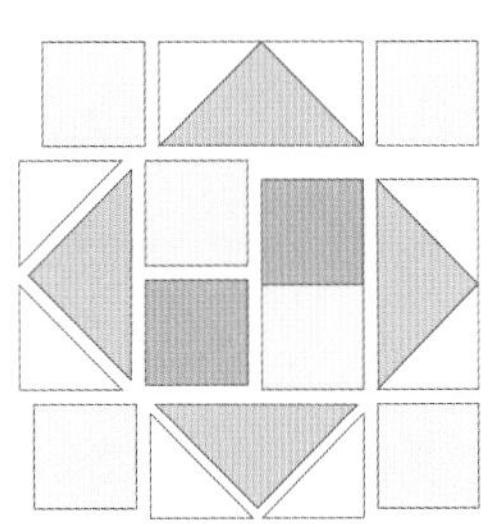

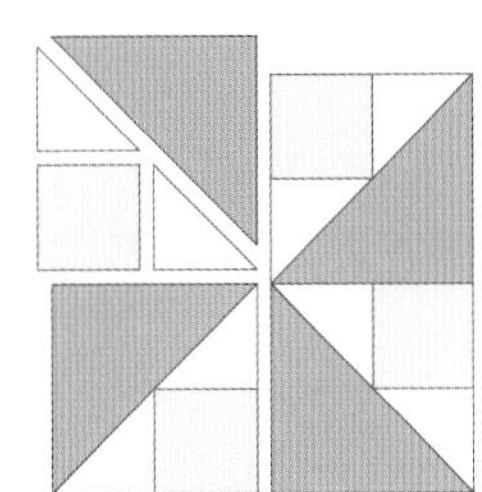

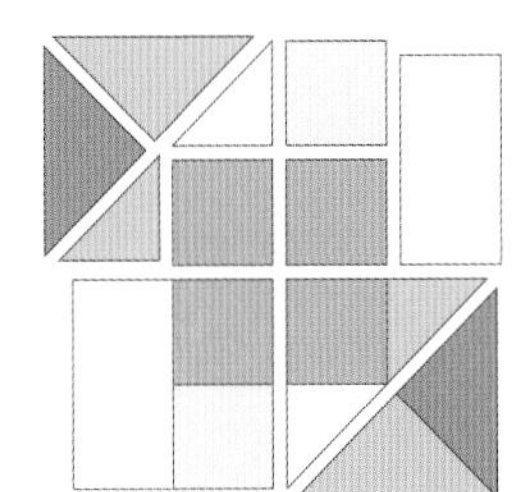

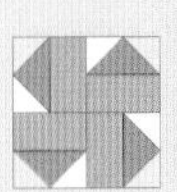

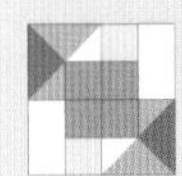

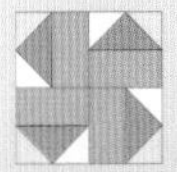

Block 13

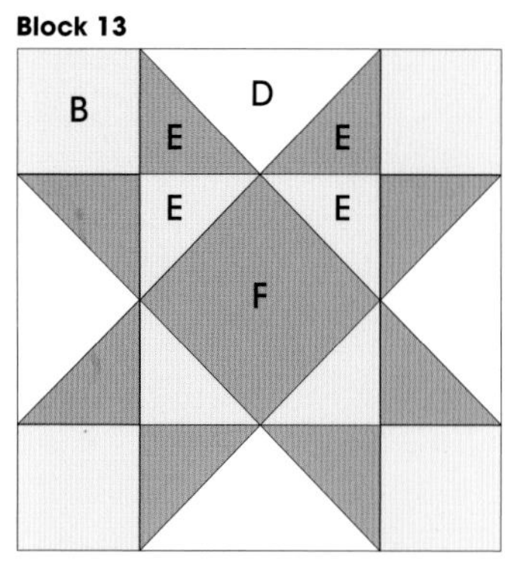


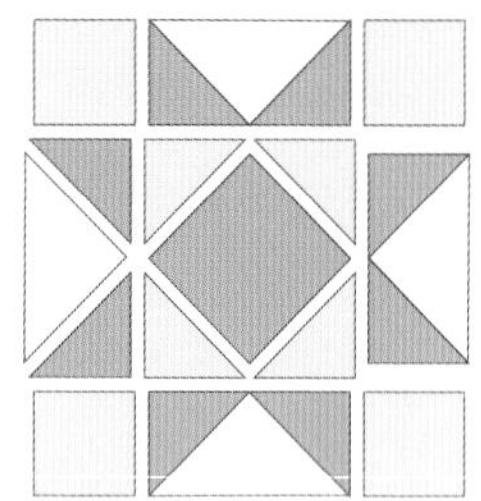

Block 14

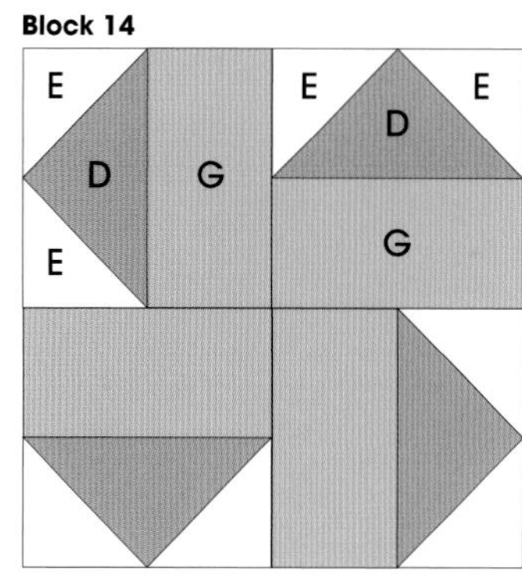


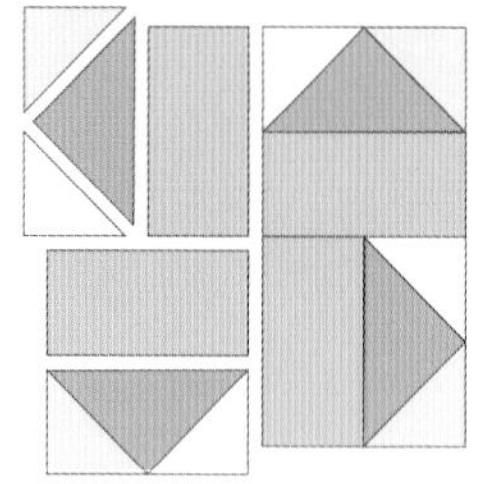

Block 15

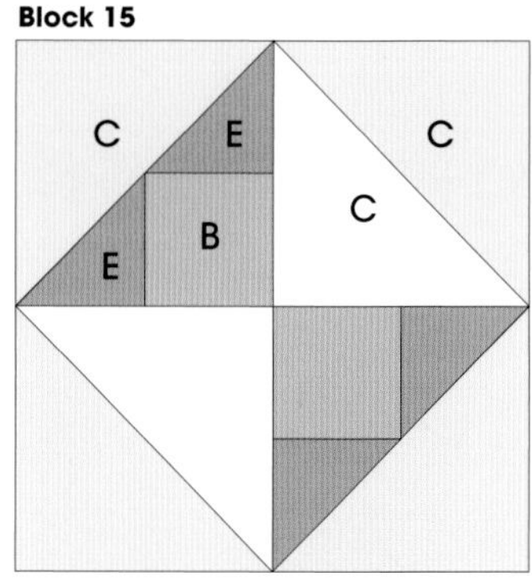


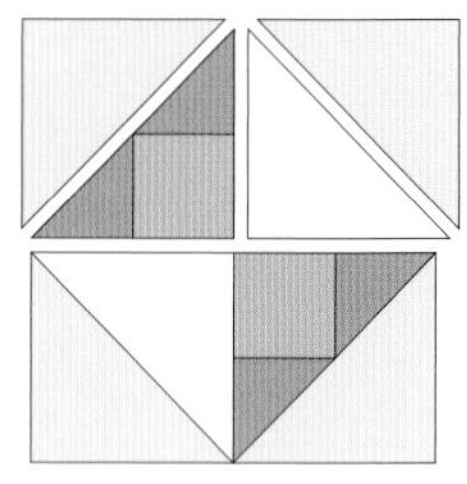

Block 16

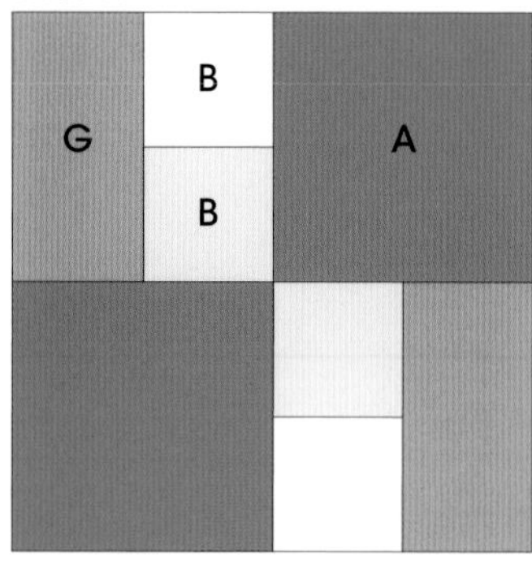


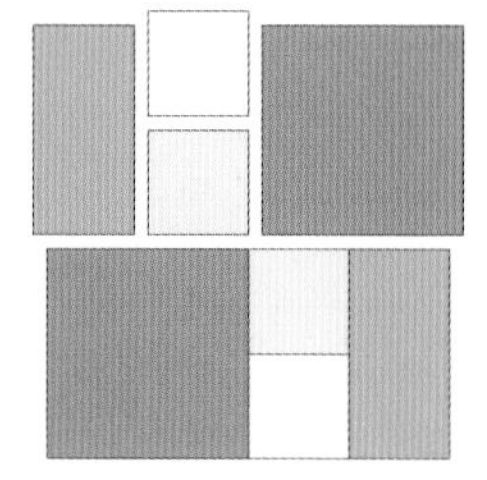

## Putting it all together

3 When you have completed all your blocks give them a light spray starch treatment and press carefully. Trim threads and check the block measurements, 8½in edge to edge, trimming and squaring up as necessary. Use a design wall or planning area to lay the blocks out and in a pleasing arrangement. See Fig 2 for my layout.

4 Cut sashing strips 1½in wide and use these to join the blocks together, making six rows of four blocks. Press the seams of each row before joining the rows together with sashing strips. Press the newly made seams before adding the sashing strips, first to the sides and then the top and bottom of the sashed blocks.

5 Cut 1¼in wide fabric strips for the narrow inner border and stitch these into position using the same sequence as the previous step (sides first, top and bottom second). Press the seams.

6 Cut 5in wide strips for the wide outer border and stitch into position, again using the same sequence. Trim threads as necessary and give the quilt top a final press.

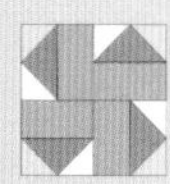

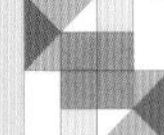

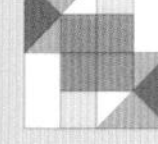

Fig 2 *Christmas Sampler layout with sashing and borders*

## Finishing off

7 Layer the quilt backing, batting and top together and baste or otherwise secure all the layers before quilting (see page 117). You could use a metallic thread for some of the quilting to add a little festive sparkle!

8 Finish by binding and labelling your quilt (see page 118) – merry Christmas!

## Colour confidence

Christmas fabrics always create a strongly traditional, very seasonal feel to any project, but see how different the same quilt looks when interpreted in a monochromatic palette of teal, soft sky blue, dark lilac and soft mauve, or in a warmer colourway of deep mango and glacier green mixed with soft blues and pinks.

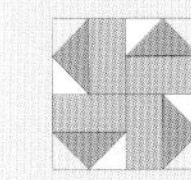

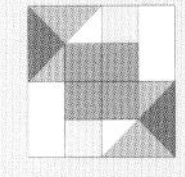

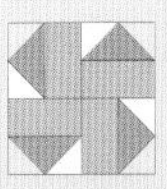

# Judi's Blues

When the piecing of this inventive strippy-style quilt was finished there was just one square of fabric remaining! Instead of arranging the cut pieces into regular blocks, Judi Mendelssohn chose to work with the simple units that are the components of so many traditional blocks – half-square and quarter-square triangles, flying geese squares, four-patch squares – and then grouped these units together in strippy vertical rows. If you have difficulty in thinking 'outside the box' this approach would be an excellent way of making a less formal, abstract or even 'arty' quilt, perhaps with a selection of hand-dyed fabrics, batiks or splashy prints. Four 1in strips of fabric were the only additions to Judi's original selection of six fat quarters. Narrow sashing strips could be inserted between the rows to make the quilt wider.

*Designed and pieced by Judi Mendelssohn, quilted courtesy of The Bramble Patch*

*"You don't need to make full-sized blocks after you have cut out all the shapes using the cutting plan – see how effectively Judi arranged very simple pieced units into a strippy-style format that is very appealing."*

**You will need**

- Six fat quarters for the blocks
- Backing fabric, 42in square
- Batting, 42in square
- Binding fabric (see page 118)

| | |
|---|---|
| **Quilt size:** | 40in square |
| **Skill rating:** | Confident beginner |

# Making the units

1 Starch and press all fat quarters carefully and then use the cutting plan (Fig 3 on page 17). Use the diagrams here as a guide to lay out all the cut shapes into simple units of flying geese, pinwheels, hourglass, four-patch and so on. Trim threads and press all the units.

2 Keeping like with like, arrange and piece all the units into eight strips of eight (see Fig 1 for the quilt layout). Press and trim the strips as required.

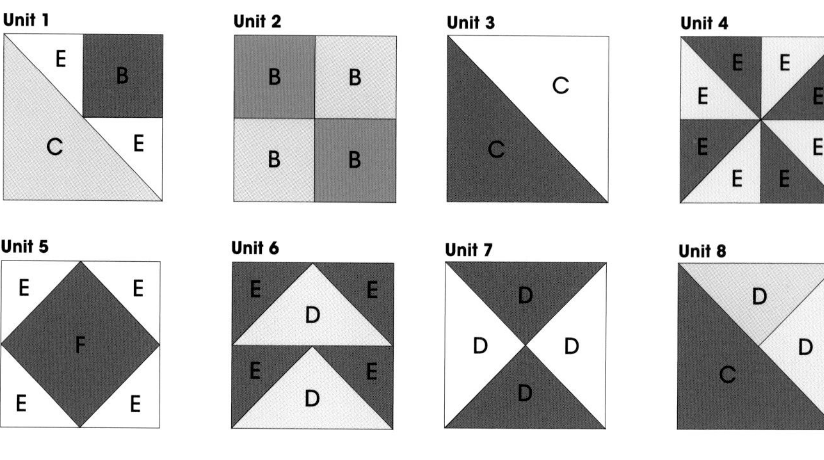


**Unit diagrams**

Judi's Blues uses eight units. Each unit is repeated eight times to make the sixty-four units that are needed for the quilt.

**Fig 1** *Judi's Blues layout*

# Putting it all together

3 Use a design wall or similar space to decide on your preferred arrangement of pieced strips. Join the strips together and press the new seams.

4 Judi inserted a slim border strip between the main portion of the quilt and its outer pieced border (not shown in Fig 2): cut strips 1in wide and stitch carefully into place using the usual sequence of sides first, top and bottom second.

5 For the wider border, piece the remaining A squares into two strips of ten squares each, and then sixteen each of the remaining G rectangles into two strips. Press and trim all four strips. Stitch these pieced border strips into position – the shorter rectangle strips at the top and bottom followed by the square strips at the sides.

## Finishing off

6 Trim threads and press the quilt top. Layer the quilt backing, batting and top together and baste together before quilting (see page 117). An all-over quilting design was used for Judi's Blues but you might have other ideas of your own – a different, simple texture for each strip perhaps or maybe designs typical of the strippy tradition?

7 Finish by binding and labelling your quilt (see page 118).

## Colour confidence

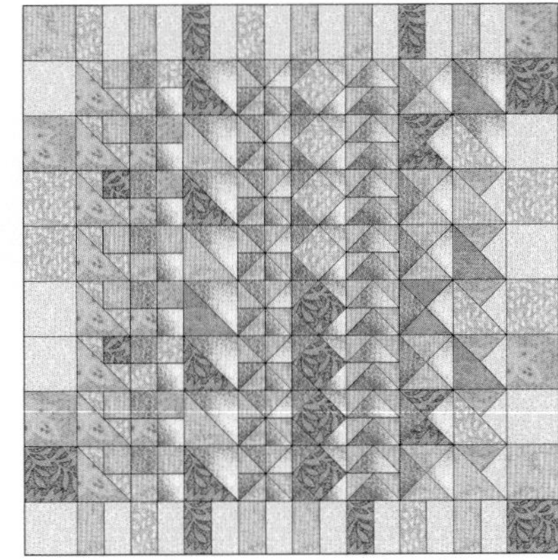

Bright sparky colours give a different emphasis to this quilt layout – medium-toned pastels reminiscent of 1930s charm or deeper tones in a complementary colour scheme. Notice how the different values of fabric affect the overall look of the border.

# Quilt Gallery

### BEWARE, BUTTERFLIES CROSSING

*Designed and pieced by Cindy Davies*
*Quilted courtesy of The Bramble Patch*

*Size: 37in x 41in*

*Begun with 8 fat quarters*

Just as Judi looked at the cutting plan and saw that she didn't have to make up formal, traditional blocks but could arrange smaller pieced units instead, volunteer Cindy Davies arrived at a similar conclusion. She decided not to make 8in or 12in blocks and opted instead for what she describes as more of a strippy look.

# Magenta Medallion

Encouraged by the first two quilts made using the cutting plan (see pages 32 and 42), I was intrigued that the plan seemed to result in a good overall spread and balance of fabrics. This time I determined to try 'difficult' fabrics (purple is not my favourite colour!) and see what happened. Way back in the 1980s puzzle quilts were very much in vogue – arrangements of pairs of blocks where the values and colour placements were radically changed around – and this concept came back to me when thinking how to arrange all the cut pieces. I made as many pairs of blocks as possible, ending up with eight pairs. The setting of four blocks on point with block borders gives the blocks a breathing space and adds drama. It also very conveniently makes the quilt a little larger!

*Designed and pieced by Barbara Chainey, quilted courtesy of The Bramble Patch*

*"Not quite a one-day wonder, however the sixteen blocks in this medallion-style quilt were fun to make and easily pieced and set together into a top ready for quilting in just three days."*

**You will need**

- Six fat quarters for the blocks
- Background fabric: one 8½in square for centre; one 12¼in square and two 6⅞in squares
- Four strips 4in x 9in and eight strips 3in x 9in
- Inner border fabric, four strips 1½in x 25in
- Narrow outer border fabric, four strips 2in x 44in
- Wider outer border fabric, four strips 4½in x 54in
- Backing fabric, 54in–56in square
- Batting, 54in–56in square
- Binding fabric (see page 118)

| | |
|---|---|
| **Quilt size:** | 52in square |
| **Block size:** | 8in square finished |
| **Skill rating:** | Improver |

## Making the blocks

1 Starch, press and stack your chosen six fat quarters and cut according to the cutting plan (Fig 3 on page 17). Take care! I was over-confident with the cutting for this project, being certain that by now I knew my way around the cutting plan and knew what the measurements were without any need to double check against my 'map'. You can probably guess the rest – fortunately the mistake could be partially rectified and I ended up with rather more B 2½in squares than in the original plan. To avoid this check, check and check again before cutting and put all the cut pieces into position on your paper map.

Block 1

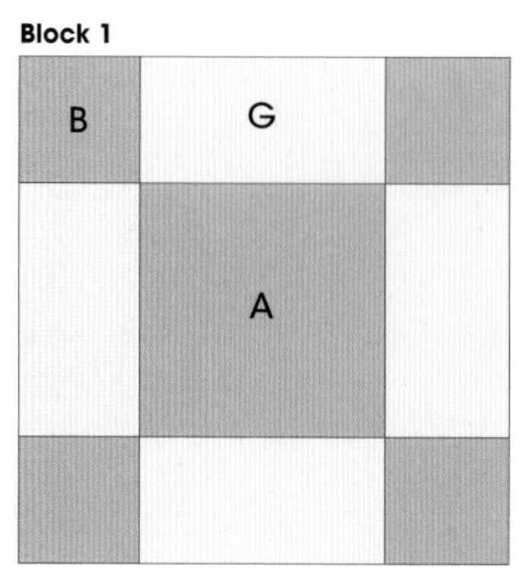


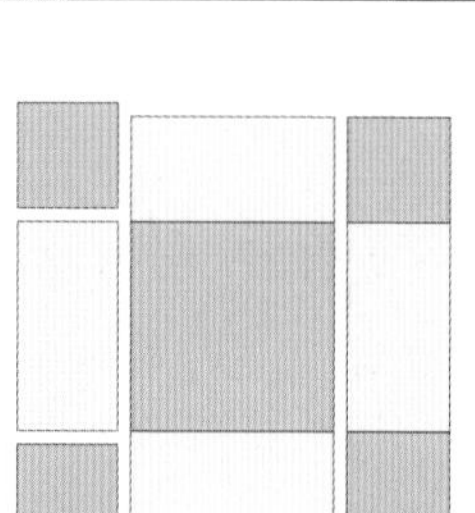

Block 2

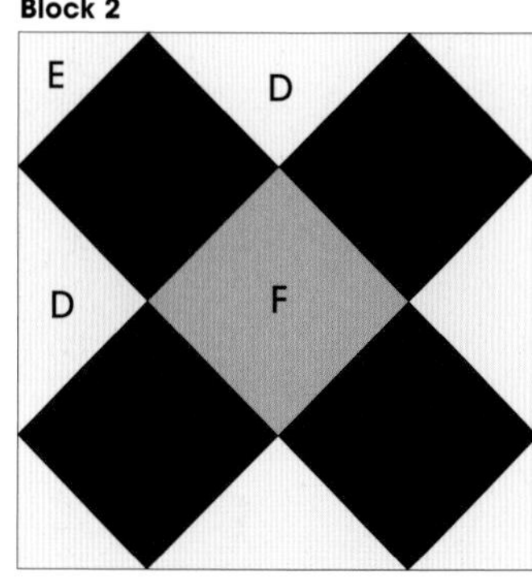

Block 3

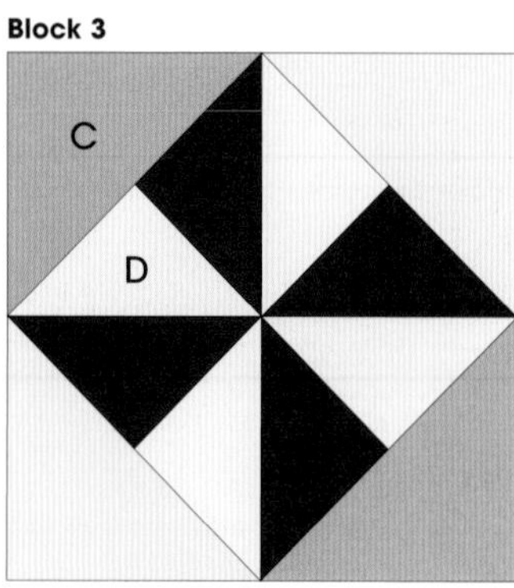

Block 4

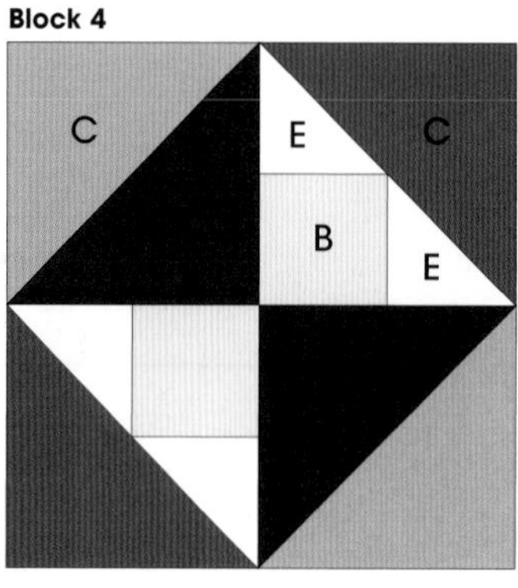

Block 5

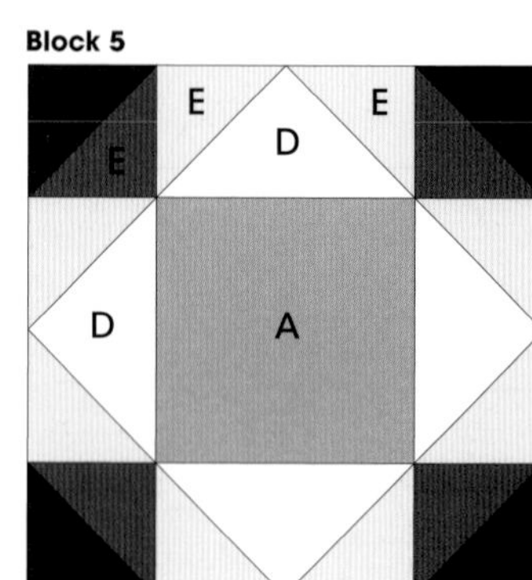


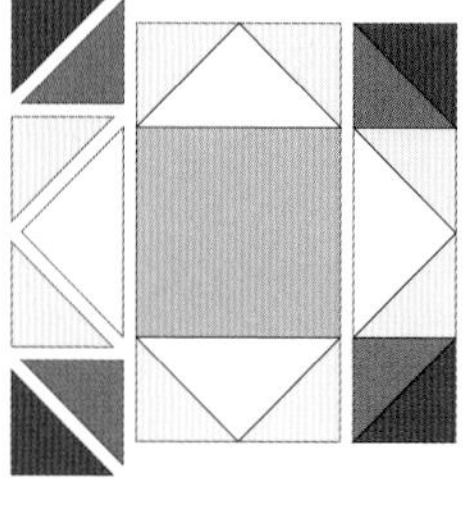

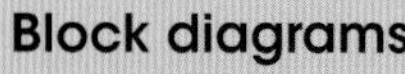

### Block diagrams

Magenta Medallion uses eight blocks, shown here. You will need two of each block (see Fig 1, opposite). See the 'exploded' diagrams for construction.

2 Use the diagrams shown on these two pages as a guide to lay out a total of sixteen blocks in eight pairs – note that there will not be sufficient of any one shape and fabric to be able to keep exactly the same value or fabric placement in these block pairs. Alternatively, you may prefer to select different blocks for your eight pairs – either make your own blocks or refer to page 24 for other suggestions.

3 Make up the blocks using the exploded diagrams as a guide and referring to page 20–23 for cutting and piecing advice. Press all blocks before measuring and trimming each block to 8½in square as necessary.

Block 6

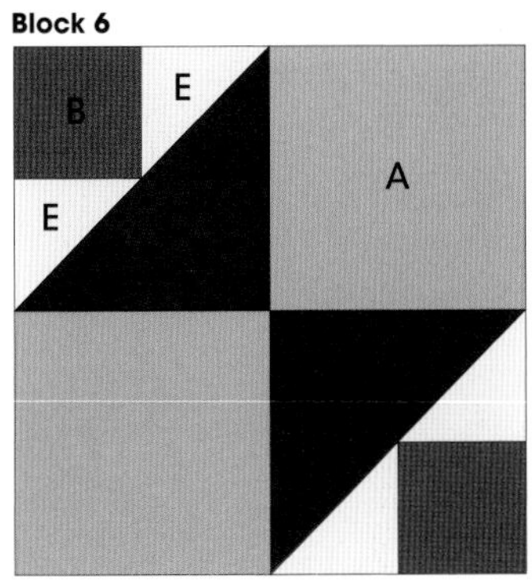


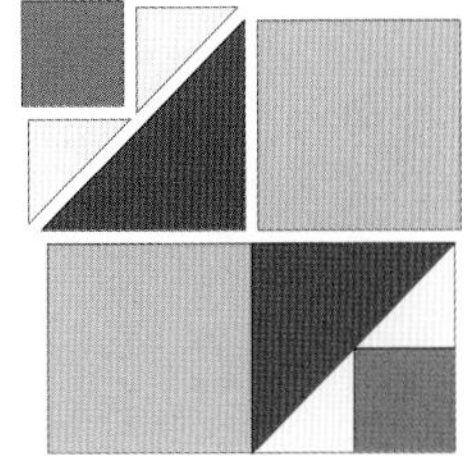

Block 7

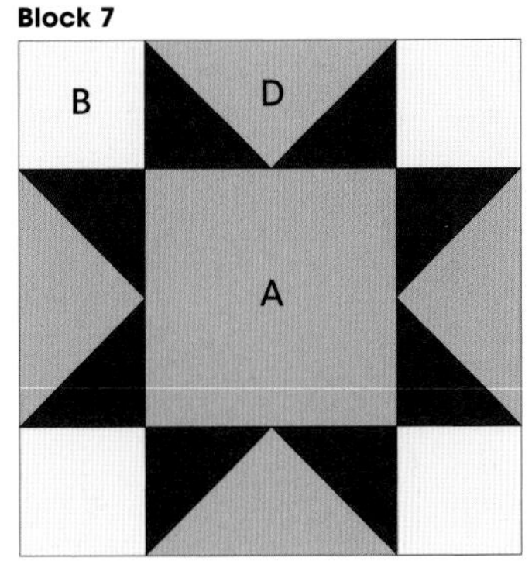


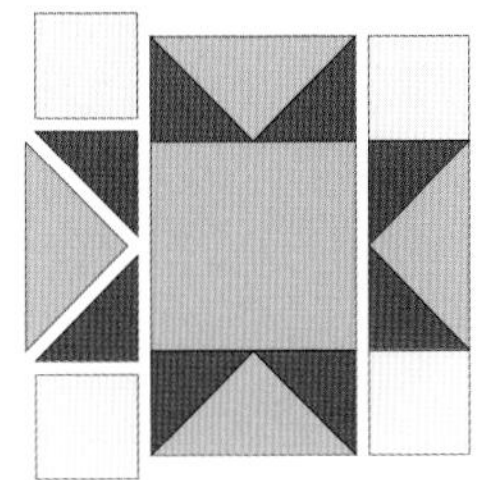

Block 8

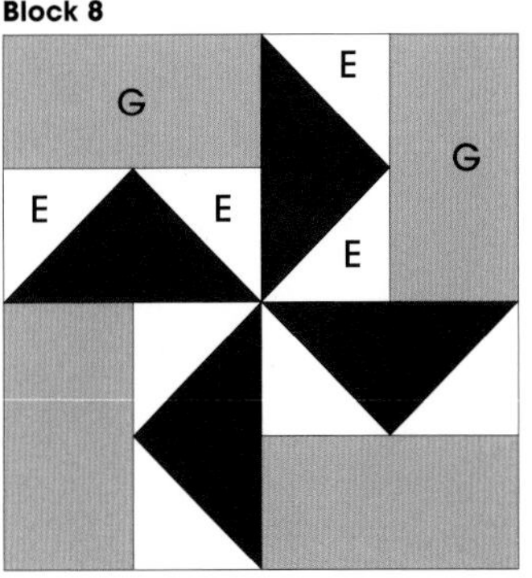

## Putting it all together

4 From background fabric cut one 8½in square – this will be the centre square of the quilt. From background fabric cut two squares 6⅞in. Cut each square diagonally once to give four half-square triangles (marked on Fig 1 as triangle a).

5 From the same background fabric cut one 12½in square then cut on both diagonals to give four quarter-square triangles (marked on Fig 1 as triangle b). Join together the four centre blocks, centre square and finishing triangles (see Fig 1 for the piecing sequence).

**Fig 1** *Piecing sequence for the four centre blocks, the centre square and the finishing triangles*

**Fig 2** *Layout of Magenta Medallion*

6 From the inner border fabric cut four 1½in x 25in strips (approximately) and use these to frame the pieced centre unit, stitching the sides strips into position first, then the top and bottom strips (see Fig 2).

7 Join blocks and spacer strips of background fabric to make the block border – wider spacer strips have been used between the blocks and narrower strips at the outside edges. You will need two strips of two blocks and three strips for the sides, and two strips of four blocks and three strips for the top and bottom. Stitch the block strips into position, the sides first followed by the top and bottom.

8 From the fabric for the narrow outer border cut four 2in x 44in strips (approximately), checking the measurements to the actual piece before cutting. Stitch into position following the sides first, top and bottom last procedure.

9 From the fabric for the wider outer border cut four 5in x 54in strips (approximately) – again, before cutting check these measurements to the piece and adjust as necessary. Stitch into position as in the previous step.

## Finishing off

10 After pressing and trimming threads from the quilt top, layer it together with the batting and backing and tack (baste) the layers together in readiness for quilting (see page 117).

11 Quilt according to your preference – an all-over pantograph leaf pattern was used for this quilt. You may prefer to highlight the blocks and background spaces with more traditional quilting choices of outline quilting and patterns in the major spaces. Bind and label your quilt to finish (page 118).

# Quilt Gallery

Magenta Medallion was one of three quilt tops I used to present the cutting plan concept to the volunteers from Cosby Quilters. Gina Cooke and Jean Waterfield chose to use a similar framed medallion-style setting for their quilts. Gina made different sized blocks and fitted them together carefully, with only a dozen or so pieces left over from her original eight fat quarters. Jean made traditional blocks and chose a strikingly dark sashing to set them off.

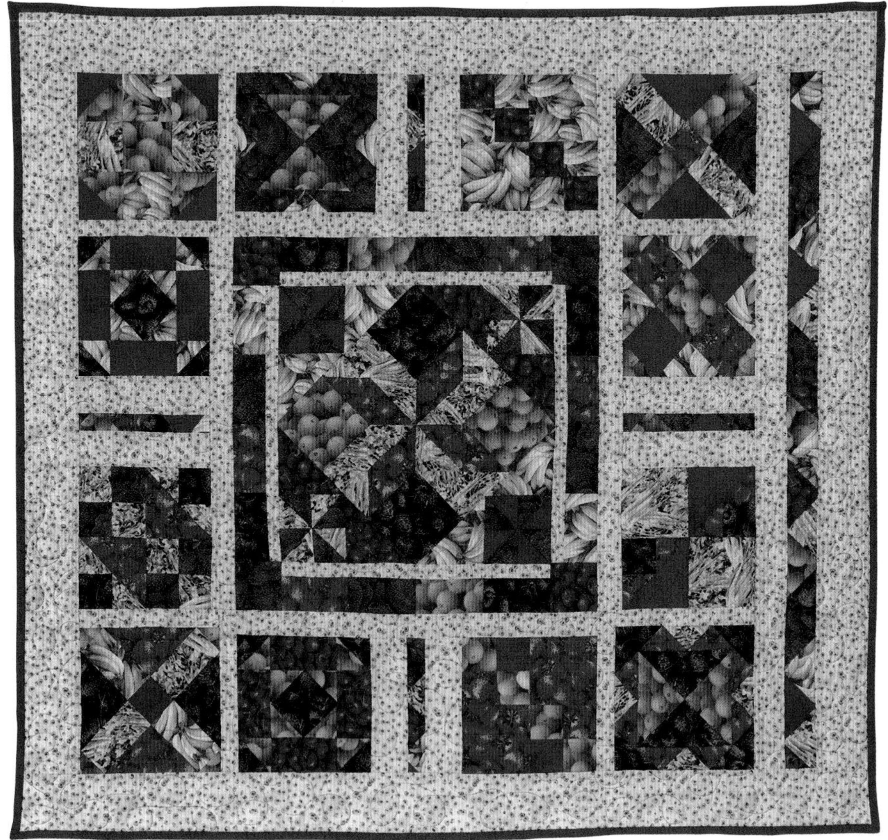

**FIVE A DAY**

*Designed and pieced by Gina Cooke*
*Quilted courtesy of The Bramble Patch*

*Size: 54in x 44in*

*Begun with 8 fat quarters*

Gina Cooke picked delicious fruit and vegetable prints, although she was not entirely sure they would work. Now she is very pleased with this fresh, bright and happy quilt.

**CARAMEL CREAM**

*Designed and pieced by Jean Waterfield*
*Quilted by Debbie Wendt*

*Size: 47in x 47in*

*Begun with 7 fat quarters*

Jean Waterfield enjoyed the 'addictive challenge' of making different traditional blocks for her medallion-style quilt. She added her own original touch to the centre by appliquéing eight leftover triangles into place to look like Flying Geese.

# Accuracy Does Madder

Debbie is without a doubt the unsung star of this book. In the early planning stages she readily agreed to work with the cutting plan and make a quilt and later found herself being volunteered by me to do a lot of the longarm quilting – to an impossibly tight timescale. Despite this huge burden, our redoubtable heroine loyally declared that this handsome medallion quilt was fast and fun to make and, most importantly, we are still friends! Fourteen fat quarters of reproduction madder prints were combined with ten fat quarters of regular muslin and Debbie (being a highly organized quilter) counted all of the cut pieces she began with and those left over at the finish: from a grand total of 1,008 cut pieces there were a mere 80 left when the quilt was complete – and Debbie is sure to have come up with a plan for these!

*Designed, pieced and quilted by Debbie Wendt*

*"The need for piecing accuracy and the reproduction madder-style prints featured in this handsome medallion quilt prompted its maker, Debbie Wendt, to come up with the tongue-in-cheek title."*

**You will need**

- Fourteen fat quarters of prints for the units
- Ten fat quarters (or equivalent yardage) of muslin or other non-printed fabric
- Batting, 70in square
- Backing fabric, 70in square
- Binding fabric (see page 118)

| | |
|---|---|
| **Quilt size:** | 64in square |
| **Skill rating:** | Beginner to confident improver |

## Making the units

1 Starch and press all fat quarters. Layer them up in four stacks of six and cut according to the cutting plan (Fig 3 on page 17).

2 Debbie made her quilt in stages by arranging and re-arranging cut pieces on a large flannel design wall and then stitching and assembling sections. You could begin by arranging pieces for the central portion using Fig 1 as a guide and when you are satisfied with the arrangement, carefully piece together all the small units (shown in Fig 2).

**Fig 1** *Use this layout as the reference for placing the small units*

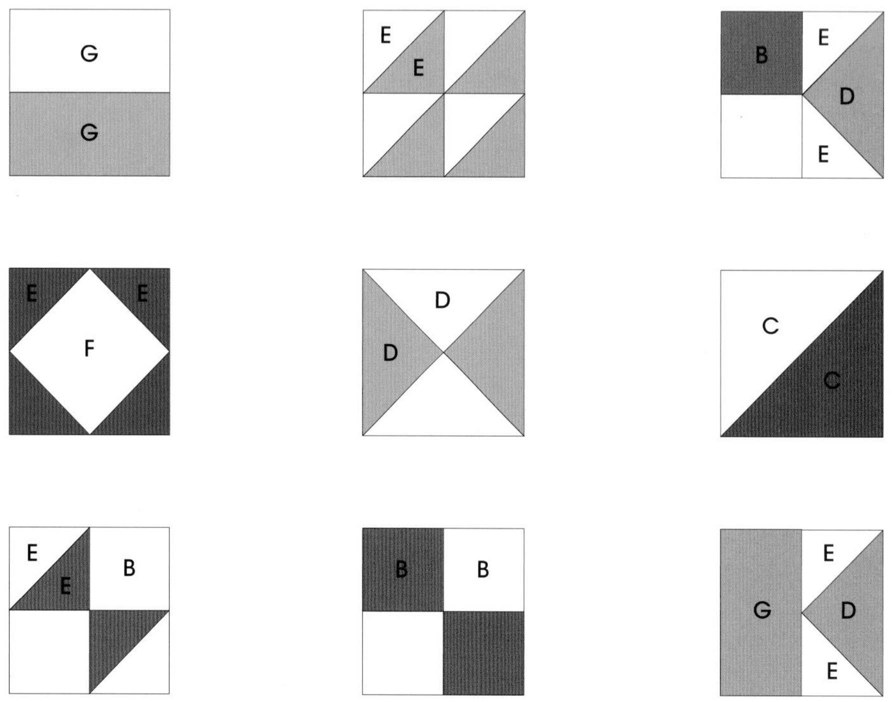


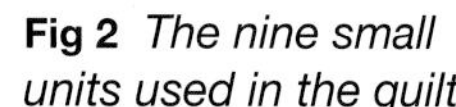

**Fig 2** *The nine small units used in the quilt*

Fig 3 *An alternative working method – assembling the units into quarters*

## Putting it all together

3 Press and trim the units before joining them into larger sections. Trim and press the completed central portion and return it to the design wall to continue the laying out and stitching of units, working in borders around the centre. Trim all threads and press the completed quilt top.

An alternative method of working might be to lay out the quilt as Fig 1, make up all the small units first and then assemble these into quarters (see Fig 3) and finally stitch the quarters together to assemble the full quilt top.

## Finishing off

4 Layer together the backing, batting and quilt top and baste to secure the layers before quilting (see page 117). Debbie chose a traditional-style Baptist Fan quilting pattern and worked this over the whole quilt. You might choose quilting lines to enhance the large star shapes, filling in the 'blank' background spaces with simple close texture.

5 Finish by binding and labelling your quilt (see page 118).

## Colour confidence

Changing the background colour and value can make a huge difference to the look of a quilt. The first colour scheme shows that black adds drama and contrast. The second uses warm cream to reduce the contrast and soften the overall effect, while a cool grey/blue background looks sharp against the warm reds and yellows.

# Quilt Gallery

Debbie knew she wanted to make a medallion-style quilt, arranging shapes outwards from a centre point, and the same idea was developed by other volunteer quilters. Ann Jermey made a delightful small medallion quilt using her own hand-dyed fabrics. Lyn Spencer delivered a dramatic framed medallion, while Jane Rimell designed her medallion on point. Sue Trangmar cut up and arranged three sets of quarters to make her nineteenth century-style quilt.

**FLAMENCO**

*Designed and pieced by Lyn Spencer Quilted courtesy of The Bramble Patch*

*Size: 36in x 36in*

*Begun with 8 fat quarters*

Lyn wanted to use as much of the vibrant fabrics as possible without using traditional blocks, and achieved her goal with this setting and just sixteen E triangles left over.

**SUE'S MEDALLION**

*Designed, pieced and quilted by Sue Trangmar*

*Size: 56in x 56in*

*Begun with 7 fat quarters, finished with a total of 19 fat quarters*

Sue planned to make a small quilt but found that she was soon overcome by the urge to cut up more and more fabric to let her quilt grow – and use as many of the cut pieces as possible.

## ANN'S FANCY

*Designed, pieced and quilted by Ann Jermey*

*Size: 48in x 39in*

*Begun with 5 fat quarters*

Ann whipped this understated and elegant quilt together in no time at all. It would look good in just about any colour scheme or style of fabrics – strong batiks, nursery pastels, jungle prints. . .

## JANE'S MEDALLION

*Designed and pieced by Jane Rimell Quilted courtesy of The Bramble Patch*

*Size: 62in x 62in*

*Begun with 12 fat quarters*

Jane has the priceless ability to work quickly to a high standard and makes samples for The Bramble Patch in Northampton. Of course, choosing fabric for this quilt was easier with a whole shop to choose from!

# Fiona's Flowers

Fiona Bowman is a keen and speedy quilter who likes a challenge, whether it be stitching through the night or the thrill of the unknown, and this made her an obvious choice to be volunteered to test the cutting plan. Typically, Fiona set herself a number of challenges during the making of this perky quilt. Starting with a photograph of colourful spring tulips from her garden as inspiration she painted and dyed most of the fabric and then had fun cutting it all up. The key to balancing her vibrant mix of fabrics was to chop them up and really mix the pieces across all the units and blocks. Few of the pieced units have any symmetry of colour placement. The three largest blocks measure 12in and have all eight fabrics.

*Designed and pieced by Fiona Bowman, quilted by Debbie Wendt*

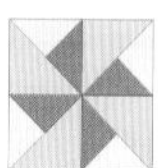

*"I wanted to create something contemporary-traditional from a photo inspiration and retain the feeling of the original picture. I also wanted to use my own fabrics and put together a top using random blocks and units to create an overall asymmetric design."*

**You will need**

- Eight fat quarters for the blocks and units
- Four strips 2½in x 44in for finishing border (the corner squares are from offcuts)
- Batting, 52in x 48in
- Backing fabric, 52in x 48in
- Binding fabric (see page 118)

**Quilt size:** 48in long x 44in wide
**Skill rating:** Intermediate

# Making the blocks

1 Starch and press all the quarters carefully and layer up either into one stack of eight or two stacks of four according to your preference (and the sharpness of your blade). Cut your fabrics following the cutting plan (Fig 3 on page 17) and put all the pieces on your paper map.

2 On a design wall or similar space lay out the pieces using Fig 1 as a guide. When you are satisfied with the layout begin to assemble the small units and then the blocks – see Fig 2 for some that Fiona used. Work systematically and take care when replacing pressed and trimmed units back in the layout.

**Fig 1** *Use this layout as a reference for placing the small pieced units*

**4in units**

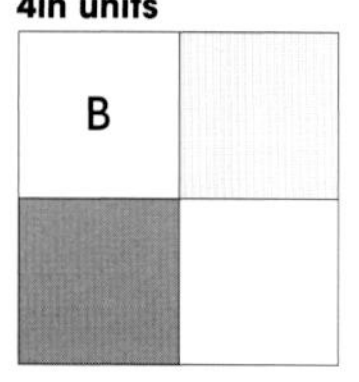


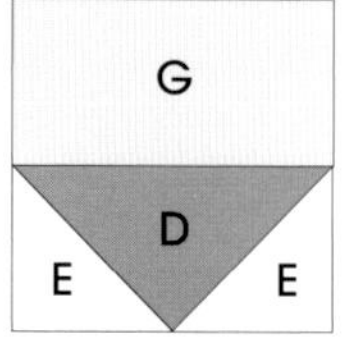


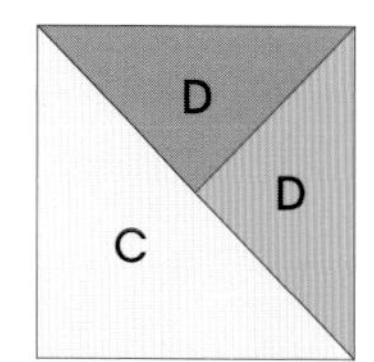


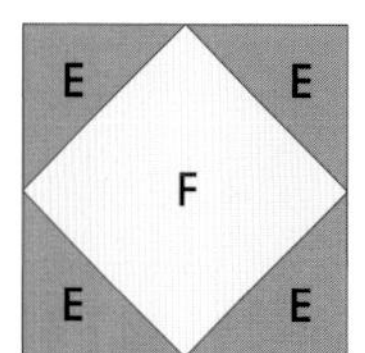


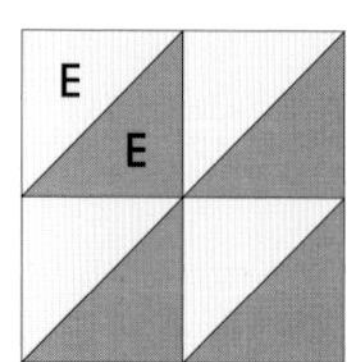


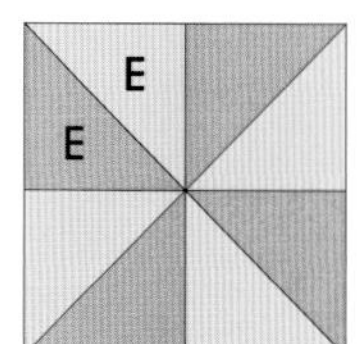


**Fig 2** *Fiona used numerous pieced units, and also four 8in blocks and three 12in blocks (see opposite)*

**8in blocks**

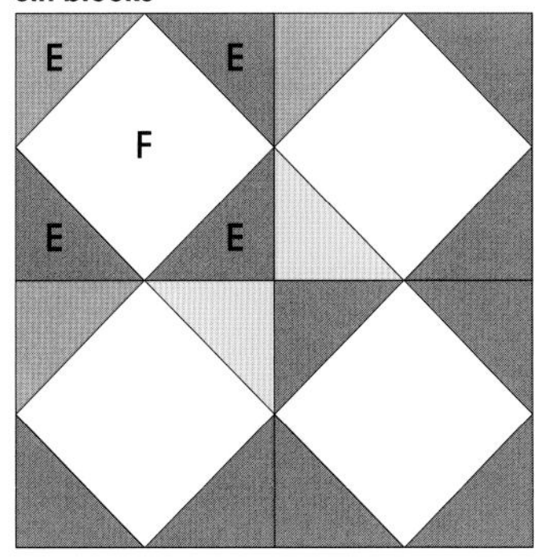


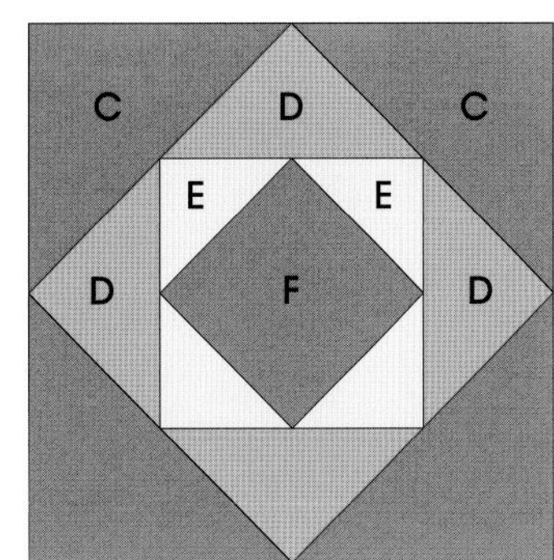


**12in blocks**

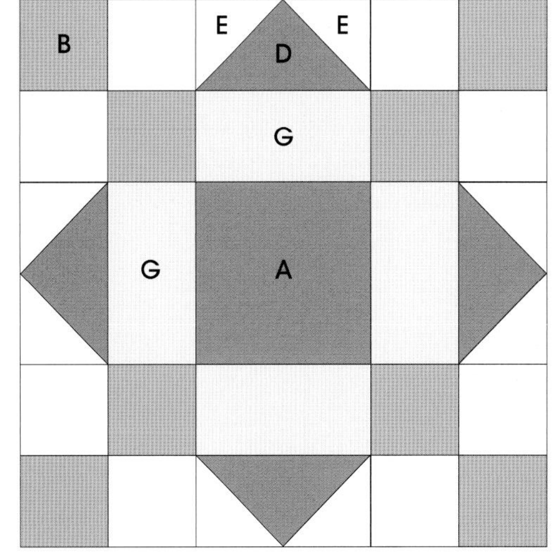


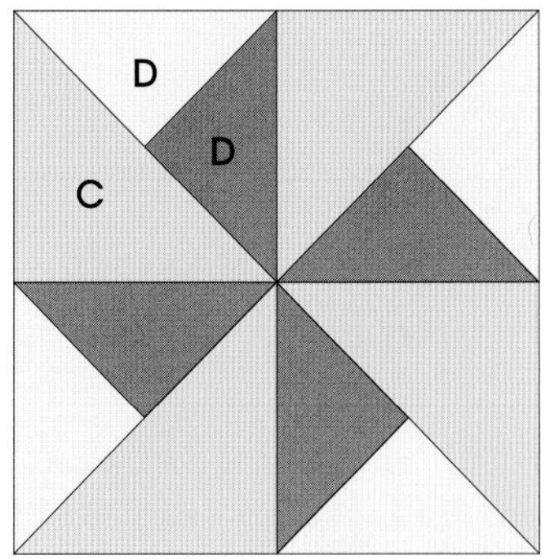


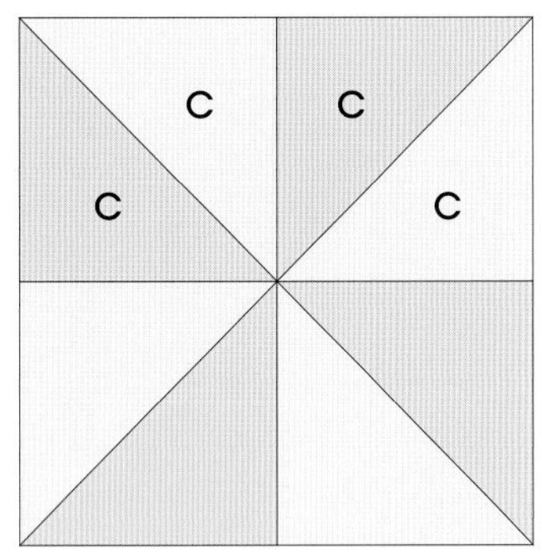


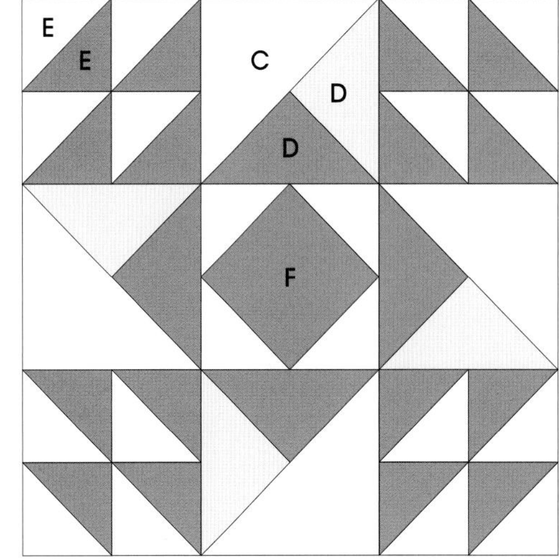


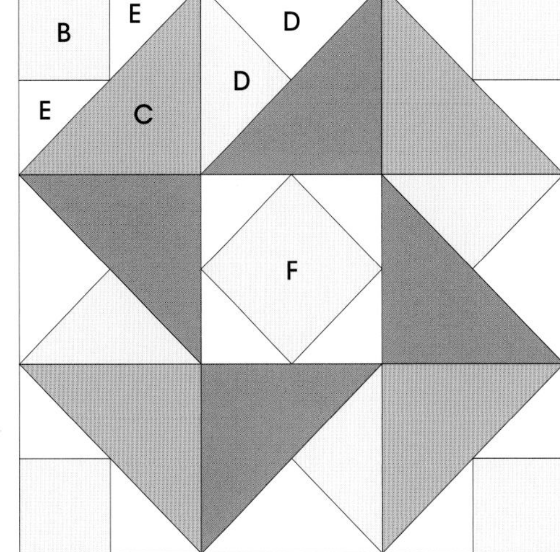


## Putting it all together

3 Look long and hard at your laid-out blocks and units and identify which can be pieced together to make larger sections – you are aiming to build up square and rectangular sections, which can then be joined together in straight, not set-in, seams. Be prepared to take a little time with this step.

4 Join the sections together, pressing seams and trimming threads as you go.

5 Using the 2½in x 44in border fabric strips, add the border strips and corner squares (from offcuts) in the usual sequence of sides first, top and bottom second.

## Finishing off

6 Press the completed quilt top and trim threads if necessary, then put the three layers of top, batting and backing together and baste ready for quilting (see page 117). Quilt according to your preference. Debbie chose a swirling all-over pattern of loops and a strongly coloured variegated thread to complement the piecing and unique fabrics.

7 Finish by binding and labelling your quilt (see page 118).

# Quilt Gallery

The impression of an overall, freeform arrangement that Fiona set as her goal in Fiona's Flowers was also evident in other quilts made with the cutting plan. Sue Hobson's quilt, Pot Luck, is similar in style and scale to Fiona's. Anne Sampson's cheerful Sunshine Team is a great arrangement of different block sizes and shapes. Gaynor Sandercock also used different sized blocks but worked out a more formal arrangement. New Zealand quilter Marj Ussher's quilt Kotare has the same 'free but structured' look.

**KOTARE**

*Designed, pieced and quilted by Marj Ussher*

*Size: 39in x 30in*

*Begun with 8 fat quarters*

From class and cutting fabric to finished quilt in two weeks – Marj used the Maori name for kingfisher as a title for her charming small quilt.

**IN MY SECRET GARDEN...**

*Designed and pieced by Gaynor Sandercock*
*Quilted courtesy of The Bramble Patch*

*Size: 58in x 50in*

*Begun with 8 fat quarters*

Many of the blocks Gaynor chose for this delightful quilt have names that continue the garden theme of the title – Spider, Weathervane, Bird House, Rosebud, Maple Leaf, Flower Basket and Nosegay.

## SUNSHINE TEAM

*Designed and pieced by Anne Sampson with additions by Judi Mendelssohn Quilted courtesy of The Bramble Patch*

*Size: 44in x 44in*

*Begun with 7 fat quarters*

Anne was not entirely sure she had done the 'right' thing with this sunny and sparky quilt. Quilt doctor Judi Mendelssohn added a couple of finishing touches and borders, so now it's hard to tell where one began and the other finished.

## POT LUCK

*Designed and pieced by Sue Hobson Quilted by Debbie Wendt*

*Size: 58in x 49in*

*Begun with 10 fat quarters*

Sue is on a personal mission to use up (her actual words are 'get rid of') lots of fat quarters and made as many different arrangements as she could – right down to the pieced border.

# Pastel Points

Just seven fat quarters provided Jacquie Durber with the starting point for this narrow strippy quilt. Designed specially for display across the foot of a king-sized bed, this elegant quilt features a pretty collection of deep pastel fabrics set off to perfection by the dark print fabric that surrounds the blocks. Jacquie decided she would use as many of the cut pieces as possible and made up a grand total of twenty full blocks with two half blocks and then did a great job of creating a balanced quilt setting. Adding in two yards of dark print from her stash, she put the blocks on point with a half shift into a streak of lightning setting, using leftover pieces for slim side borders and also at the four corners.

*Designed and pieced by Jacquie Durber, quilted by Debbie Wendt*

*"It was a very satisfying and enjoyable method, once cut to the plan. The blocks were very easy to sew together and the sorting was a breeze. I would certainly use the plan again and again and again."*

**You will need**

- Seven fat quarters for the blocks
- Setting and borders, 2yd fabric
- Batting, 46in x 86in
- Backing fabric, 46in x 86in
- Binding fabric (see page 118)

**Quilt size:** 42in long x 82in wide
**Block size:** 8in square finished
**Skill rating:** Intermediate

## Making the blocks

1 Starch and press the seven quarters and stack them ready for cutting. Decide whether to work with one single stack of seven or divide the quarters into one stack of three and another of four. Cut the stack(s) according to the cutting plan (Fig 3 on page 17) and set the cut pieces out on your paper map.

2 Lay out and piece a total of twenty blocks – the ones Jacquie used are shown here and overleaf but you could make different choices according to your preference. Jacquie laid out the pieces for each of her blocks almost randomly to achieve a non-symmetrical effect. Remember to press and trim seams and threads as you work through the construction of the blocks. Give all completed blocks a final press and trim. Blocks should measure 8½in edge to edge (approximately).

Block 1

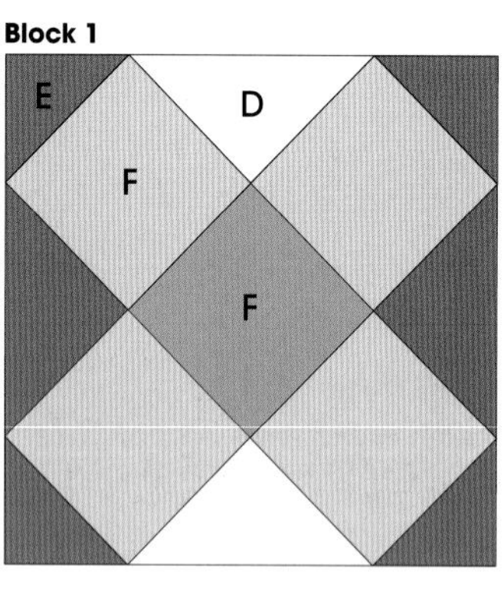

Block 2

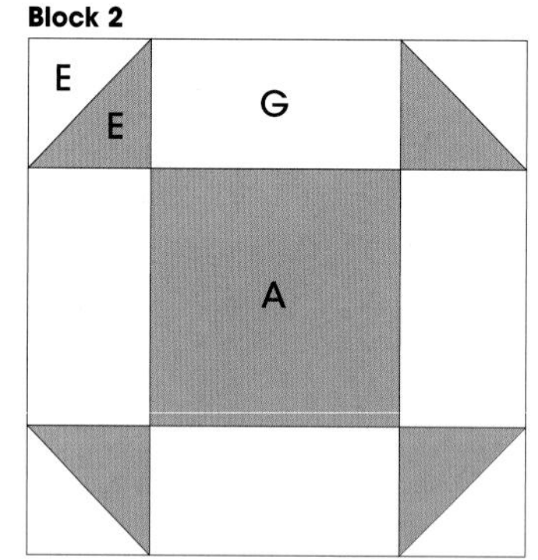


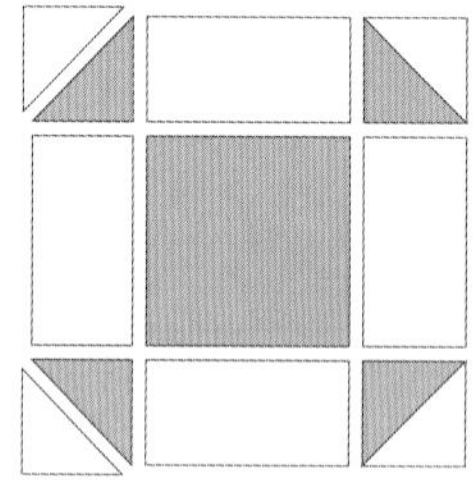

Block 3

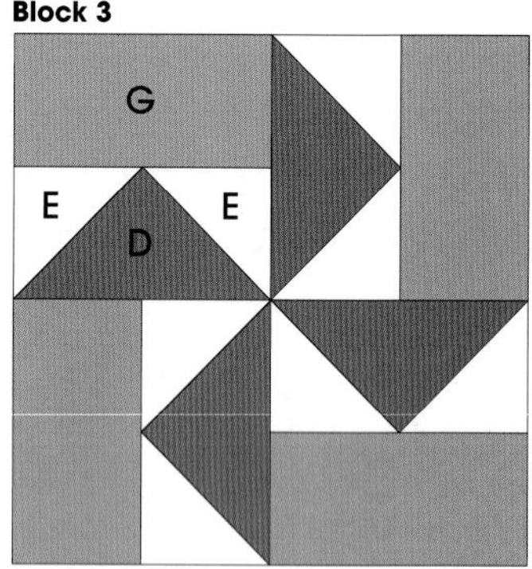

Block 4

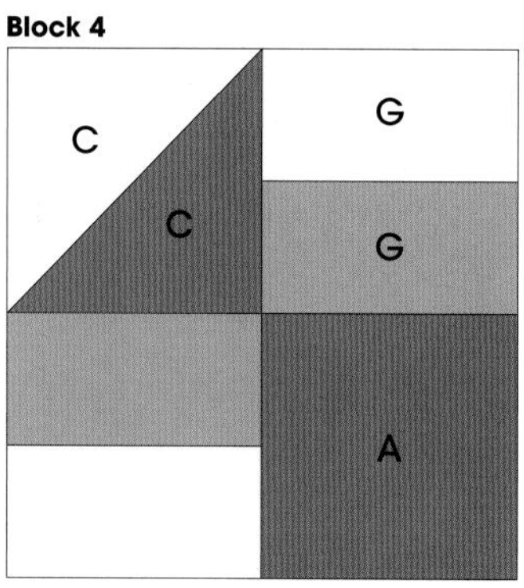


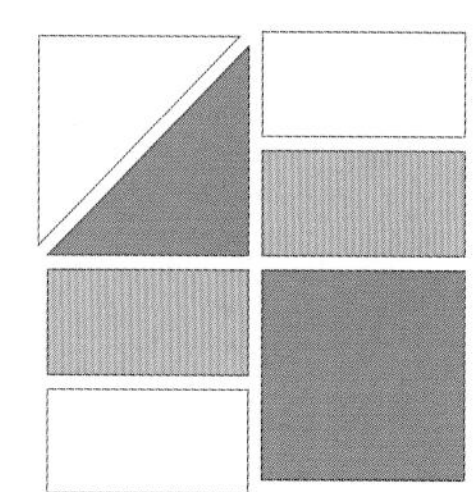

Block 5

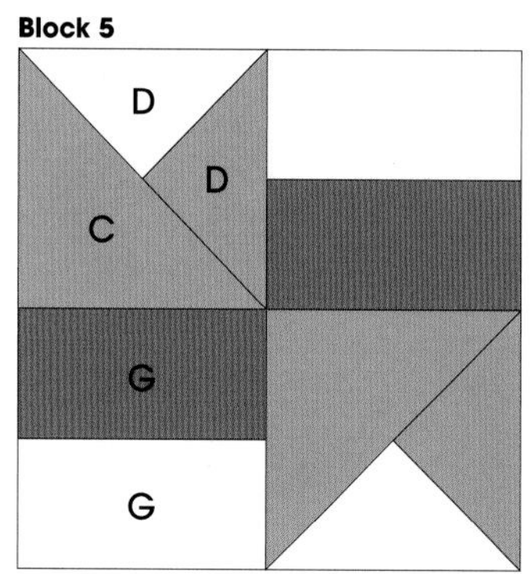


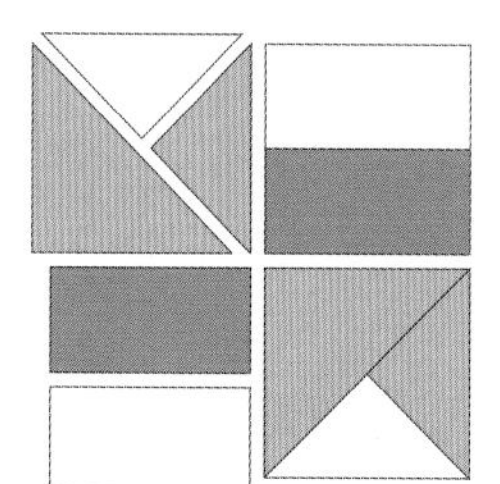

Block 6

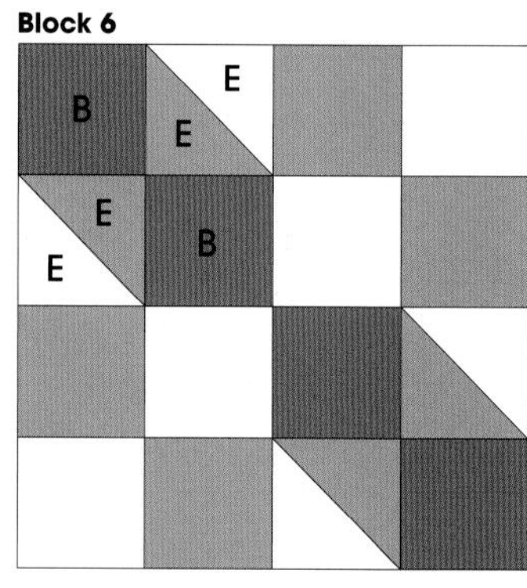


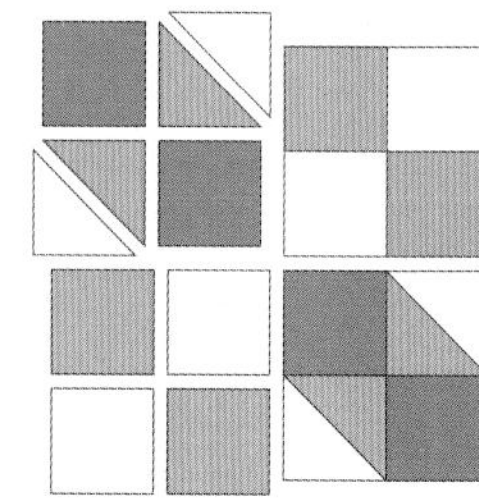

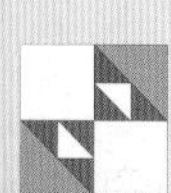

## Block diagrams

Pastel Points uses eighteen blocks, shown here and overleaf. Blocks 1 and 2 are repeated, to make up the total of twenty blocks.

3 Jacquie also made two half blocks from leftover pieces, to set at the top and bottom of the centre strip and fill that particular space. You could either use A squares and C triangles following Jacquie's example, or devise your own according to the leftovers that you have.

Block 7

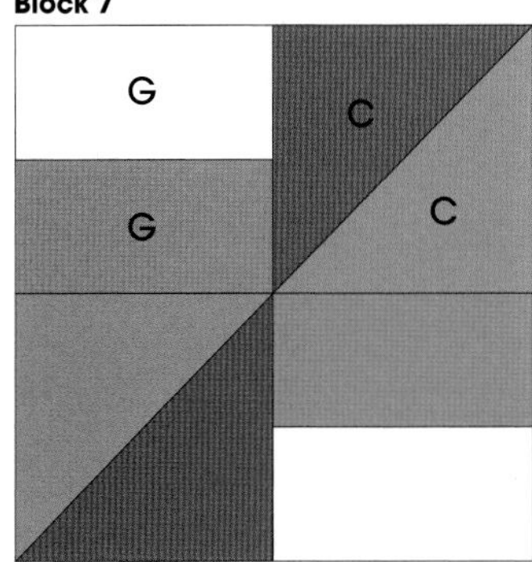


Block 8

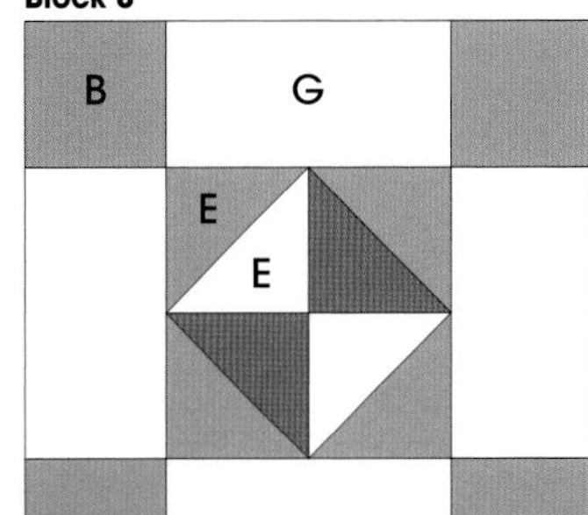


Block 9

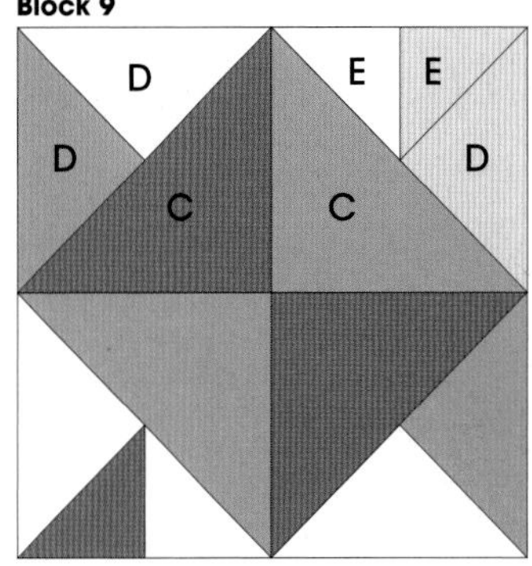


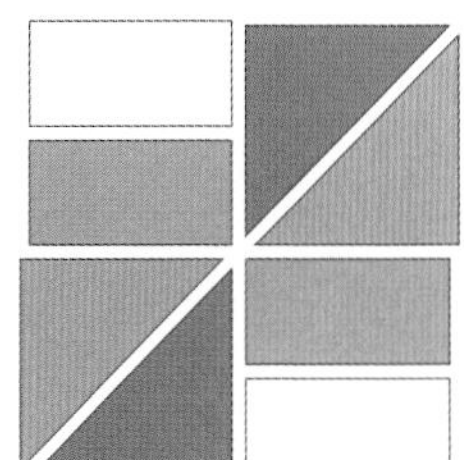

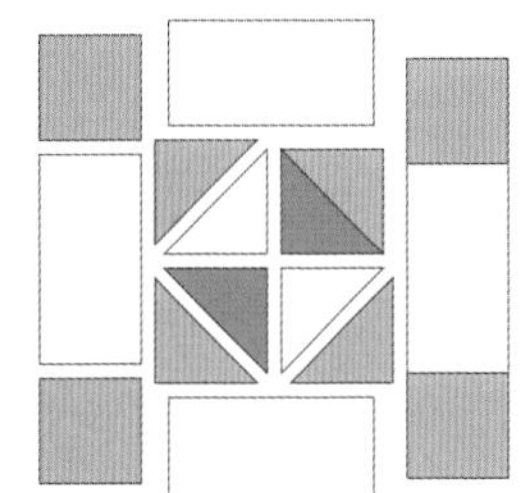

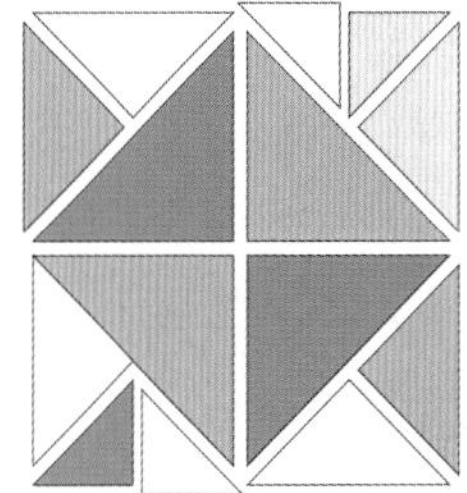

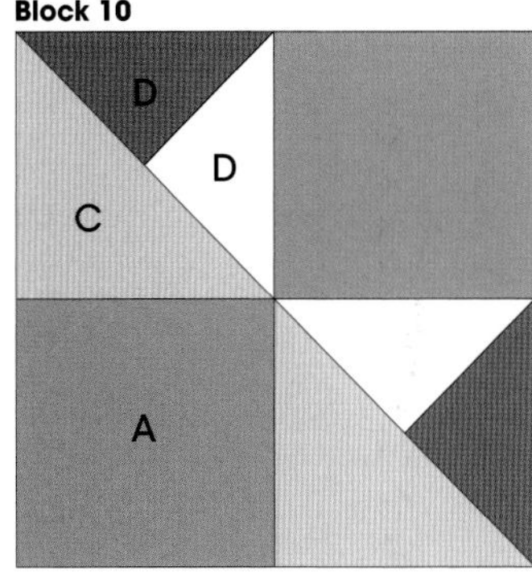


Block 11

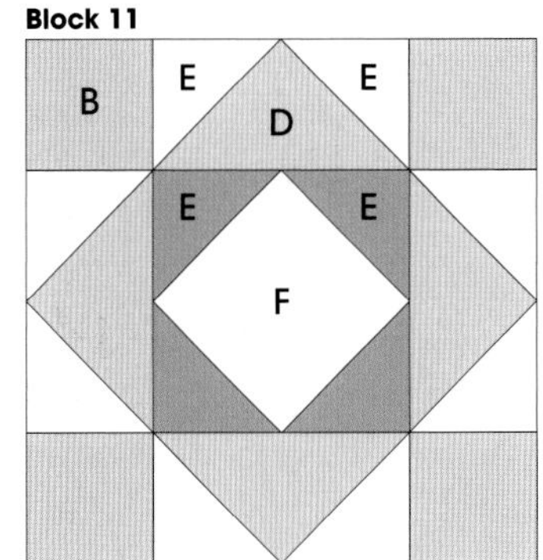


Block 12

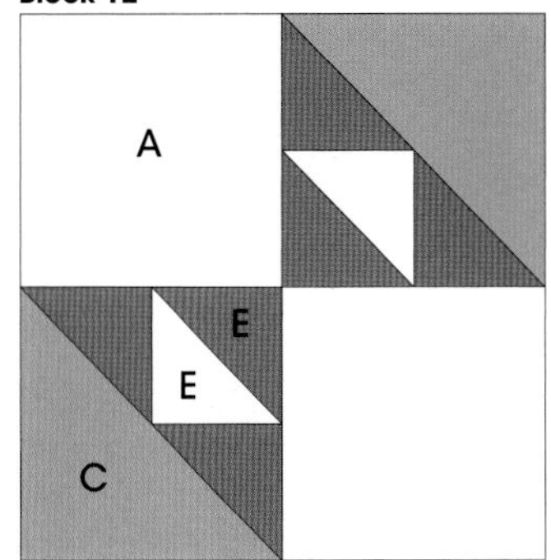


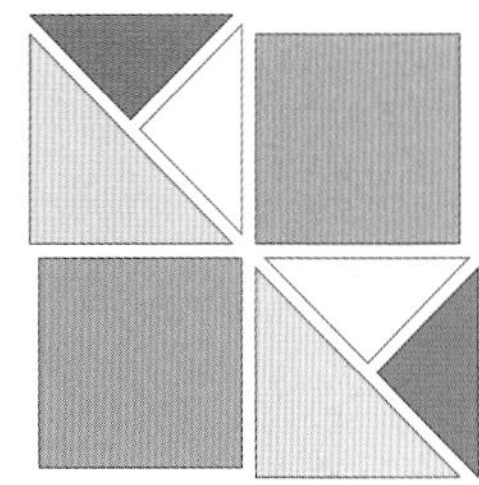

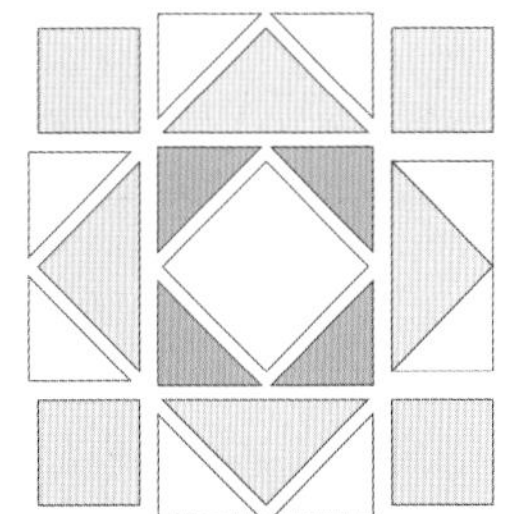

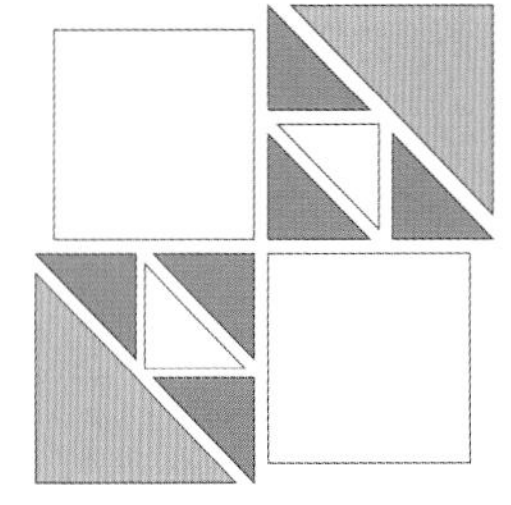

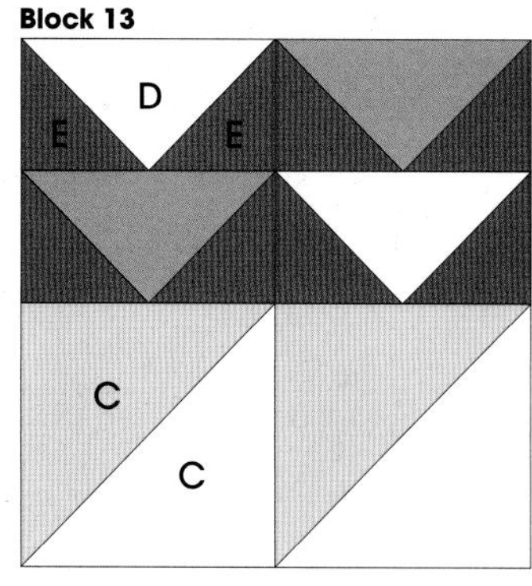


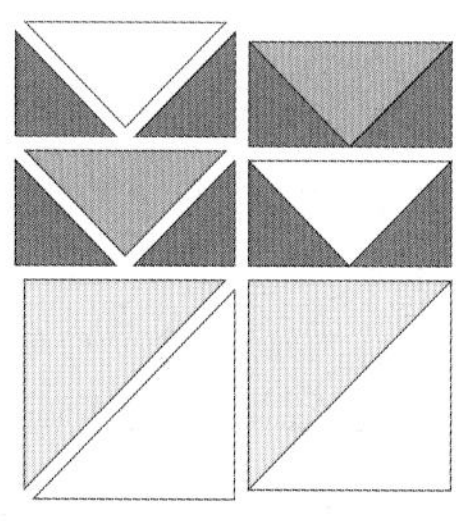

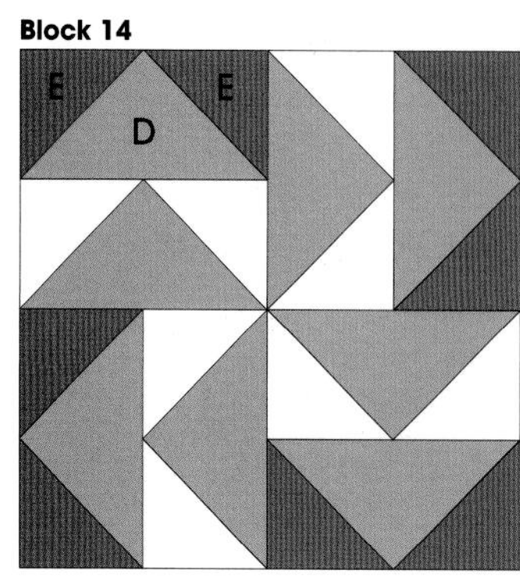

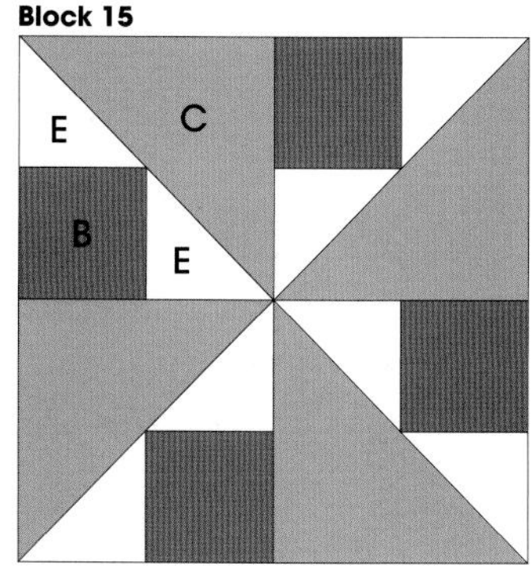


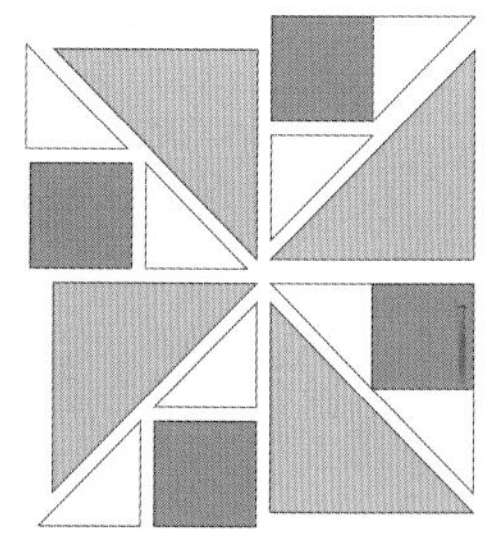

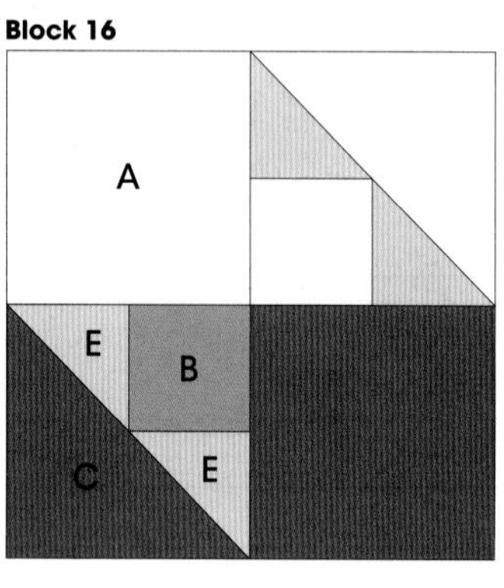


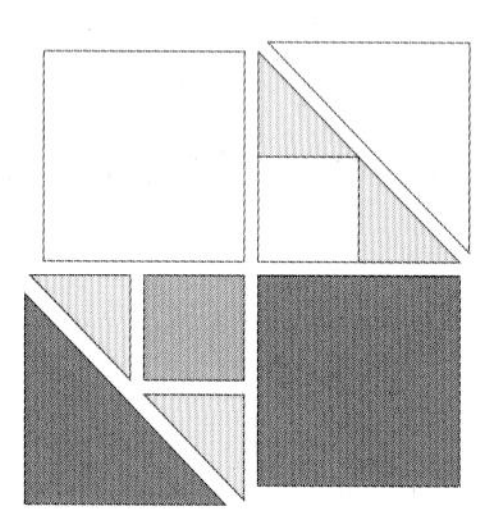

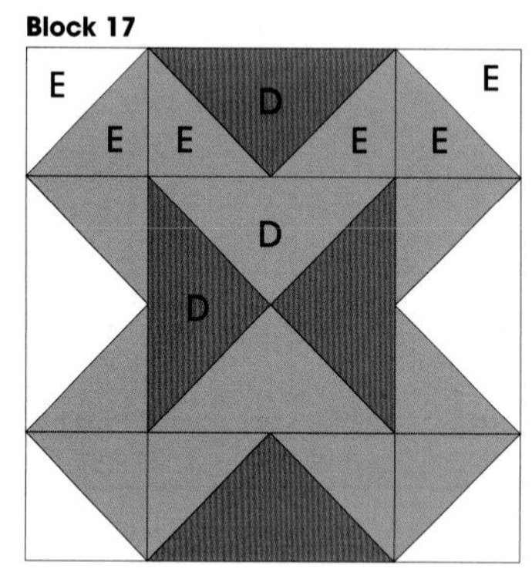

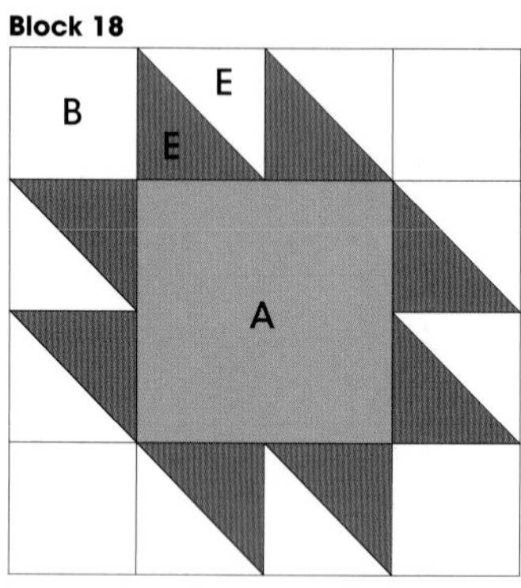


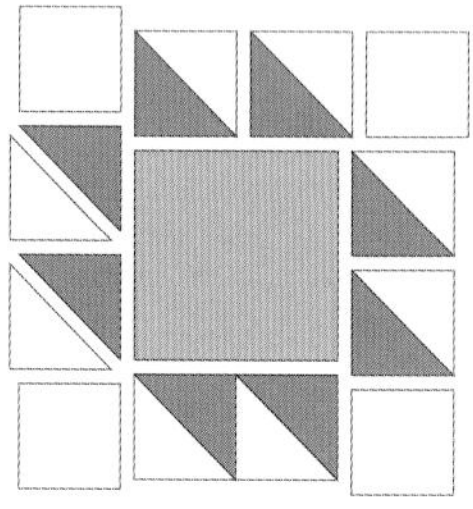

## Putting it all together

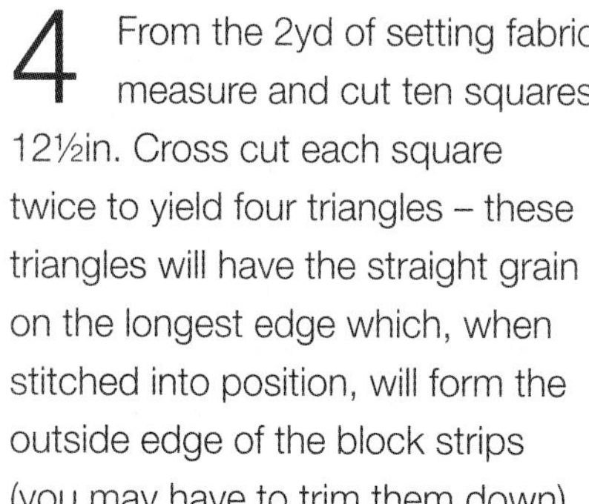

4 From the 2yd of setting fabric measure and cut ten squares 12½in. Cross cut each square twice to yield four triangles – these triangles will have the straight grain on the longest edge which, when stitched into position, will form the outside edge of the block strips (you may have to trim them down).

You will need a total of thirty-eight triangles (shown in Fig 2). From the setting fabric also measure and cut four squares 6¼in. Cross cut each square once only to yield eight triangles. These smaller triangles will be placed on each side of the top and bottom of the left and right strips (see Fig 2 opposite).

5 Join blocks and triangles into three strips following Fig 2. Press the strips carefully before joining them together. Pin at the seams and midway between seams to ensure good matching.

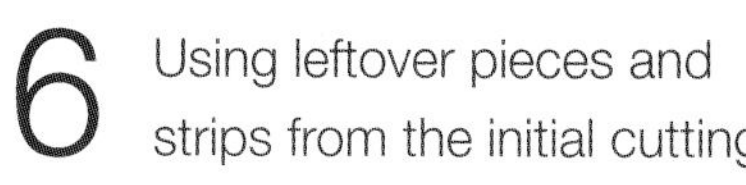

6 Using leftover pieces and strips from the initial cutting,

piece together two narrow strips for side borders and press before stitching into position. Measure and cut 3½in strips for the outer borders, piecing these together as necessary to make the required lengths. Make four pieced units (Jacquie used B squares) for the outer corners if desired.

7 Join corner units to both ends of each of the short top and bottom final border strips. Add side borders first, followed by top and bottom borders. Press all new seams.

## Finishing off

8 Layer up the quilt top, batting and backing and baste ready for quilting (see page 117). Quilt as desired – the zigzag spaces between blocks would be a great for simple but showy hand or machine quilting

9 Finish by binding and labelling your quilt (see page 118).

**Fig 2** *Piecing blocks and setting triangles together into long strips*

# Quilt Gallery

The on-point setting Jacquie used so successfully was also used by Anne Broughton for Festive Cheer.

**FESTIVE CHEER**

*Designed and pieced by Anne Broughton*
*Quilted by Debbie Wendt*

*Size: 75in x 63in*

*Begun with 7 fat quarters*

Anne made a total of twenty 8in blocks and used an on-point setting to show them to best advantage. She chose a warm-toned fabric for the setting squares and inner border and two further borders complete the seasonal theme. There were a number of border options and I finally added two further borders in appropriate colours.

# Debbie in De Nile

A teaching trip to Cairo in 2004 gave me the opportunity to conduct a trial class, using a very early development of the main cutting scheme, for the aptly named local group, 'Quilters in De Nile'. Debbie Wendt (who has a number of credits elsewhere in this book) had first asked me to teach for this exciting and eclectic group of quilters back in 2000 when she was their organizer-in-chief. Since then it has been a huge pleasure and privilege for me to return each year. It seemed appropriate therefore that I should ask Debbie if she would quilt this lively sampler-style quilt, which was designed and pieced by her organizing successor, Debbie Fetch. This super quilt, with its jaunty twist-and-turn setting, represents our long-distance and truly international quilting friendships, which span the distance all the way from Cairo to Iowa, via Boston and England.

*Designed and pieced by Debbie Fetch, quilted by Debbie Wendt*

 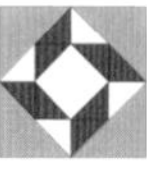  

*"Tradition with a contemporary twist! Well-travelled quiltmaker Debbie Fetch came up with this lively quilt after she had organized and participated in the inaugural class for the main cutting plan. The quilt was begun in Cairo, quilted in the US – who knows where this quilt will go next?"*

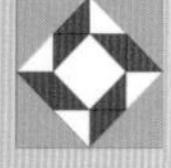

**You will need**

- Six fat quarters for the blocks
- Twist-and-turn setting, forty-eight 9in x 2in strips
- Inner border, four 1½in strips
- Outer border, four 4in strips
- Batting, 52in x 42in
- Backing fabric, 52in x 42in
- Binding fabric (see page 118)

**Quilt size:** 48in long x 38in wide
**Block size:** 8in square finished
**Skill rating:** Intermediate

## Making the blocks

1 Starch and press all the quarters and stack them in readiness for cutting. Cut according to the cutting plan (Fig 3 on page 17) and set out the cut pieces on your paper map.

2 The twelve traditional blocks that Debbie chose are shown in the block diagrams here – you can follow these or make different choices. The quilt plan is shown in Fig 2 overleaf.

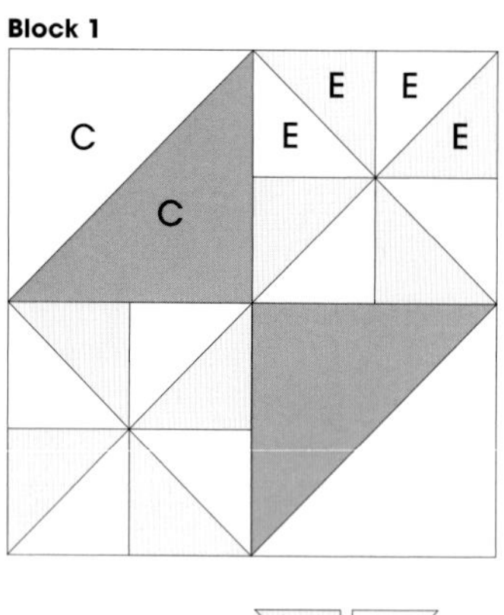


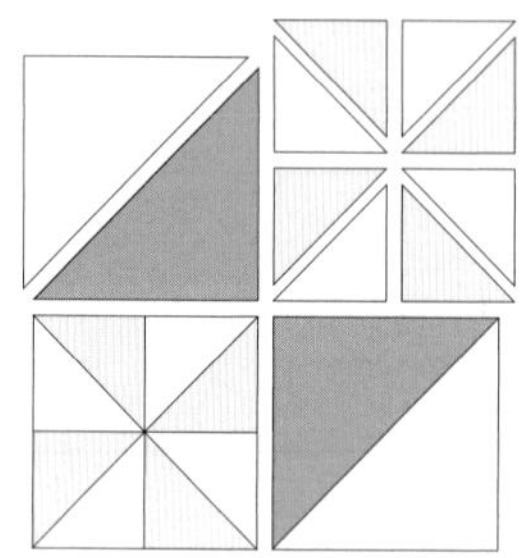

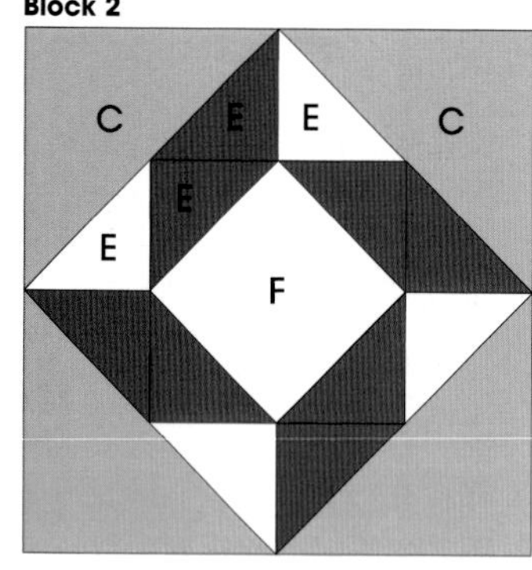

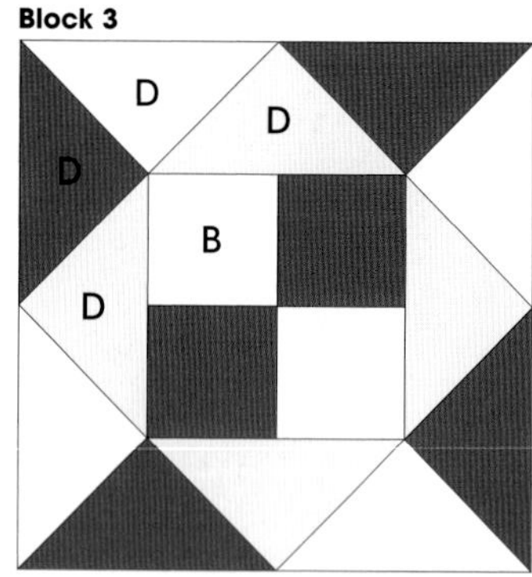

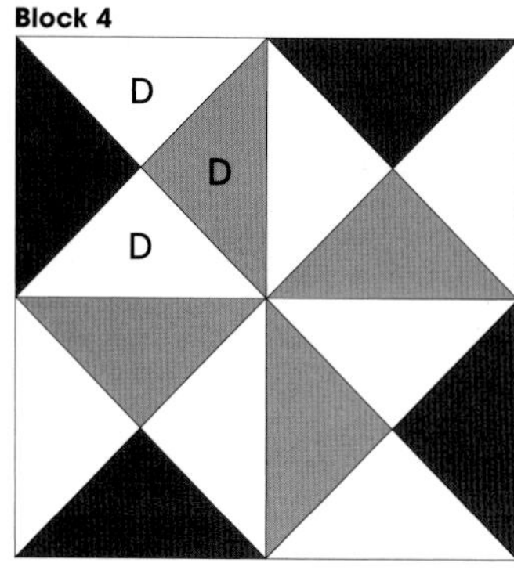

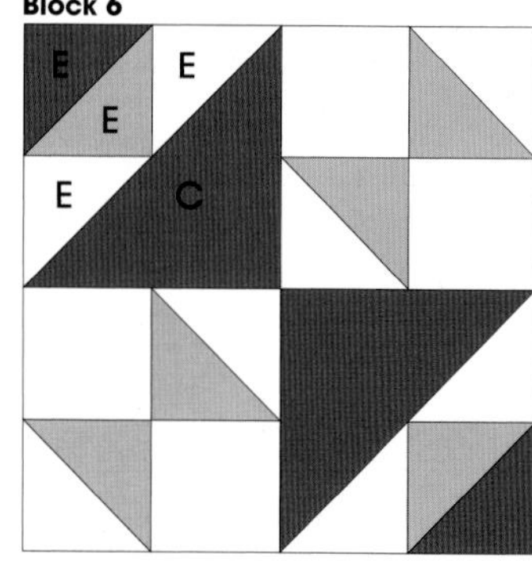

## Block diagrams

Debbie in De Nile uses twelve blocks, shown here. See the 'exploded' diagrams for construction.

Block 7

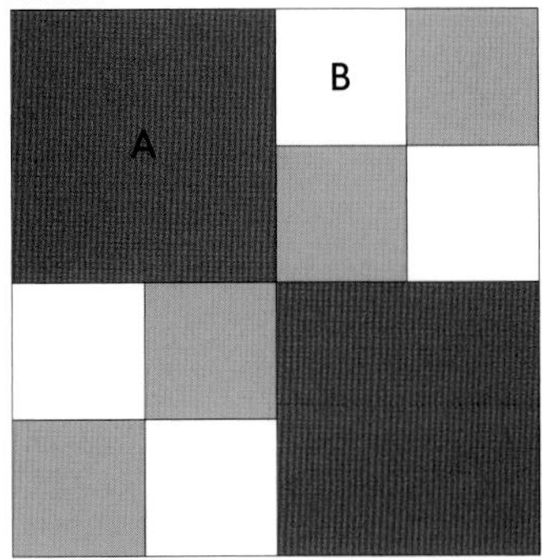

Block 8

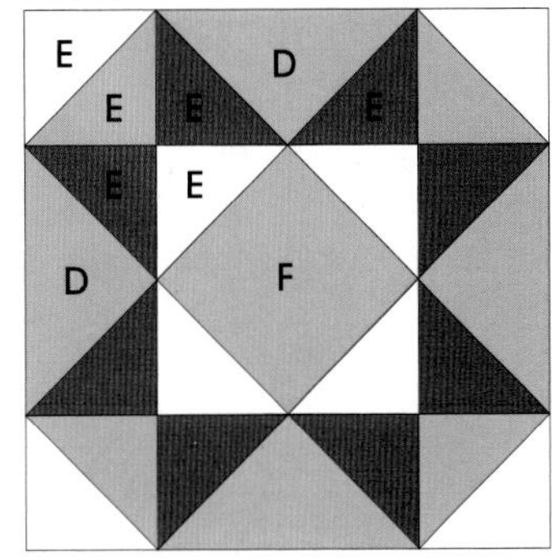


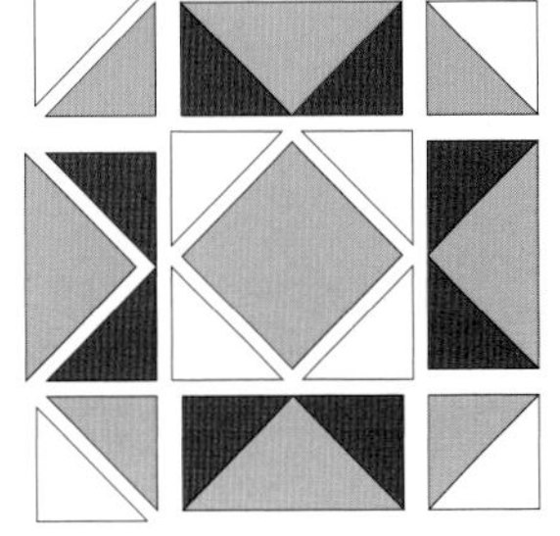

Block 9

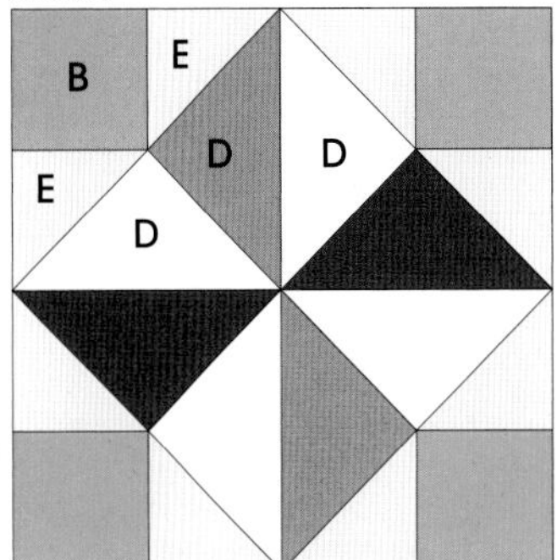

Block 10

Block 11

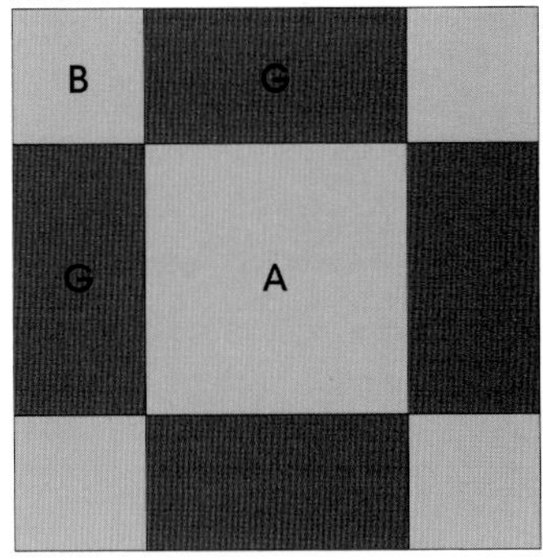

Block 12

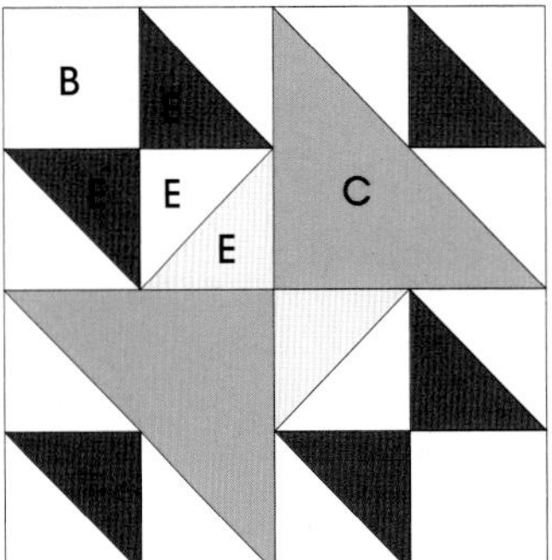


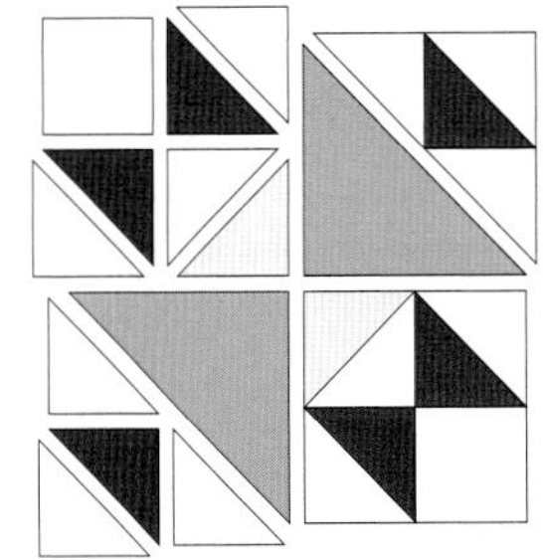

**Fig 2** *Layout of Debbie in De Nile with borders*

## Putting it all together

3 The twist-and-turn setting can be achieved by stitching strips to all four sides of a block then skewing it around and trimming the edges to make a 'new' block – see Fig 3. Debbie carefully changed the direction of twist on the blocks for maximum impact and movement.

4 Join the newly skewed blocks together in three sets of four and then join the three sets together.

5 Add the narrow inner border strips in the usual sequence of sides first, top and bottom second, and press the new seams before adding the outer border strips in the same way. Press again.

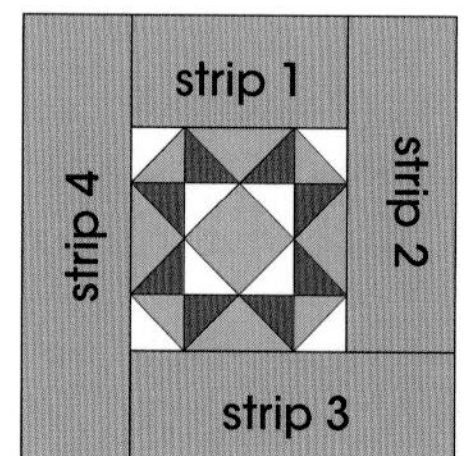


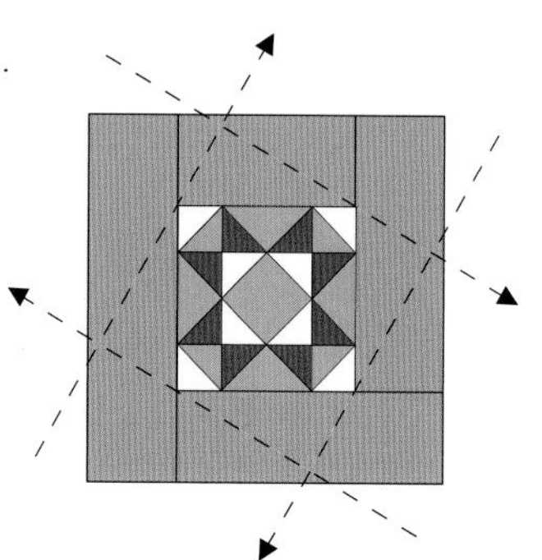

**Fig 3** *Make a twist-and-turn setting for the blocks by first adding strips and then re-cutting the block square*

## Finishing off

6 Layer the quilt top, batting and backing together and baste in preparation for quilting (see page 117).

7 Quilt according to your preference (see page 118) – Debbie used a swirly, all-over floral design of her own devising to complete this all-Debbie special.

8 Finish by binding and labelling your quilt (see page 118).

## Colour confidence

Debbie's lively quilt lends itself to many colour choices and changes. You might try combining outdoor shades of cool blue and soft greens with summery touches of lilac and pink. For a completely different, but equally effective look, choose jaunty red and blue prints with accents of black and strong yellow.

# Quilt Gallery

Debbie's choice of a twist-and-turn setting shows just how effective simple block framing and setting can be. Jan Holland chose an equally graphic Attic Window setting for her quilt – she made sixteen blocks and only had twenty-eight pieces left over! See pages 111–113 for other framing examples.

**THROUGH THE SQUARE WINDOW**

*Designed and pieced by Jan Holland*
*Quilted by Debbie Wendt*

*Size: 57in x 57in*

*Begun with 6 fat quarters*

Jan tried to make as many simple blocks as possible from her warm-toned fat quarters and used an Attic Window setting to frame them.

# Wow!

Shirley Smith's deliciously bright quilt made from twenty 8in blocks may be traditionally based but has a sharp contemporary feel to it, with its strongly contrasting sashing and setting squares and confident handling of clear and strong colours. The eight fat quarters of eye-catching prints that Shirley selected actually made a total of twenty-four blocks – she hasn't yet revealed what happened to the remaining four! There are several repeats but this is not immediately obvious because different colourways can change the appearance of a block so effectively. Shirley said she thoroughly enjoyed making the quilt and found it went together really quickly. When the quilt top arrived, I felt that an extra border would add even more of a 'wow' factor and took the liberty of adding a simple but bright piano key-style border.

*Designed and pieced by Shirley Smith, quilted by Debbie Wendt*

 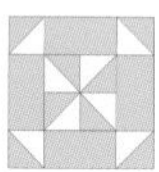 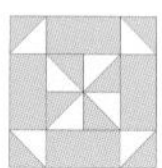 

*"The title is exactly what everyone said when they saw Shirley Smith's confident and vibrant sampler quilt. Shirley's enjoyment in making the quilt using the cutting plan certainly shows in the finished piece."*

**You will need**

- Eight fat quarters for the blocks
- One fat quarter for the setting squares
- Sashings, ¾yd fabric
- Border fabrics, ½yd lengths of six fabrics
- Batting, 65in x 55in
- Backing fabric, 65in x 55in
- Binding fabric (see page 118)

**Quilt size:** 61in long x 51in wide
**Block size:** 8in square finished
**Skill rating:** Intermediate

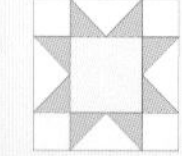

# Making the blocks

1 Starch and press all quarters before making two stacks of four quarters and cutting according to the cutting plan (Fig 3 on page 17). Transfer all the cut pieces to your paper map.

2 The blocks Shirley chose are shown in the diagrams on these two pages. There are eleven different blocks but some have been repeated (blocks 4, 5 and 9 are each repeated twice and block 3 seven times). You can follow Shirley's blocks or make some different choices of your own, depending on your preference. As you make up the blocks, remember to press and trim the seams at each stage.

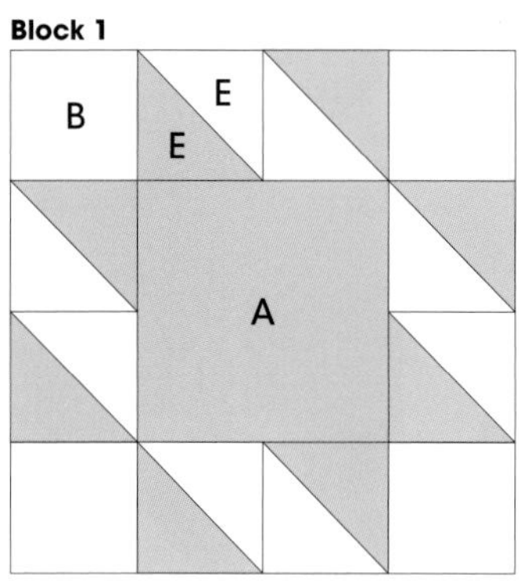


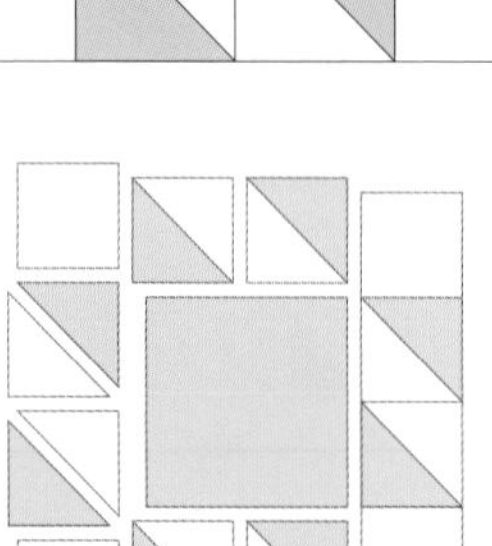

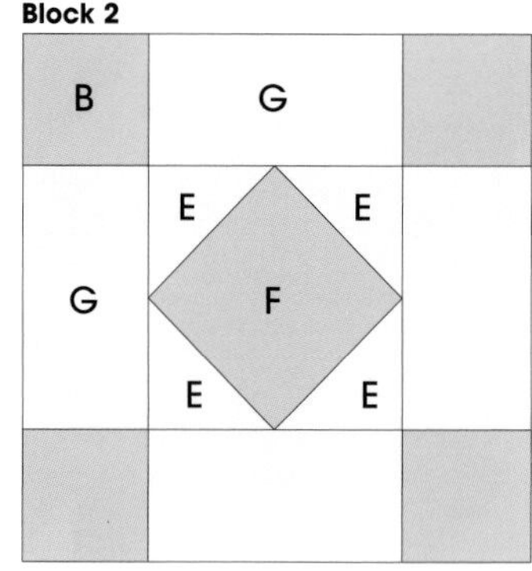


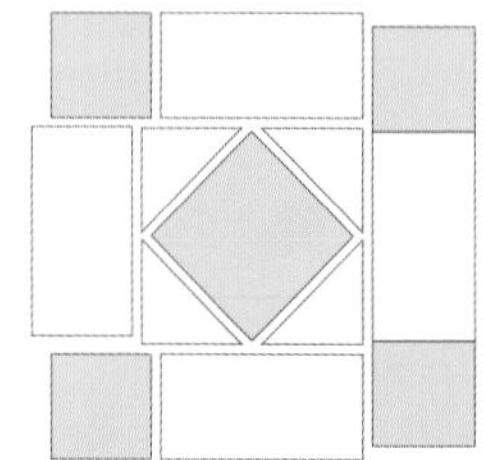

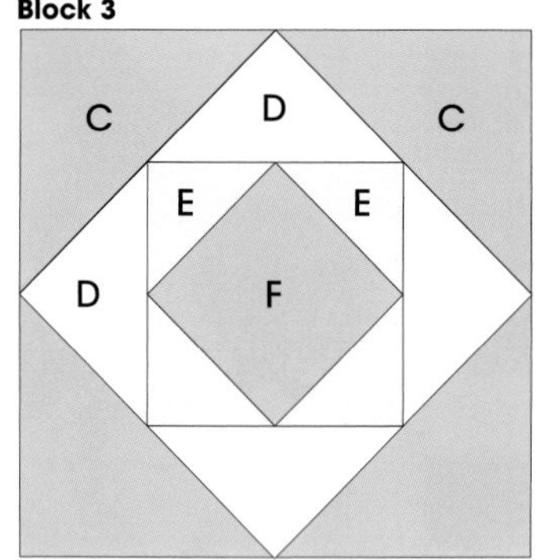

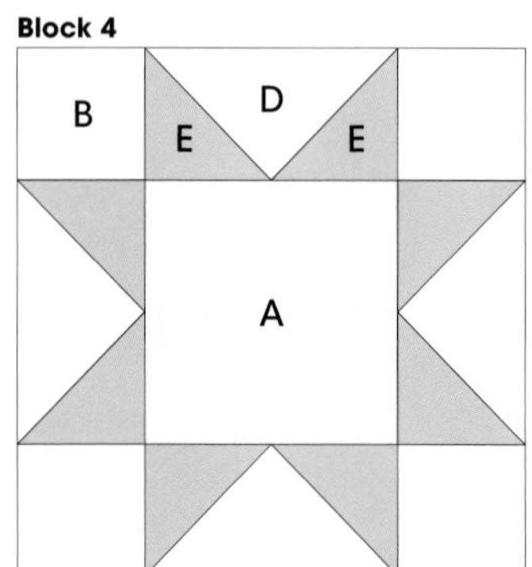


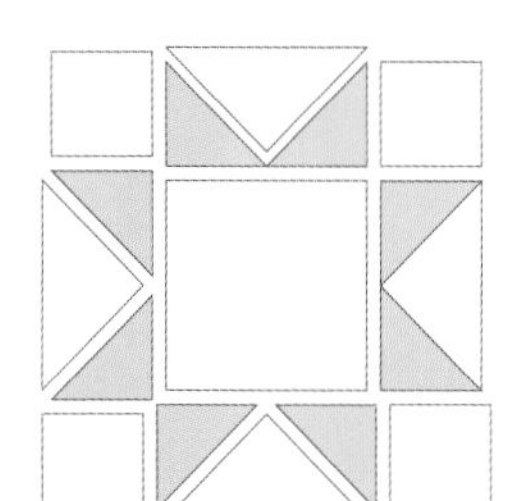

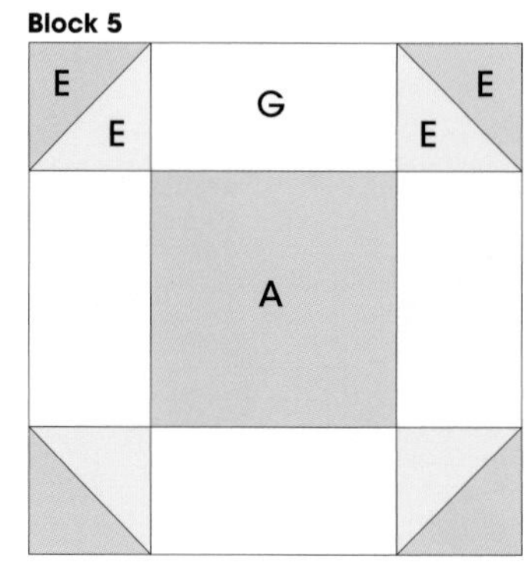


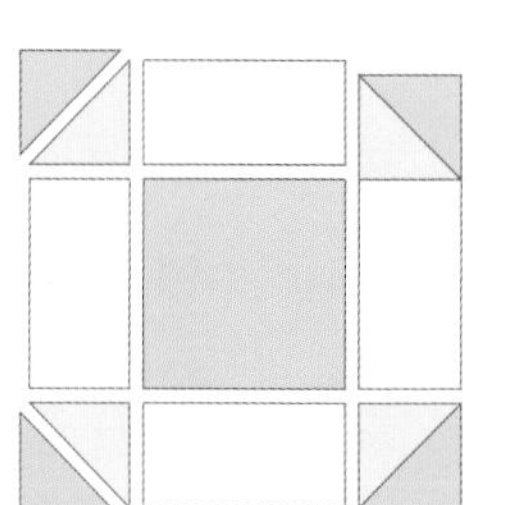

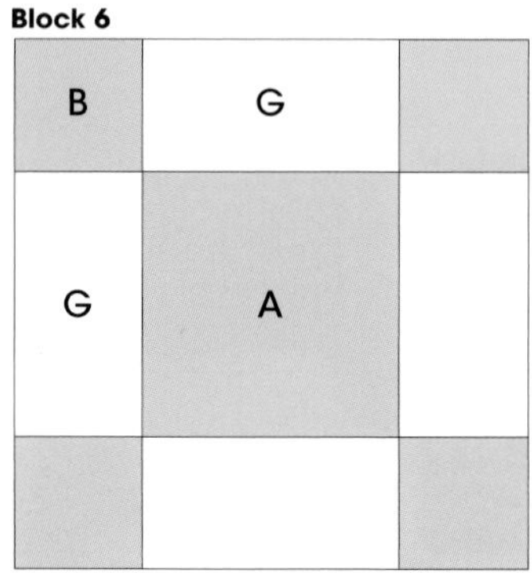


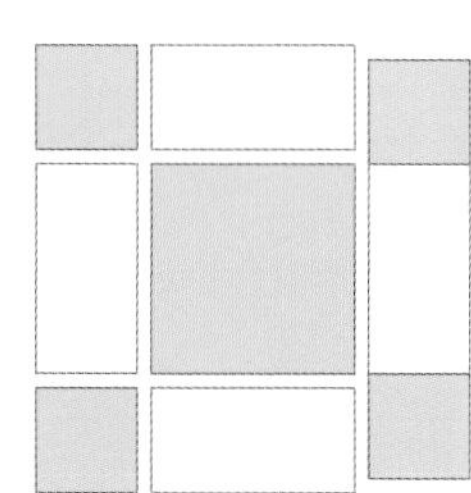

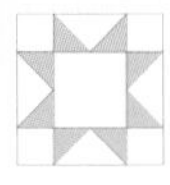

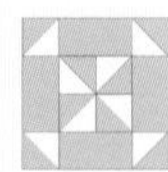

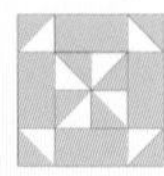

**Block 7**

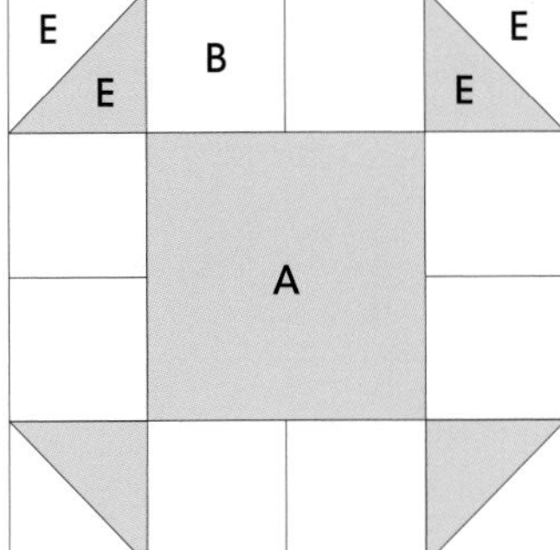


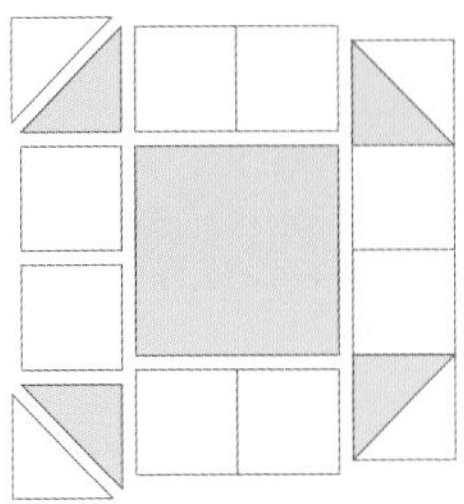

**Block 8**

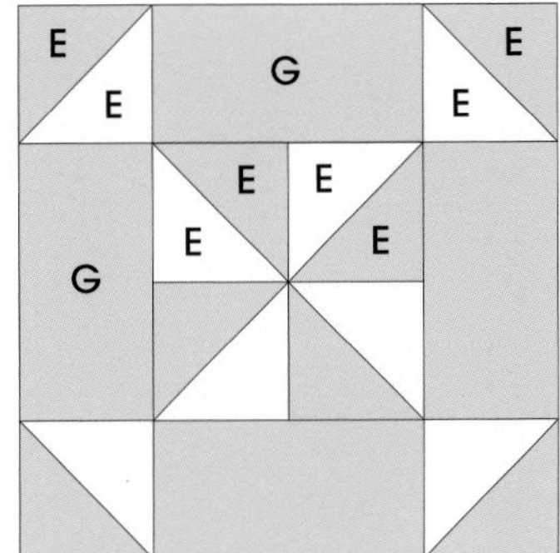


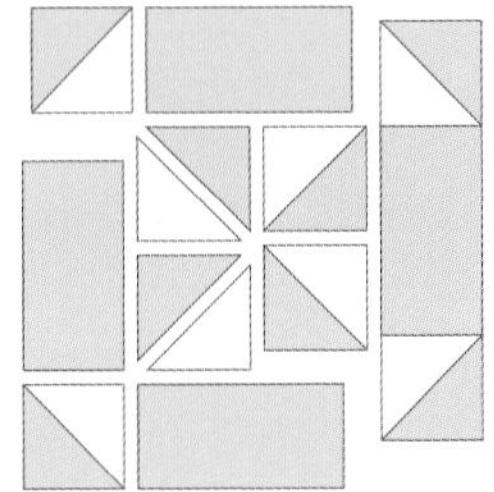

**Block 9**

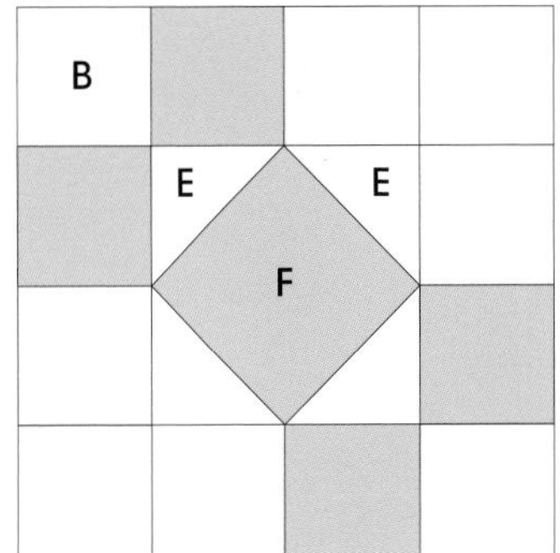


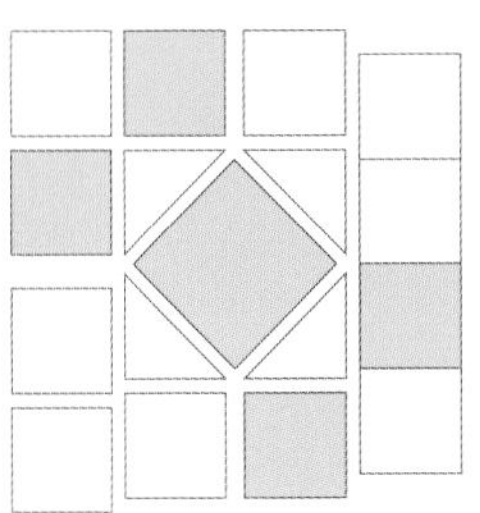

## Block diagrams

Wow! uses eleven blocks, shown here. See the 'exploded' diagrams for construction. Shirley repeated at least four blocks and made variations to others to make up the total of twenty blocks.

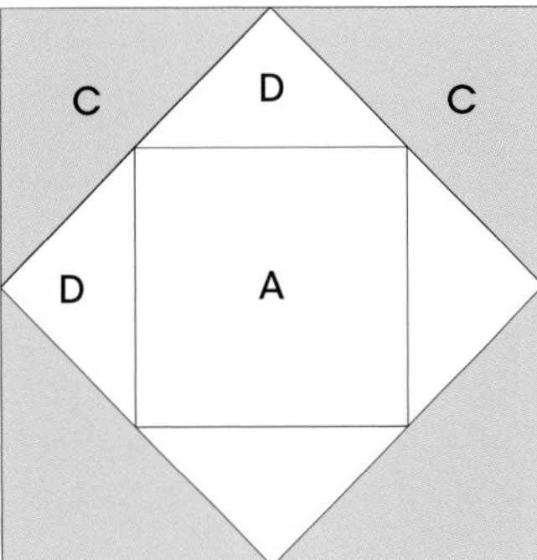


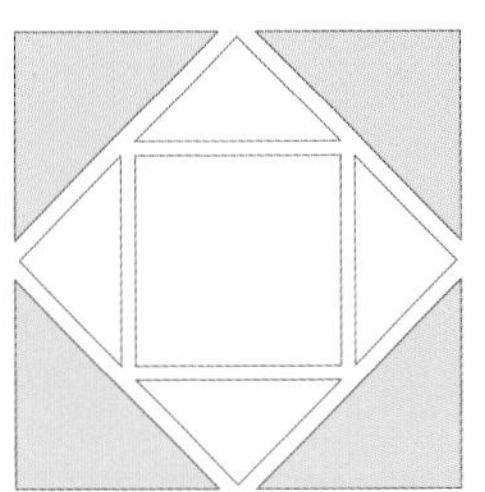

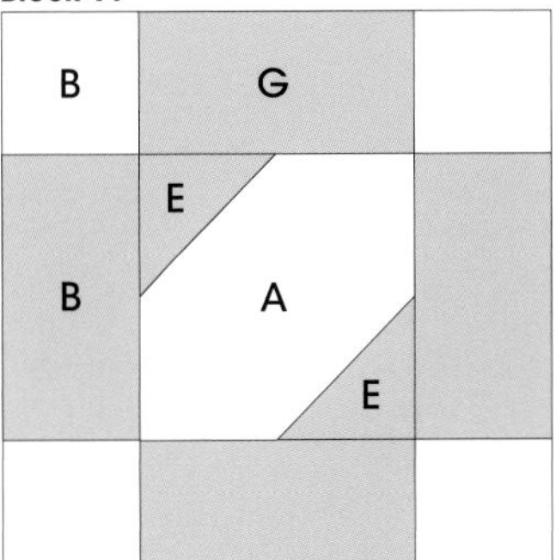


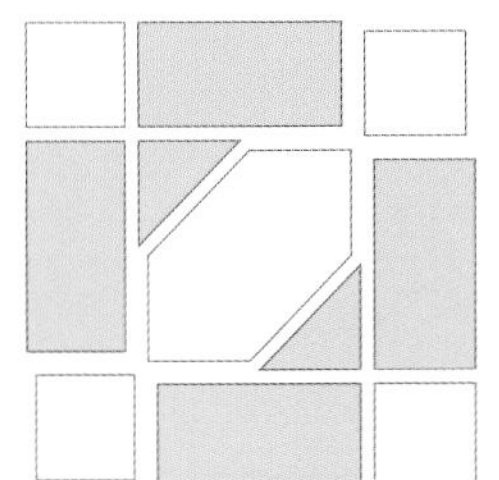

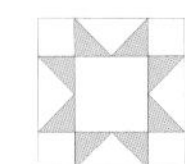

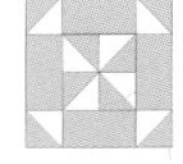

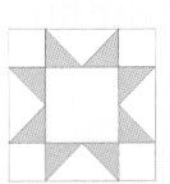

**Fig 2** *Layout of Wow!*

## Putting it all together

3 Use a large design space to lay out all your blocks (see Fig 2). If, like Shirley, you have made more than the twenty blocks required for this quilt, select which you will use and which you will set aside, for matching cushions or pillows perhaps?

4 Follow the usual sequence for putting the blocks, sashings and setting squares together. The blocks are joined into strips of four with short sashing strips cut 2½in wide. The block strips themselves are then joined together with long strips of sashings and squares, either cut 2½in square or using leftover B squares. Press all new seams.

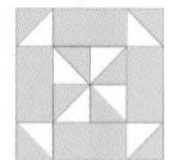

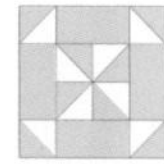

5 Add the inner border strips of sashing and squares, cut 2½in, in the usual sequence of sides first, top and bottom second. Press the work again.

6 To make the wider outer border, first cut and stitch assorted strips into a long pieced band. Cut and re-join this band until you have four pieced strips of suitable length for borders. For this quilt these strips were cut 5in wide but you can, of course, vary the width of the strips if you wish. Join these strips in the same sequence as before, adding in the four corner setting squares.

## Finishing off

7 Press and trim the quilt top carefully before layering together with the batting and backing, then basting in readiness for quilting (see page 117).

8 Quilt according to your preference and then finish your quilt by binding and labelling (see page 119).

# Quilt Gallery

Many volunteers made a selection of different blocks and, like Shirley, arranged them in a traditional-style sampler setting. This selection illustrates the variety – narrow sashings, wide sashings, narrow borders, wide borders, pieced borders, plain borders and blocks on point, plus a variety of colour schemes.

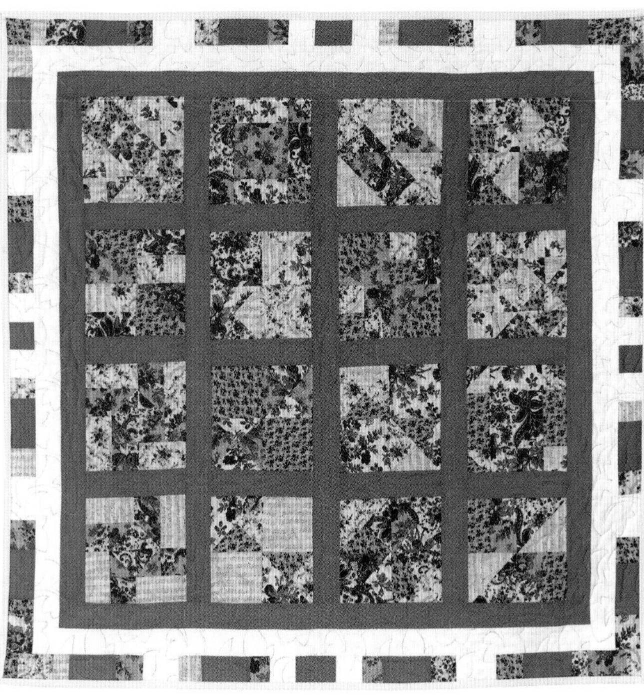

**SO EASY SAMPLER**

*Designed and pieced by Margery Blundy Quilted by Debbie Wendt*

*Size: 48in x 48in*

*Begun with 6 fat quarters*

Margery is a speedy stitcher but even she couldn't believe how quickly and easily this quilt came together.

**SUMMER SONG**

*Designed and pieced by Jan Gamble Quilted by Debbie Wendt*

*Size: 45in x 45in*

*Begun with 6 fat quarters*

Jan made as many blocks as she could and then used what was left to make the final pieced border.

**IF THE FUTURE'S ORANGE, I'M A BANANA**

*Designed, pieced and quilted by Jennie Walker*

*Size: 51in x 51in*

*Begun with 9 fat quarters*

This zingy quilt rejoices in a title that reflects Jennie's humorous take on life. The sashed setting may be traditional in style but looks as sharp and fresh as the fruit prints she used.

# Quilt Gallery

## LAST MINUTE SAMPLER

*Designed and pieced by Audrey Ball*
*Quilted by Debbie Wendt*

*Size: 59in x 59in*

*Begun with 8 fat quarters*

Audrey used the strips left over from the cutting plan to make two Log Cabin blocks, and, despite rushing to finish (hence the title), enjoyed the challenge of using as many pieces as possible.

## EILEEN'S SAMPLER

*Designed and pieced by Eileen Jenkins*
*Quilted by Debbie Wendt*

*Size: 66in x 48in*

*Begun with 7 fat quarters*

Having already made a sampler quilt block by block in the 1980s, Eileen said this went together much faster!

**SUMMER MEADOWS**

*Designed and pieced by Sue Mee*
*Quilted by Debbie Wendt*

*Size: 59in x 59in*

*Begun with 8 fat quarters*

For this quilt Sue bravely used fabric she had kept and loved for some time. It took her just ten hours from start to finish.

**CHALLENGE BC**

*Designed and pieced by Bette Williams*
*Quilted by Debbie Wendt*

*Size: 56in x 47in*

*Begun with 8 fat quarters*

After choosing colours well outside her usual comfort zone, Bette found an addictive quality in the additional challenge to herself of using as many pieces as possible.

# All Things Bright

Cosby Quilters hold Pat Screaton entirely responsible for their role as testers of this book's main cutting plan. We arranged a meeting where volunteers, marshalled by Pat, could collect their instructions and discuss fabric choices for their projects. It was no surprise to anyone to find that Pat was armed with three sets of fabrics, all set to make three sizeable quilts! Pat jumped right into the project and came up with this stunning quilt using mostly nine-patch blocks. She made twelve different 12in blocks and still had enough cut pieces left to make the small units at the centre of the setting squares. In keeping with the bright, funky fabrics, Pat opted for an equally bright and funky approach to the blocks and their setting. The clever use of spacer blocks with small pieced units at the centre is particularly successful.

*Designed and pieced by Pat Screaton,*
*quilted by Debbie Wendt*

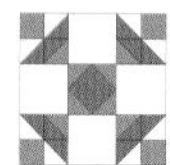

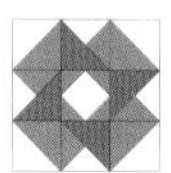

*"I enjoyed making this quilt. I made my first four blocks and then decided to lay all the remaining blocks out so I could be sure they were all different."*

**You will need**

- Ten fat quarters for the blocks
- Settings and borders, 2½yds of fabric
- Batting, 79in x 55in
- Backing fabric, 79in x 55in
- Binding fabric (see page 118)

| | |
|---|---|
| **Quilt size:** | 75in long x 51in wide |
| **Block size:** | 12in square finished |
| **Skill rating:** | Intermediate |

# Making the blocks

1 Starch and press all the quarters and make two stacks of five to cut according to the cutting plan (Fig 3 on page 17). Transfer all the cut pieces to your paper map.

2 Lay out and piece twelve blocks – the blocks Pat chose or devised are shown in the block diagrams on these pages. Press and trim seams as you go.

Block 1

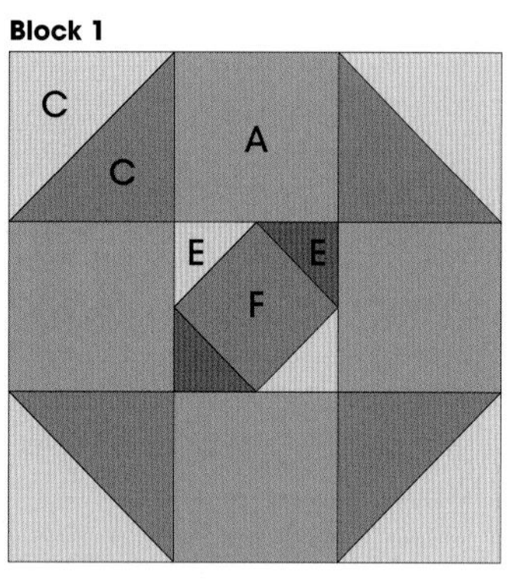


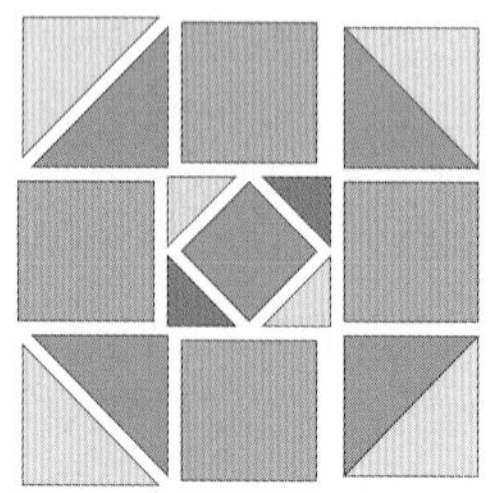

Block 2

Block 3

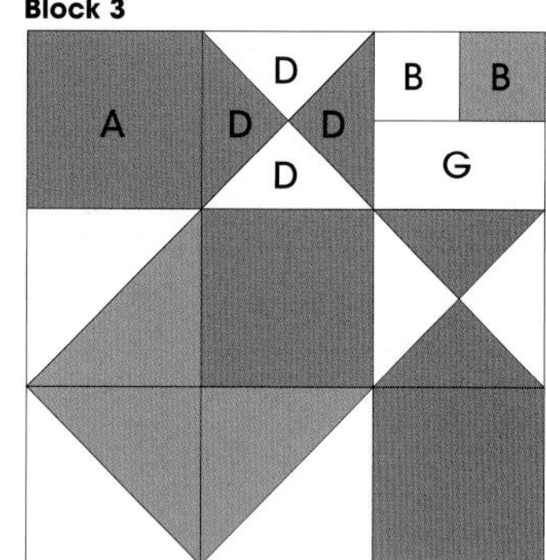


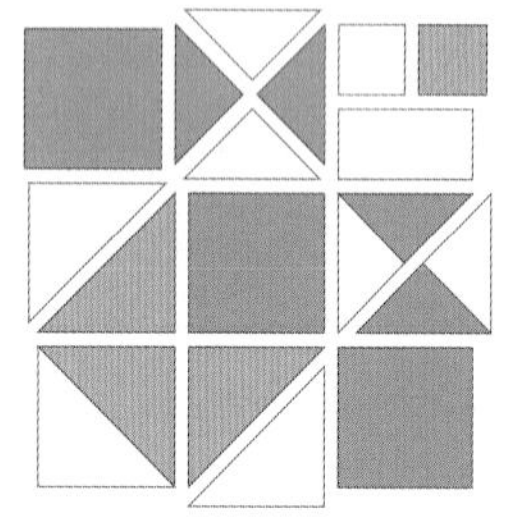

Block 4

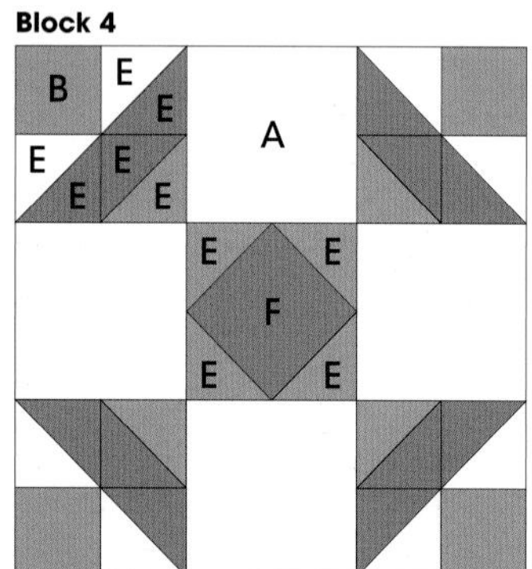


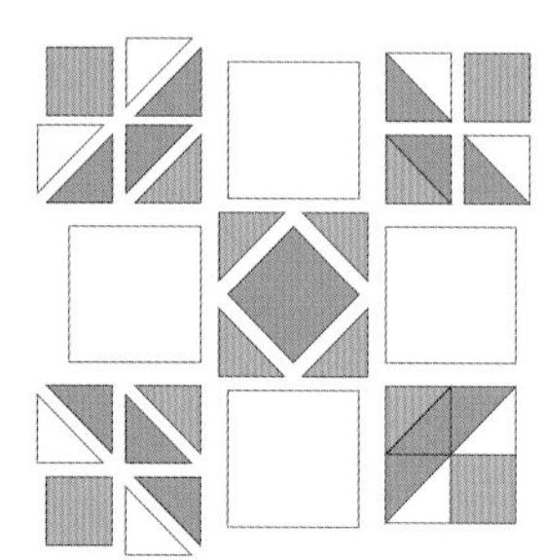

Block 5

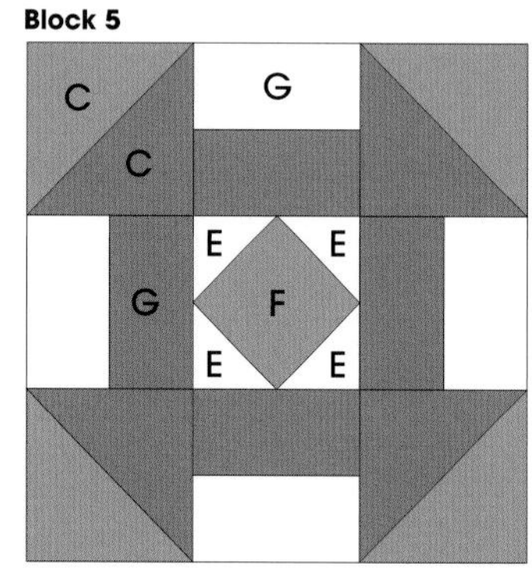


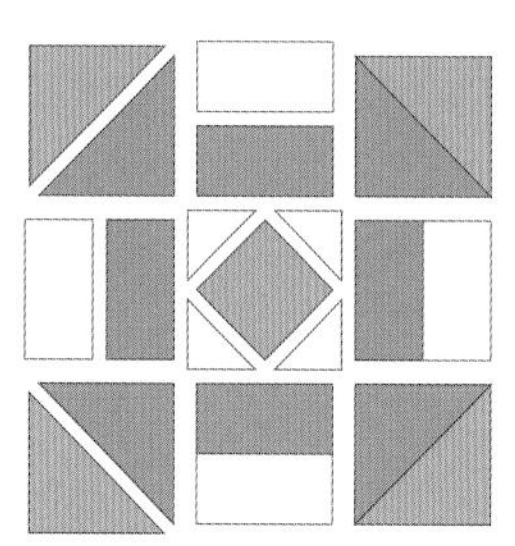

Block 6

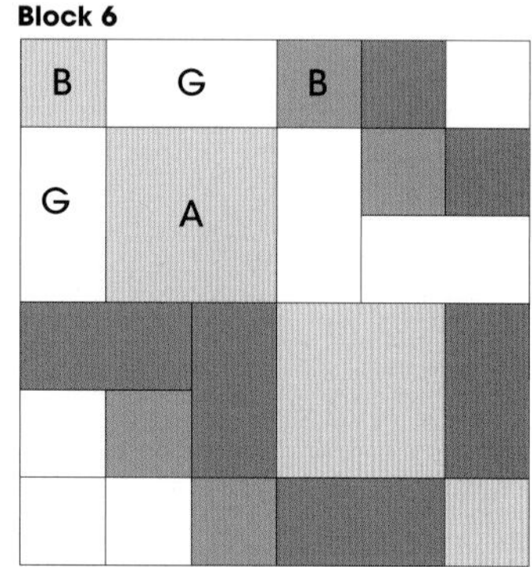


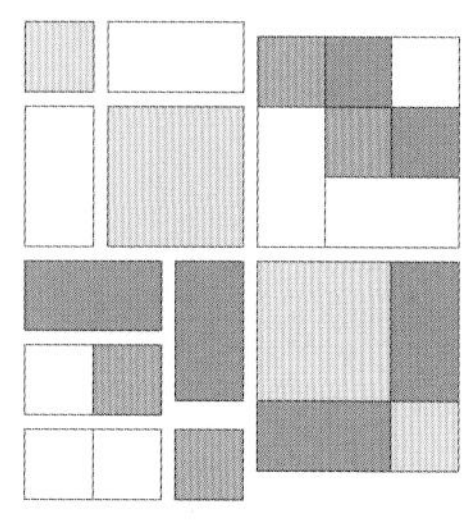

## Block diagrams

All Things Bright uses twelve nine-patch blocks, shown here. Block 7 is a repeat of block 5 but with a different value placement. See the 'exploded' diagrams for construction.

**Block 7**

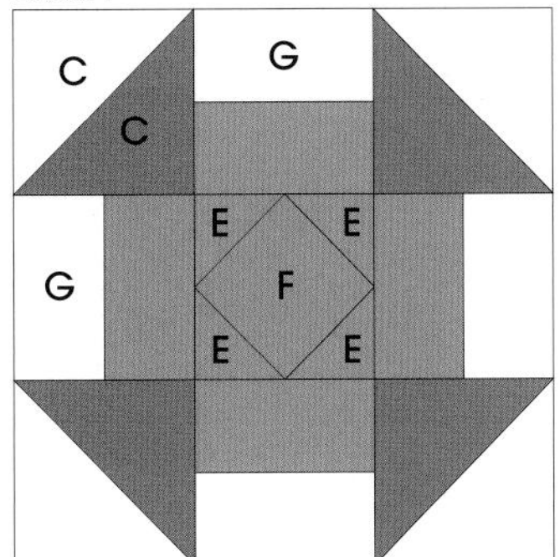

**Block 8**

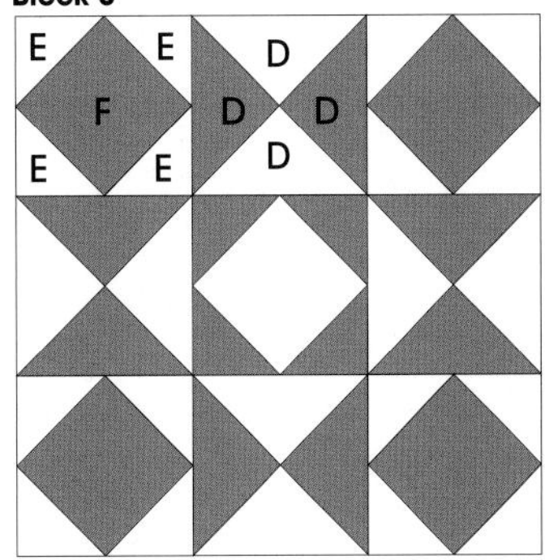

**Block 9**

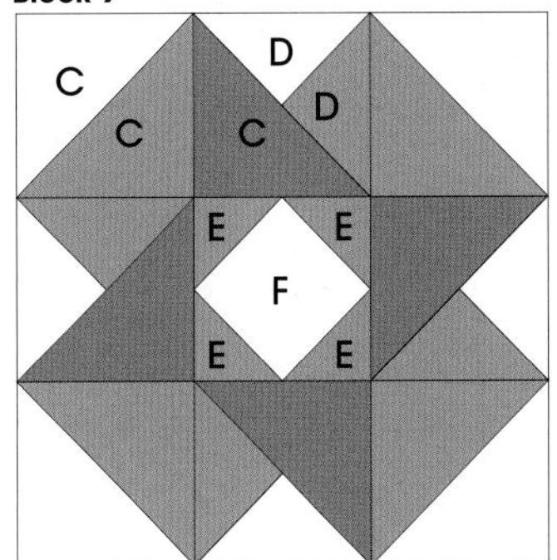

**Block 10**

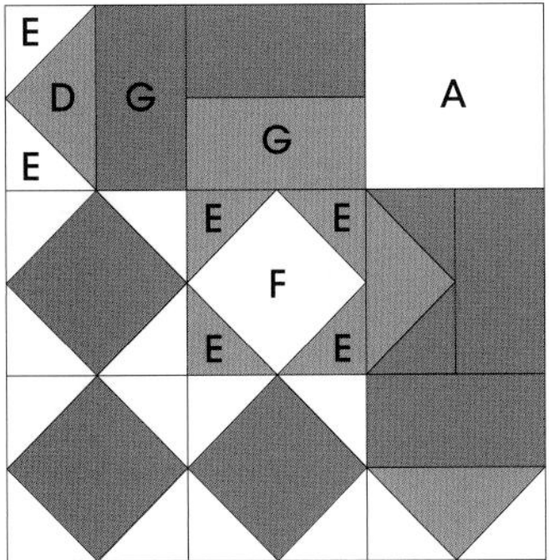


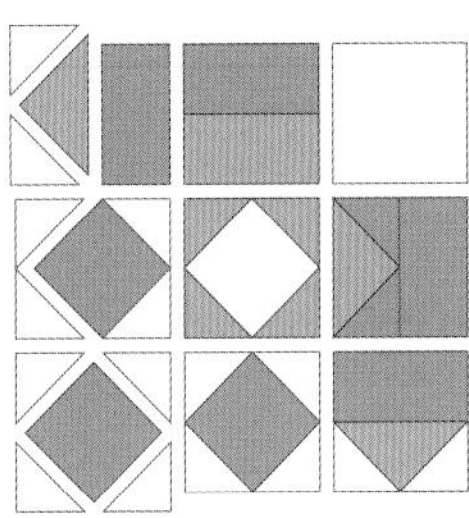

**Block 11**

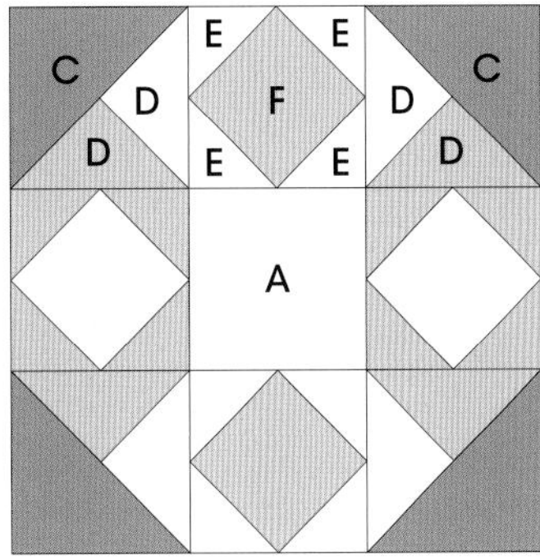


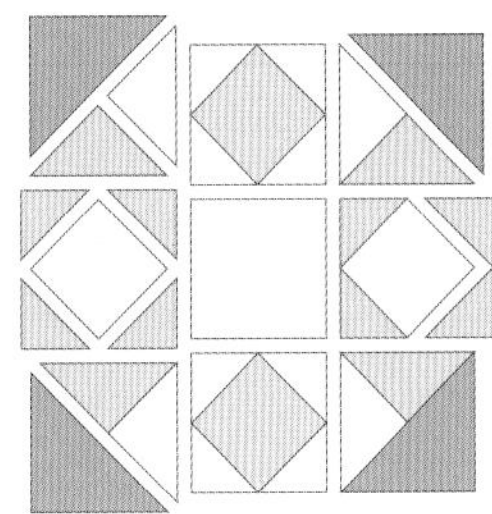

**Block 12**

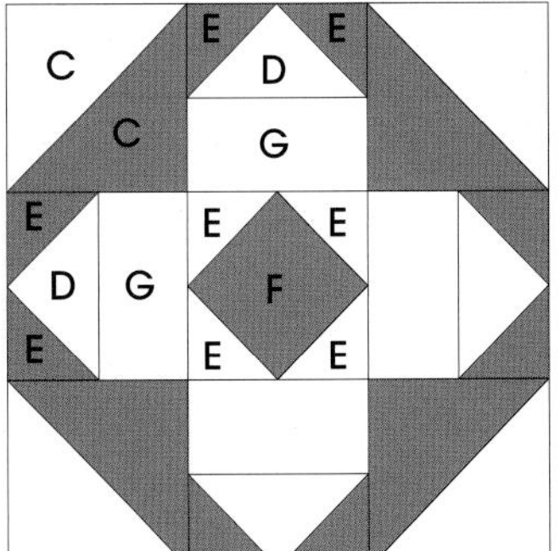


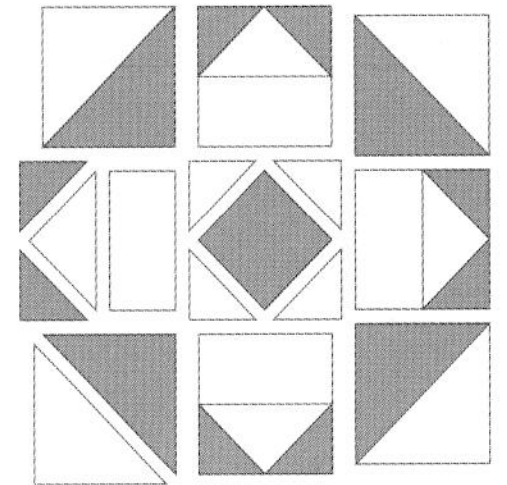

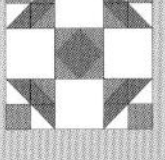

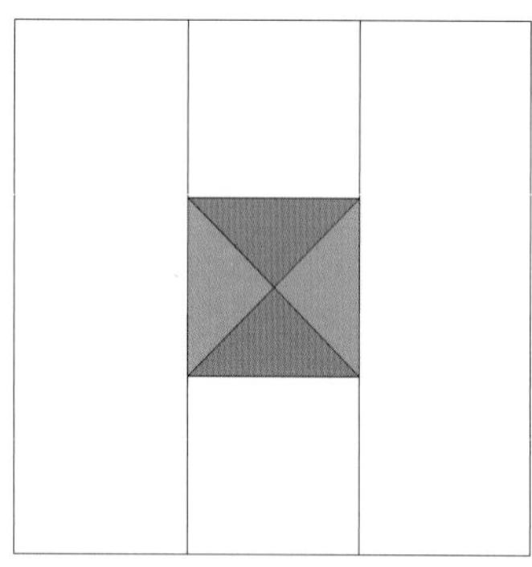

**Fig 1** *Frame a small pieced unit with setting strips to build a larger block that matches the main blocks in size*

3 From the remaining pieces make twelve pieced units, each finishing 4in square. Cut setting strips 4½in and use these to frame the small units and make a larger block – see Fig 1.

**Fig 2** *All Things Bright layout*

## Putting it all together

4 Use a design wall or similar planning space to lay out all the main blocks and the setting blocks and move them around until you find an arrangement that pleases you. The layout Pat used is shown in Fig 2, above.

5 Join the blocks together in six strips of four blocks and press new seams before going on to join the block strips together. Press again before adding narrow outer border strips in the usual sequence of sides first, top and bottom second.

## Finishing off

6 Press and trim the completed quilt top before layering it together with batting and backing and basting the layers together ready for quilting (see page 117). Quilt according to your preference.

7 Finish your quilt by binding and labelling (see page 118).

## Colour confidence

Either of these two alternative colourways – hazy sunset shades of pinks and lilacs or café-au-lait with cream and dusty blue – would offer a completely different look to the strong colours and values of Pat's original quilt. In these examples the contrast between the values of the alternating and main blocks is much reduced.

A third colourway, with black, aqua, sky blue, cool green and acid yellow, looks sharp when set against very light values, yet appears more muted when set against a medium value of lilac.

# African Adventure

This large quilt began with fat quarters of eight African style-prints plus cream, sand and black. Instead of using the main plan on page 17 I wondered what might happen if all the fabric was cut up into squares and then stitched into half-square triangles. I set myself a basic rule that at least two squares of each print would be paired with each of the three plain colours and then set to work stitching, cutting apart and pressing. The idea of cutting and stitching without any specific plan was very appealing – so much so that I decided to cut up additional fabric to increase the size of the project (whatever it was). It was great fun to put together the basic block and the variations and the whole thing went together very quickly.

*Designed and pieced by Barbara Chainey, quilted courtesy of The Bramble Patch*

   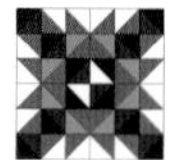

*"The idea was to see what happened after cutting fat quarters up into squares and making lots of half-square triangle units from jungle-style fabrics. It was so much fun cutting and stitching the units and making different blocks that the quilt finished considerably larger than intended."*

### You will need

- Eight fat quarters of African-themed prints plus three fat quarters each of cream, sand and black – be prepared to use more quarters as you go along (see fabric guide overleaf)
- Fabric to frame blocks, 1½in strips
- Fabric for sashings and inner border, 3in strips
- Fabric for outer border, four strips 3¾in x 100in
- Batting, 102in square
- Backing fabric, 102in square
- Binding fabric (see page 118)

**Quilt size:** 98in square
**Block size:** 18in square finished
**Skill rating:** Confident beginner

# Making the blocks

1 Spray starch all your fabrics before layering them into two piles for cutting. Cut each layered pile, first into 3⅞in strips then into 3⅞in squares. Sort and stack all the squares.

2 On the wrong side of all the cream and sand squares mark three diagonal lines ¼in apart, as shown in Fig 1. Similarly, use a light-coloured marker to make the same lines on the wrong side of all the black squares. Pair a print with a background square, right sides together and stitch on both marked outer diagonal lines. Make a second identical pairing of a print and background square and stitch on both outer diagonals again. Chain piecing will help eliminate lots of stopping and starting for this step (see page 22). I worked through this step making pairs this way – print and cream x 2, same print and sand x 2, same print and black x 2, next print and cream x 2, next same print and sand x 2 and so on. This way, I made sure that there would be even and roughly equal numbers of half-triangle squares to arrange as blocks.

### Fabric guide

As a rough guide an average fat quarter should yield twenty 3⅞in squares, maybe more depending on the actual size of the quarter, and each square gives two pieced half-triangle squares. There are thirty-six half-triangle squares in each block, and there are sixteen blocks in the quilt – so you will need to cut a grand total of 288 of those 3⅞in squares. I aimed to have only approximately similar height stacks of print squares and 'background' (cream, sand and black) squares but if you prefer the rough maths then you should finish up cutting with a total of 144 assorted print squares and forty-eight cream, forty-eight sand and forty-eight black squares.

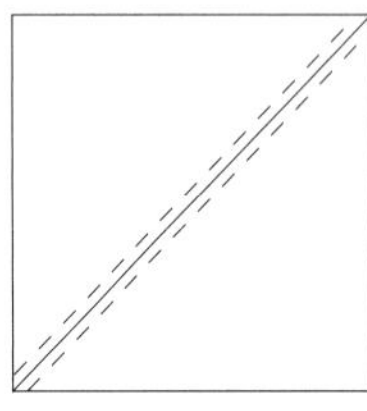

**Fig 1** *The mark-and-cut-apart method for making paired half-square triangles: mark the diagonal and stitch ¼in away on both sides, then cut on the marked diagonal to yield two paired half-square triangles*

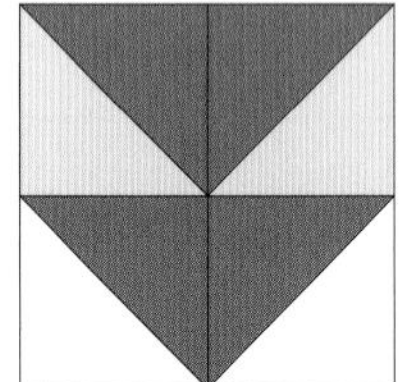
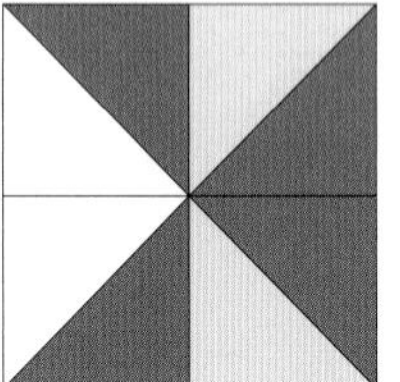

**Fig 2** *Some of the simple pieced units used to make the blocks*

3 Press all stitched seams flat before snipping the squares apart. Cut on the marked diagonal and press the two units into individual half-triangle squares.

4 Each block in this quilt is laid out in a basic nine-patch grid of simple four-patch units. Fig 2 shows some of the pieced units I used. The first diagram in Fig 3 shows the block I began with, followed by some of the many variation blocks used (given numbers for ease of identification). These variations were created by fabric and value placement. Refer to these as a starting point for your own African adventure and see what happens. The blocks are easy to piece but for beginners I have provided exploded diagrams for three of the blocks.

Block 1

Block 2

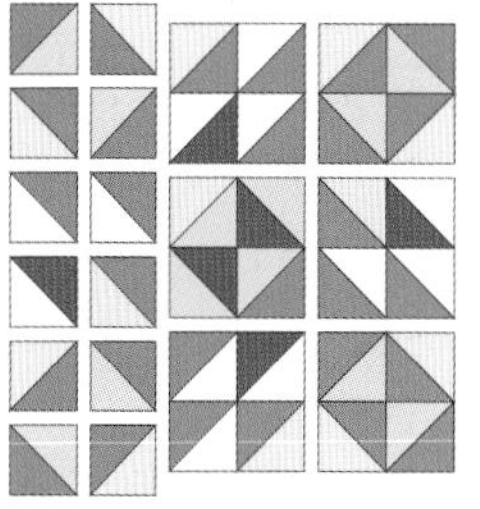

Block 3

Block 4

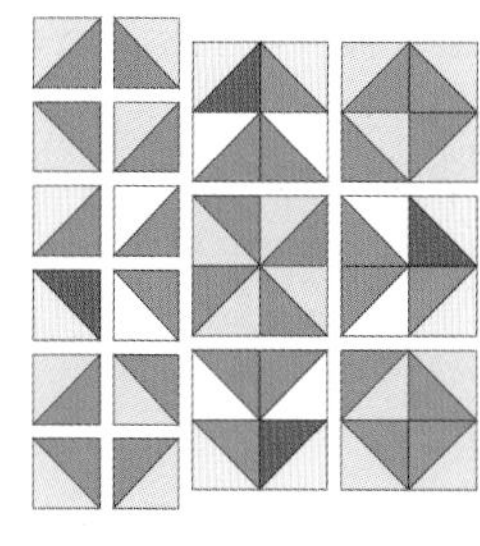

Block 5

Block 6

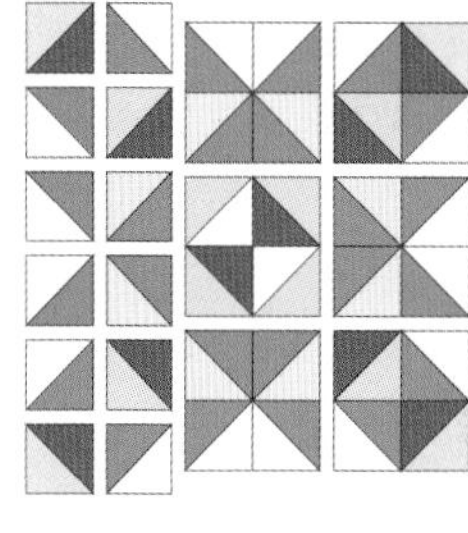

**Fig 3** *Six example blocks from the total of twenty used (block 1 being the starting point). Following a nine-patch format, no two blocks are absolutely identical. Three 'exploded' blocks show construction*

## Putting it all together

5 Starch, press and trim all blocks carefully – they should measure 18½in edge to edge approximately. Cut 1½in wide strips of black fabric and frame each block. You can use the sequence of sides first, top and bottom second, or a rotational Log Cabin sequence, but preferably not a mixture of the two.

6 Find a large space to lay out the blocks and put them into a pleasing arrangement. Cut 3in wide strips of sashing fabric and join the framed blocks into four rows of four blocks. Press the new seams before joining the four rows together using strips of the same width. Using the sequence of sides first, top and bottom second, stitch 3in wide strips into place as an inner border.

7 Cut 3¾in wide strips of border fabric and stitch these into place using the same sides first, top and bottom second sequence as above. Press and trim the completed quilt top with care.

## Finishing off

8 Layer the backing, batting and quilt top and baste together carefully, keeping all the layers smooth (page 117). Quilt by hand or machine before moving on to those all-important final steps of binding and labelling (see page 118).

# Tessellating Ts

The graphic traditional blocks for this quilt go together quickly and have great versatility, and the result is always pleasing, whether you arrange all the Ts in the same direction as in the quilt shown here or alternate the direction row by row, or put four blocks together to make a larger block. The cutting plan (Fig 1 overleaf) is specific to this block – from each fat quarter, paired with a fat quarter of background fabric, there will be sufficient pieces to make about six 6in T blocks. Unlike the main cutting plan used for the majority of the quilts in this book, this block-specific plan uses only about two-thirds of the fat quarter, so you will have ample fabric left over for piecing borders.

*Designed and pieced by Barbara Chainey, quilted courtesy of The Bramble Patch*

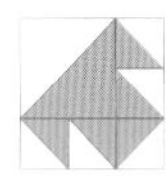 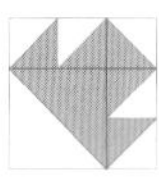 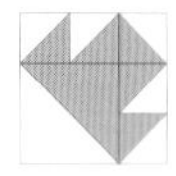 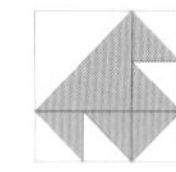

*"One print quarter partnered with a background quarter yields six 6in T blocks. With five prints and five backgrounds you can quickly cut and piece the thirty blocks that make up this appealing traditional-style quilt."*

**You will need**

- Five fat quarters of main fabrics and five fat quarters of background fabrics (try to choose background fabrics that are similar in value whilst strongly contrasting with your main fabric choices)
- Fabric for inner border, four strips 2in x 40in
- Fabric for outer border, four strips 5in x 48in
- Batting, 53in x 43in
- Backing fabric, 53in x 43in
- Binding fabric (see page 118)

**Quilt size:** 48in long x 43in wide
**Block size:** 6in square finished
**Skill rating:** Intermediate

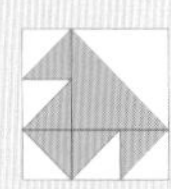
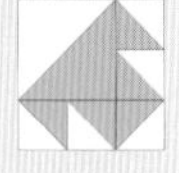
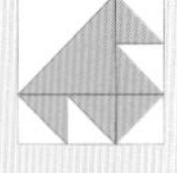

## Making the blocks

1 Starch and press all your fabrics. Layer the five main fabrics together and make a second stack of the five background fabrics. Follow the cutting plan shown in Fig 1 to cut 4⅞in squares and 2⅞in squares from both stacks. Set aside the surplus fabric.

2 Pairing the 4⅞in main and background fabric squares first, use the quick method of making half-square triangle units (see step 2, page 102). Do the same with pairings of all the 2⅞in squares. Press the stitching flat as it comes from the machine before cutting the triangle units apart and pressing them.

3 Lay out the pieces for one block as a reference and then lay out all the remaining pieces in the correct alignment on top of this. Take care to check the position of the half-square triangle units as you are stacking pieces in this way. Using the sequence indicated in Fig 2 as a guide, work systematically down the layers of block pieces to make a total of thirty blocks.

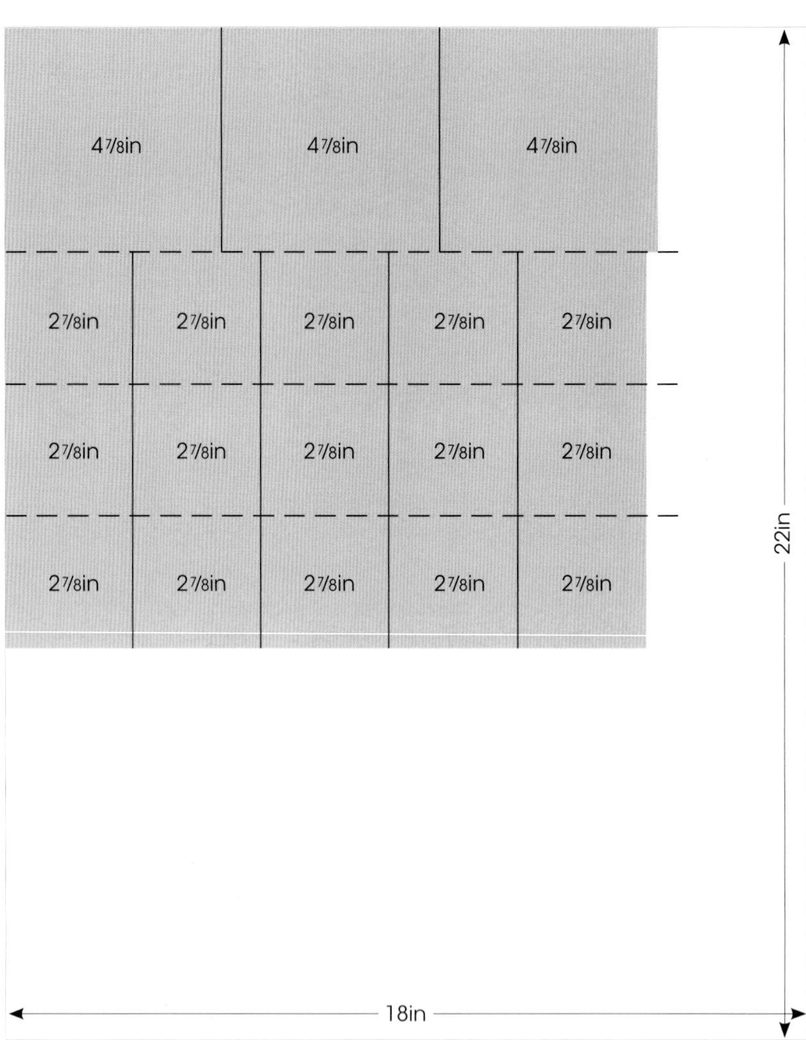


**Fig 1** *The cutting plan for the pieces that make the Tessellating T block – notice how much fabric is left over to use for borders or other blocks. The main cutting lines (shown as dashed lines) create four strips – one at 4⅞in wide and three at 2⅞in wide*

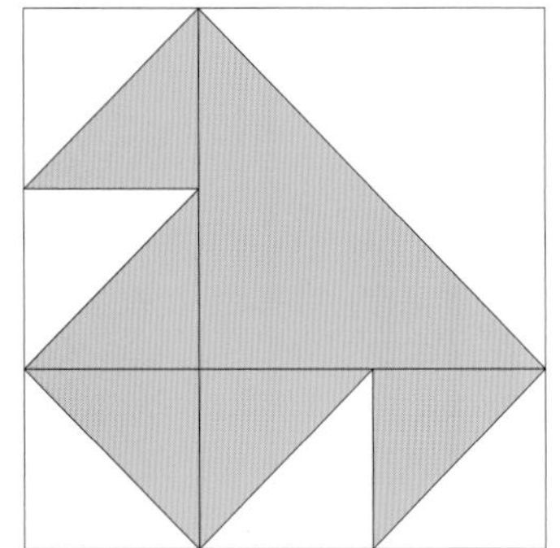

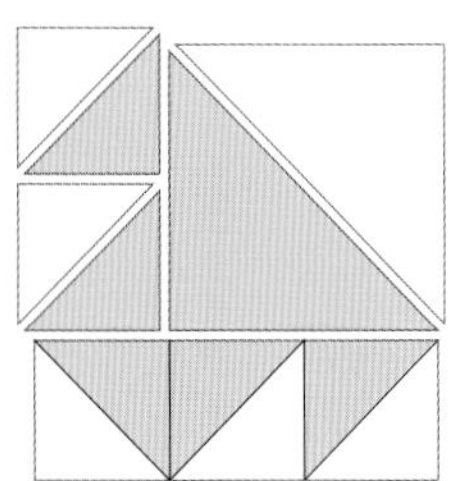

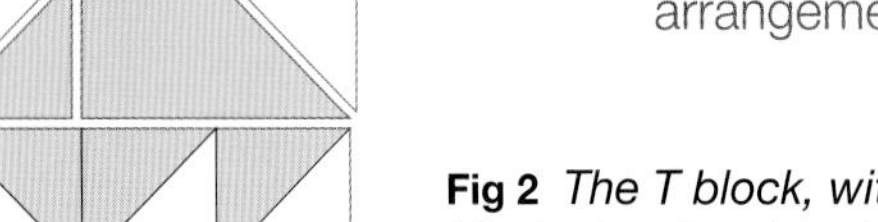

**Fig 2** *The T block, with the 'exploded' block showing the piecing sequence*

## Putting it all together

4 Press and trim all the blocks (they should measure 6½in edge to edge approximately) before trying out some different settings on a design wall or similar space. Fig 3, opposite, shows the block arrangement I used.

Fig 4, opposite, shows some different ways of arranging the T block, with some alternative layout suggestions. If preferred, you could rearrange all the triangles to create a completely different block but with similar versatility.

5 Once you have determined on an arrangement that you like, join the blocks together – first into pairs, then into fours and so on. This is often an easier strategy than making long strips of blocks and joining them together.

6 Cut four strips 2in x 40in of your chosen fabric for the inner border and stitch them into position in the usual sequence of sides first, top and bottom second.

7 Cut four strips of fabric 5in x 48in for the outer border and stitch these into position in the same way. Press the quilt top carefully and trim any remaining threads.

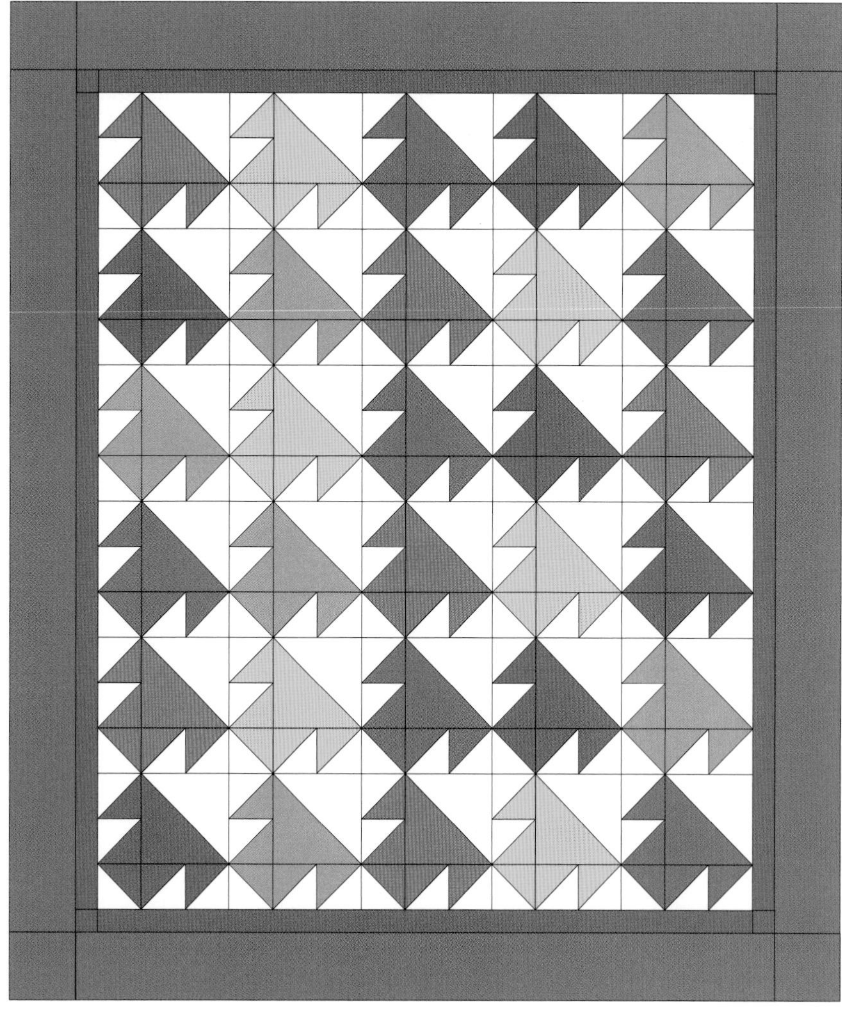

**Fig 3** *Layout of Tessellating Ts with borders*

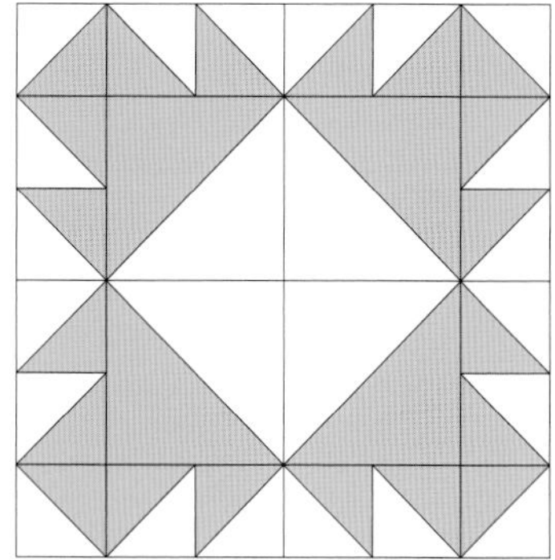

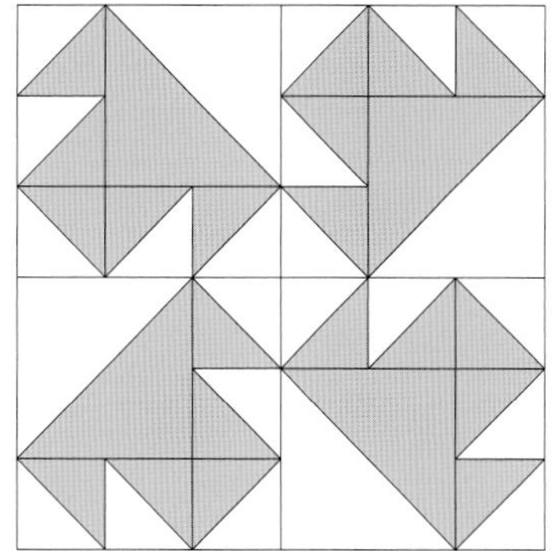

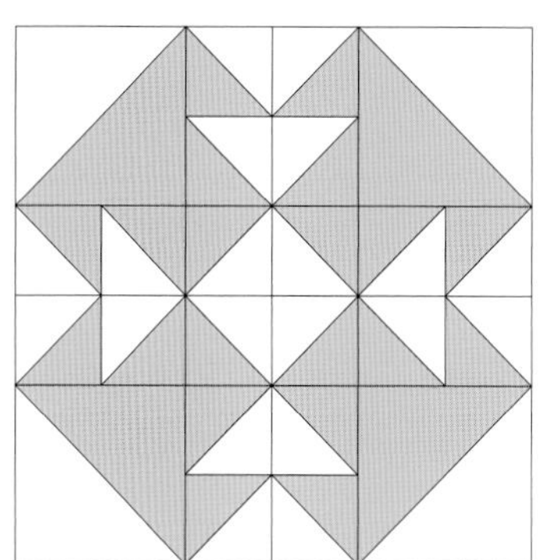

**Fig 4** *Arrange the T block in different ways and play with the block positions within the rows to find some effective alternatives*

## Finishing off

8 Layer up the backing, batting and top and baste together before quilting according to your preference (see page 117). The quilt shown has an all-over quilting pattern – you might want to consider simple outline quilting and filling in other spaces with echo quilting or various arrangements of straight lines, such as grid, parallels and so on (see page 118).

9 Finish by binding and labelling your quilt (see page 118).

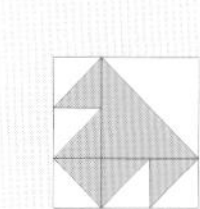

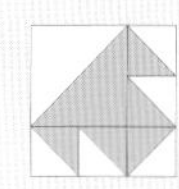

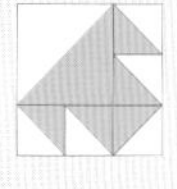

# Churn Dash

Just six fat quarters, a well-judged dash of contrasting fabric for a narrow inner border and a few hours of happy stitching is all that inventive quilter Jean Ann Wright needed to come up with this charming quilt. She cut only triangles and squares from her fat quarters to make a total of sixteen 7in blocks. The blocks were laid out with different fabric combinations although one is repeated – can you spot which one? Jean Ann used the remaining small squares to make a balanced checkerboard border with the darker-value squares placed at opposing corners. Much of the appeal of this quilt lies in the clever combination of a soft sunny yellow with the clear jewel colours of pink, teal and amethyst, teamed with an eye-catching black-and-white print.

*Designed, pieced and quilted by Jean Ann Wright*

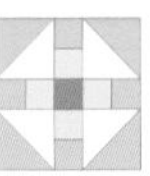  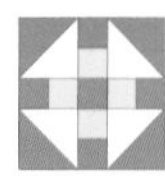 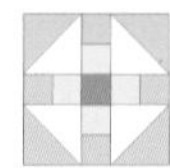

*"Triangles and squares are the only two shapes needed to make this bright Churn Dash variation. Expert quilter Jean Ann Wright had great fun laying out first the blocks and then the quilt to get the effect she wanted – notice how two opposite corners are slightly darker than the rest."*

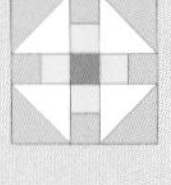

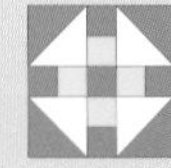

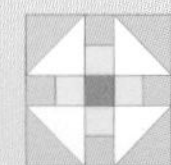

**You will need**

- Seven fat quarters for the blocks and pieced border (two of these quarters are identical, so you will have five single quarters of different prints and two repeat quarters of a sixth print)
- Inner border fabric, 2in strips
- Batting, 40in square
- Backing fabric, 40in square
- Binding fabric (see page 118)

| | |
|---|---|
| **Quilt size:** | 37in square |
| **Block size:** | 7in square finished |
| **Skill rating:** | Intermediate |

## Making the blocks

1 Starch and press the quarters before layering them ready to cut. Cut three strips 3⅝in x the width of the quarter, then cut these strips once again into 3⅝in squares to yield four squares per strip, a total of twelve squares per single quarter – seventy-two squares overall. Cut all these squares apart diagonally to make half-square triangles.

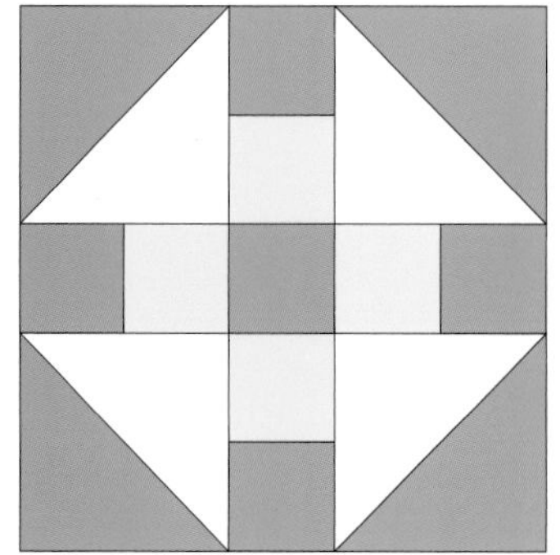

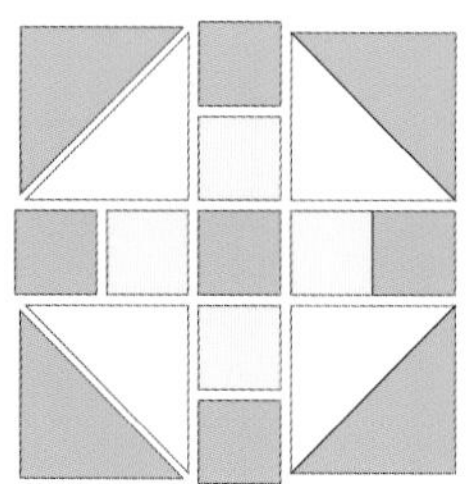

**Fig 1** *Churn Dash block and 'exploded' piecing sequence*

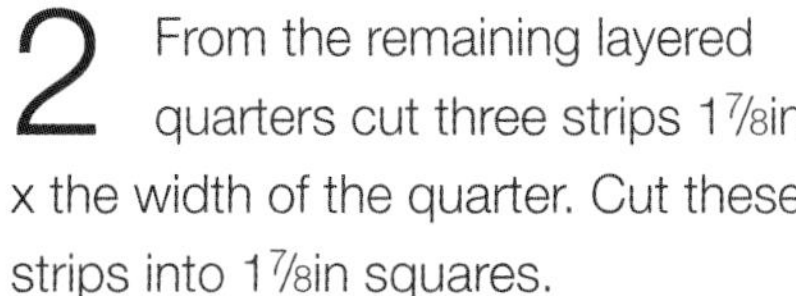

2 From the remaining layered quarters cut three strips 1⅞in x the width of the quarter. Cut these strips into 1⅞in squares.

3 Lay out a total of sixteen blocks, aiming to keep actual repeats of fabric placement to an absolute minimum.

4 Piece the blocks together, trimming threads and pressing as you go. The blocks should measure approximately 7½in edge to edge.

## Putting it all together

5 On a design wall lay out the blocks in a pleasing arrangement – Fig 2 shows the layout used for this quilt. Join the blocks together in four rows of four then put the rows together. Alternatively, join the blocks together in pairs, then fours, then two sets of eight and finally join these two halves together. Trim threads and press.

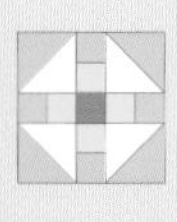

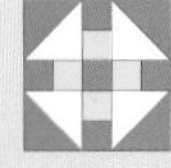

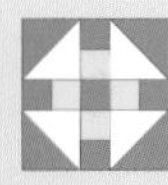

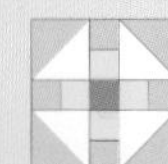

6 Cut four strips 2in wide and stitch these into position for the inner border using the usual sequence of sides first, top and bottom second.

**Fig 2** *Churn Dash layout with borders*

7 Now piece pairs of the remaining squares into four-patch units. Press the units carefully before arranging them to your liking and joining them together to make four border strips. Stitch these border strips into position, using the same sides first, top and bottom second sequence as before. Trim any remaining threads.

## Finishing off

8 Press the quilt top, then layer together the backing, batting and top and baste to secure (see page 117). Quilt by hand or machine according to your preference.

9 Finish your quilt by binding and labelling (see page 119).

# Finishing Your Quilt

This final section gives useful information on finishing, including advice on settings and sashings, adding borders, quilting, binding and labelling.

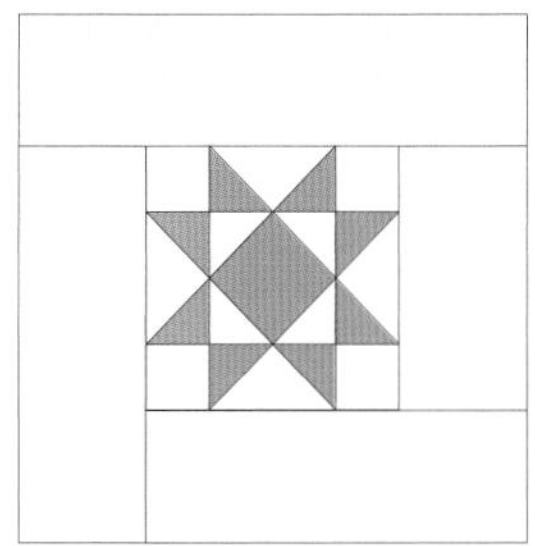

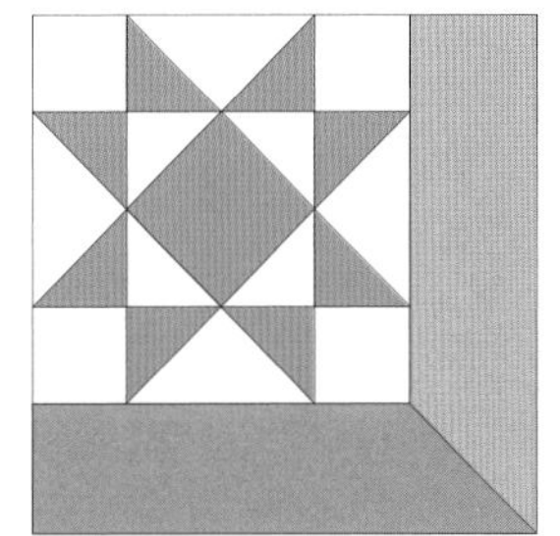

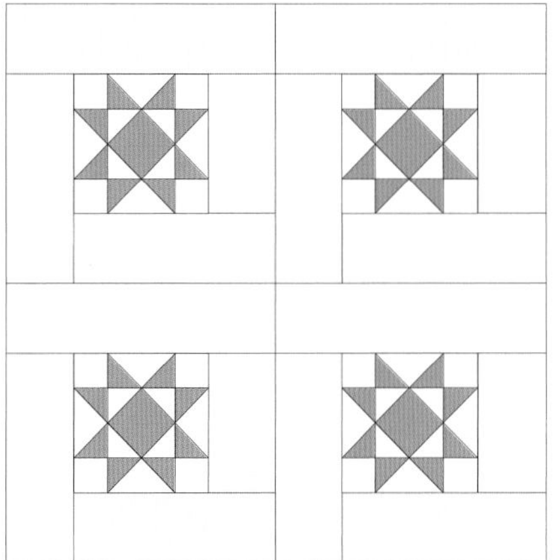

*Make a quick and easy frame with strips Log Cabin-style – here the strips are all the same width. You could use different width strips at random for a funkier look*

*Attic Window framing relies on careful placement of light and dark value strips for its three-dimensional effect*

*One of the easiest ways to frame a block is to set it on point*

## Framing Blocks

There are so many ways to extend and enhance pieced blocks and you may like to consider some of these possibilities as you are making up your own blocks with pieces from the main cutting plan. In the diagrams here and overleaf you can see individual framed blocks and then four of the newly framed blocks set together edge to edge. Do as some of the quilters in this book did and use fabrics from your stash, leftovers from the main cutting plan or (horrors!) buy more fabric to frame and set your blocks.

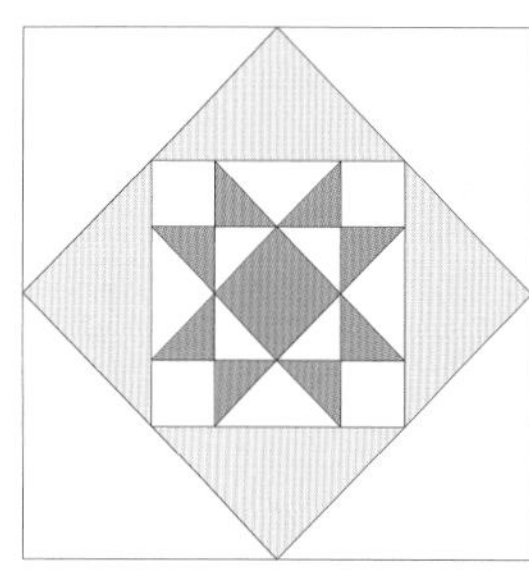

*Set a block on point once and then do it again for the more complex look of a square within a square*

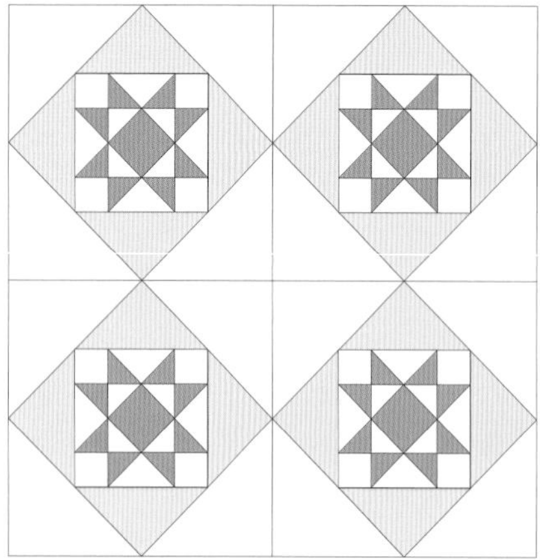

*Four square-within-a-square blocks set together*

*Consider alternating two framing ideas – here on point and square-within-a-square framed blocks are combined. A secondary star pattern appears to frame the central block*

*All done with triangles! With careful value choices you can achieve a lively effect when four or more of these framed blocks are set together*

*Framed by simple triangles and corner squares, it's almost a new block. When four blocks are set together edge to edge, secondary patterns appear*

*Make each block a star! Exactly the same pieces make this frame as the previous diagram – it's all down to placement and value*

*Sharper angles and more pieces make up this block frame*

*A Storm at Sea frame is not difficult, just more pieces*

*Use up leftover strips of different widths and corner squares for this easy (and economical) frame*

*A framing of easy triangles and squares makes another block and creates a secondary pattern in the centre*

*Returning to the on-point framing, divide up the corners into squares and triangles*

# Simple settings and sashings

If you have opted to make blocks from your cut quarters you will probably already have some setting or arrangement ideas of your own. Will you use a single sashing, stripped sashing or pieced sashing? Will you surround each block with narrow strips of two or more different fabrics? What if you don't use sashing at all and join the blocks edge to edge? Could you set the blocks into vertical rows and separate them with wide strips? What about setting blocks in horizontal rows, again separating them with wide strips, or perhaps with simply pieced strips? Strong graphic settings such as Twist and Turn, (see quilt on page 81) and Attic Window (page 85) can add lots of character and personality to a collection of blocks. Try turning some or all of the blocks on point, with or without sashings – setting blocks on point can be a very easy and effective way of beefing up the size of a quilt. Some settings are shown in the diagrams here. See also pages 111–113 for ideas on block settings.

*Traditional sashed setting examples showing the effect of narrow or wide sashing strips, simple pieced setting squares, which can add interest as can simply pieced sashing strips, or a complete sashing and squares setting, which has a strong design of its own*

### General assembly

If you are joining blocks or units together edge to edge or with regular sashing strips, work systematically to join them into lengthways strips. Think about the direction of seams as you press the strips and plan this so that the block-joining seams oppose each other strip to strip. This makes matching seams simpler when the long strips are pinned and stitched together. The usual joining sequence is sides first, top and bottom second.

If you have chosen an on-point setting, follow the same advice but work with strips of different lengths and join them in diagonal rows. Join rows in pairs and then pairs together rather than one row after another.

*Here is a framed medallion setting arrangement but with border treatments that range from four narrow strips through some easy-to-piece options, which add a more defined frame to the quilt*

*Surround the blocks with additional strips, Log-Cabin style, set them on point, add strips then re-cut for a twist-and-turn effect, or use spacer blocks and/or strips – there are so many possibilities!*

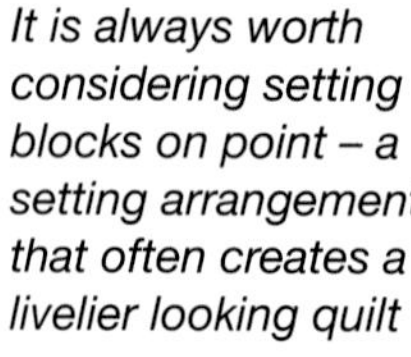

*It is always worth considering setting blocks on point – a setting arrangement that often creates a livelier looking quilt*

## Borders

Almost every quilt benefits from a well-judged border. A border not only frames a quilt, it enhances and highlights the piecing and fabric or colour choices. It is worth taking time to consider your choices – the colour of the border fabric can radically change the overall look of a quilt.

One border or two? A narrow inner border can provide a contrast, accent or highlight, which will give the finished quilt some extra sparkle rather than just adding a basic four-strip border.

What about piecing the border? It may not be the fastest of the various finishing options but is often the most effective – think of repeating one of the main shapes, perhaps a square or strips to create a piano key border, stripped border or squares on point. You may have leftover pieces from cutting the stack of fat quarters, so consider making small units to make corner squares or border midpoints.

It is always advisable to err on the side of safety and cut border strips rather longer than the required finished length. The measurements given for each of the projects have this built-in safety factor. To determine the length of border strips measure the finished quilt top at the centre rather than the edges as these may have stretched with handling. Mark the midpoint of each side of the quilt top and the midpoint of each border strip and align these as you pin each strip into position in its turn. On a technical note, it is usually advisable to stitch border strips into place working from the midpoint of the length of the border rather than from top to bottom as this reduces any potential slippage and distortion. Before trimming away any excess fabric wait until all the border strips are in place and checked.

**Press, press and press again**

Time spent pressing and trimming blocks, units and quilt tops is seldom time wasted. It means that everything is properly in place before proceeding to the next step and you will see that pressing features strongly in all the project instructions. Give the quilt top its final pressing, first from the wrong side and then the top side.

## Backing

Whatever fabric you choose for the backing of your quilt be sure that you cut or construct it to exceed the measurement of the completed quilt top by at least 2in on each side. For smaller quilts you will be able to use a single width of regular fabric; for larger quilts you can choose from the selection of extra wide backing fabrics (100in–108in) or piece lengths of fabric to the required measurement. If two lengths are required, consider halving one length and seaming either side of the full width rather than have a single centre seam.

## Battings

The type of batting (often called wadding in the UK) you use is very much a matter of personal preference. Make your choices based on how you will be quilting, by hand or machine, and whether you will be quilting a lot or a little. It really is worth buying a branded quality rather than an anonymous package – the old adage of getting what you pay for certainly holds true in batting matters.

For hand quilting it is usually best to choose a batting that will be easy to needle, probably not a needlepunched one. Cotton and cotton/polyester/dacron blends are all popular choices. All-polyester battings, together with those made with wool, are probably the easiest to stitch through.

For machine quilting, battings that are mostly cotton and needlepunched are extremely popular, being very easy to work with and giving a pleasing medium-loft texture.

## Basting

The three layers of a quilt – the top, batting and backing – need to be smooth and secured to prevent shifting during the quilting process. For most quilters this can be a totally tedious process. However, close attention to good basting practice is time well spent if it avoids unsightly and unplanned lumps and wrinkles in the finished quilt.

For hand quilting, thread basting is a main option. Smooth out all three layers of the quilt and baste systematically with long, even stitches into a grid or sunburst shape.

Tack basting with a special gun tool is a method suitable for either hand or machine quilting. Keeping everything smooth, shoot the tacks through the three layers and remove all the small tacks carefully when you have finished quilting.

Spray basting is fast and almost painless, perfect for machine quilters in a hurry to get to the quilting. Work in an open or well-ventilated space to avoid fumes. Lay out the backing, wrong side up and spray it, put the batting in position on top of the backing, spray the top of the batting or the wrong side of the quilt top before smoothing the quilt top into position on top of the batting. This method can also be used by hand quilters, but it may be preferable to add some regular thread basting if a lot of quilting (and thus a lot of handling) will be done.

Machine basting also works well and could be done with water-soluble thread so that it can be dissolved away upon completion. Set an extra long stitch length to put in regularly spaced lines that will hold the three layers together – this is even easier to do on a longarm machine, and many commercial quilting services offer this facility at a very reasonable rate.

## Quilting

Quilting is of course a major part of the quiltmaking process, but for most of us deciding what to quilt where can cause as much heart searching as deciding what colours/fabrics to use at the outset. The general rules are to keep it simple and, if you will be doing the quilting yourself, keep it well within your capabilities. If you plan to send the top out to be quilted, be prepared to be guided to some extent by the quilter who will be doing the work – perhaps the two first major points to consider are do you want an all-over pattern and texture, or would you prefer custom work with selected quilting designs?

### Quilting patterns

If you choose an all-over texture for your quilt there is really no need to do outline or in the ditch quilting. However, some outline quilting to work with the main shapes and blocks is best done before moving on to custom quilting based on specific selected designs. There is always the fear that our quilting skills are not up to the quality required by the job in hand. If you feel this way resolve to keep things manageable and simple by using mostly straight lines and easy curves connecting points/seams – described in much greater detail in *Quilt It!* (D&C, 1999).

### Hand quilting basics

Hand quilting is a running stitch worked through the three layers. If you are new to hand quilting, consult one of the many excellent titles on the subject and remember that it is not the size of the stitch that matters – you are aiming to have all your stitches look more or less even. If you are using a quilting hoop or frame choose a short needle, usually a betweens 8–10, and an 18in–24in length of thread.

Make a flat knot near the end of the thread, take the needle in through the top fabric and bring it out where you wish to start. With a gentle tug, pop the knot through the top fabric so that it lies just beneath the surface. It is not essential to take multiple stitches – just keep the stitches roughly similar in size. When you are ready to finish the thread, make your last stitch and bring the needle back up to the top of the work. Make a flat knot as close as you can to the work surface, then push the needle back down through the fabric, along the batting and back up through the top. As you pull the thread through you will pop the knot again in the same way as you did to start. Clip both starting and finishing threads.

### Machine quilting basics

Your motto here should be keep it simple and make it manageable. For straight lines and shallow curves use a walking foot or even-feed setting. For free-motion quilting drop or cover the feed dogs and use a darning foot. If you are new to quilting or your machine, take time to read the manual to familiarize yourself with these procedures. Put together several practice blocks about 16in–20in square using plain muslin for the top and back and your chosen batting. Use a walking or even-feed foot and thread of your choice and experiment with straight line variations. Drop the feed dogs, change to a darning or open embroidery foot and experiment with different curves, following marked lines, doodling.

### Threads for quilting

Monofilament or colourless used to be the thread of choice for many machine quilters – it produced the texture without drawing undue attention to itself. However, huge improvements in quality, count (thickness) and colour of thread mean that we now have a wonderful choice of exciting threads and the finished effect is often more visually appealing than the gleam of monofilament. An appropriately coloured variegated thread will work well in most cases and give a good degree of definition – for instance, if your quilt is mostly blues and greens, look for a variegated thread that has either or both of these colours. These variegated threads are also a good choice for many hand quilters as they go such a long way towards solving the dilemma of which colour thread(s) to use to complement the fabrics.

### Starting and finishing

Start machine quilting by putting the needle down and up to bring up the bobbin thread to the top of quilt. Hold bobbin and top threads at the back of the needle out of the way. Make three or four stitches at the shortest setting, so they are virtually one on top of the other. Change the stitch length to the required setting and proceed. Finish off in a similar way, making a few stitches on the spot and then clip threads.

### Quilt management

Manipulating a large and bulky quilt in a small space is not straightforward. Rolling up the sandwich to either side of the portion to be quilted is one solution, but can be heavy and unwieldy. Many quilters prefer instead to bunch the quilt up around the portion to be quilted and then re-group and re-bunch as necessary.

## Binding

This is a process you can learn to love! It is an important final step for any quilt, and time and care taken with binding really does make a difference. Too much binding is always better than too little – I measure twice the length and twice the width and then add a generous 12in, to allow for mitring the corners and to make general handling of the quilt easier.

So, for a single bed size quilt (70in x 100in) 70in twice is 140in and 100in twice is 200in: 200 + 140 = 340in + 12in allowance = a total binding length of 352in.

Double-fold binding makes an excellent finish with good endurance and may be cut either on the straight of grain or on the bias, according to your preference – I mostly work with straight of grain, saving bias bindings for use on curved edges.

Cut the strips four times the width of the finished binding plus a ½in seam allowance – you will find that a 2½in width works in most situations. Join the strips together to make the required length, making crosswise joins. Align the two cut edges and press the folded strip. Pin the binding in position with raw edges aligned with the edge of the quilt, and stitch into place (see the diagram below). It's a good idea to use a walking or even-feed foot for this step to prevent the layers from shifting. Butt or mitre the corners – the convention is that if you have added a border with mitred corners then mitre the corners of the binding too. Similarly, match butted borders with butted corners for the binding. Carefully trim away any excess fabric and batting once all the binding is correctly in position, and then bring the folded edge of the binding over to the back of the quilt and stitch neatly into place.

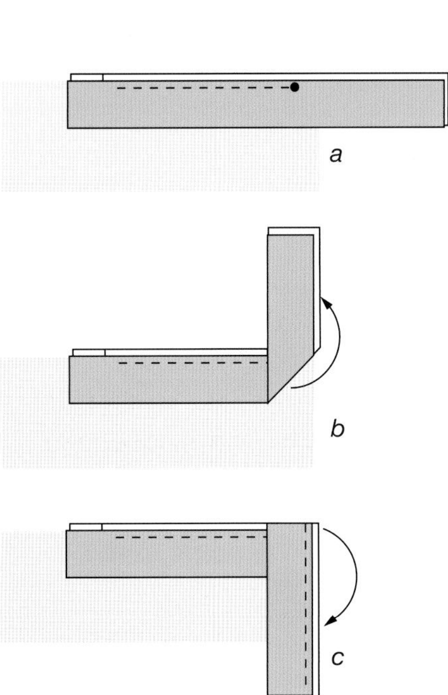


*To turn neat mitred corners for your binding stop stitching the width of your seam in from the aligned raw edges. Now carefully fold the binding strip back at 45 degrees. Fold it back over the angled fold and begin stitching again the width of your seam in from the aligned raw edges*

## Labelling

All quilts should be labelled, whether they are intended as short-life casual gifts or major heirlooms to be cherished for years. If you use a computer you can easily design and print your own labels or acquire dedicated software that will almost do the whole job for you. Non-computer folk can usually call on a willing friend to help. Hand-written labels can easily be made by using a fine-tipped permanent marker on fabric that has been temporarily stabilized with freezer paper. Also, think of those leftover pieces – could you perhaps make a label with some of these? Remember that the basic information you need to include on any label is: the title of the quilt (if you've thought of one), your name, the name of the recipient, the date or the year. Use a neat blindstitch to attach the label to the back of the quilt.

### Hanging sleeve

If you intend to hang the quilt then a hanging sleeve is quick and easy to make – and if more quilters included this step as a basic finishing process there would be far less last-minute stitching before quilt show deadlines! It's a great touch if the hanging sleeve matches the backing but this may depend on availability of fabric. A 4in sleeve seems to be the accepted convention. Begin by cutting a strip of fabric 8½in wide and 1in shorter than the width of the quilt. Double hem the short edges before folding the strip in half lengthways, wrong side out and aligning the two long edges. Stitch ¼in from the raw edges, press the seam open and flat before finally turning the tube to the right side and stitching it into place at the top of the quilt.

## Acknowledgments

The tolerance of my family and friends has been considerably stretched, not for the first time, during the relatively short period it has taken to bring this book into print. Grateful thanks to Derek, who keeps things on an even keel, my mother for great forebearance, Jean Ann for giving me her original idea to play with, Anna, Pat and Mike, Chris, Pat, Maggie and Alan, Di Huck, paid-upmembers of the Old Lags Society, Roberts Reliable Reservations, and others too numerous to mention.

Many quilters have willingly involved themselves in making quilts, testing instructions and generally being supportive – thanks particularly to Debbie and Bob Wendt, Sue Trangmar, Pat Screaton, Cosby Quilters, Anne Willcox and everyone at The Bramble Patch, Debbie Fetch and the Quilters in De Nile, Diane Anderson and Auckland Quilters Guild.

It has been the greatest of pleasures to be re-united and work on this book with the incomparable Vivienne Wells – there is no substitute! Lin Clements has brought great charm and fortitude to the thorny task of turning script into page. At David & Charles, Ame Verso and Sarah Underhill have done sterling work.

The Electric Quilt Company, whose excellent design software is an essential tool for so many teachers and quilters worldwide.

## About the Author

In twenty-five years of teaching, writing, designing and judging nationally and internationally, Barbara Chainey has inspired and encouraged countless quilters of all skill levels. Her books *The Essential Quilter* and *Quilt It!* are widely regarded as standard references.

# Index